NEHRU

Celebrating
30 Years of Publishing
in India

Praise for the Book

'*Nehru: The Debates that Defined India* is an important contribution to the continuing evaluation of Nehru's role in the crafting of modern India. Examining four key debates between Nehru and the leading figures of his age on religion, foreign policy and civil liberties, Tripurdaman Singh and Adeel Hussain allow Nehru and his interlocutors to express themselves in their own words. Delving lucidly into the most significant ideological battles of the era, this book deftly outlines the thinking and dialogue that laid the foundations of the Republic – and which remain deeply relevant and contentious today.'

– **Shashi Tharoor**, Member of Parliament, Lok Sabha, and author of *Inglorious Empire*

'In contemporary India, Jawaharlal Nehru has become a polarizing figure. Worshipped by his admirers and rubbished by his detractors, the complexity of the man and his ideas has increasingly been buried. In exploring four controversies through the exchanges between Nehru and his main challengers, Tripurdaman Singh and Adeel Hussain have brought to life the intellectual vibrancy and excitement that surrounded the debates. These were not mere political arguments but cerebral duels that enriched public life. Resurrecting these for today's audiences is a public service.'

– **Swapan Dasgupta**, Member of Parliament, Rajya Sabha, and author of *Awakening Bharat Mata*

'This innovative book allows us to understand Nehru's legacy by focusing on some of the most important debates of his career. Putting together his correspondence and conversation with powerful rivals and colleagues, ranging from Jinnah to Sardar Patel, the authors have for the first time made available in a single volume the intense arguments that went into the making of modern India. The result is a nuanced exploration of the strengths and weaknesses of the country's first Prime Minister.'

– **Faisal Devji**, Professor of Indian History, University of Oxford, and author of *Muslim Zion*

'[A book that] Reminds us of an era when Indian politics thrummed with ideas and arguments, articulated with conviction and civility. There is much to learn from, and in turn to argue with, in this timely anthology of some of modern India's most contentious – and still continuing – debates.'

– **Sunil Khilnani**, Professor of Politics and History, Ashoka University, and author of *The Idea of India*

'This insightful volume foregrounds hitherto little-trodden dimensions of Nehru's political ideology. It is likely to broach new debate on interesting issues like Nehru's perception of Islam, Muslims and communism. Therefore, it is an endeavour to open up a new vista of perception about Pandit Nehru's vision which makes it an exciting read.'

– **Tahir Kamran**, Professor of History, Beaconhouse National University and author of *Colonial Lahore*

NEHRU

THE DEBATES THAT DEFINED INDIA

TRIPURDAMAN SINGH

AND

ADEEL HUSSAIN

FOURTH ESTATE · *New Delhi*

First published in Hardback in India by Fourth Estate 2021
An imprint of HarperCollins *Publishers*
4th Floor, Tower A, Building No. 10, Phase II, DLF Cyber City,
Gurugram, Haryana – 122002
www.harpercollins.co.in

This edition published in India by Fourth Estate 2022
An imprint of HarperCollins *Publishers*

2 4 6 8 10 9 7 5 3 1

P-ISBN: 978-93-5629-413-4
E-ISBN: 978-93-5422-820-9

Cover design: Gavin Morris
Front cover photo: Getty images
Authors photos: Alessandra Malussa
Mariam Chauhan

Typeset in 11.5/16 Garamond at
Manipal Technologies Limited, Manipal

Printed and bound at
Thomson Press (India) Ltd.

To our parents

Contents

Introduction

JAWAHARLAL NEHRU HAS loomed like a colossus[1] over modern India – his life and legacy intimately intertwined with both its history and its present. As one of the leading lights of the nationalist movement, as one of the principal actors in the drama of Independence and Partition[2] and as India's first Prime Minister – Nehru fashioned the destiny of an entire subcontinent and left an indelible stamp on the history of South Asia. In the words of one biographer, he truly was 'among the tallest figures of the twentieth century'.[3] From his election as interim Prime Minister in 1946 to his end in 1964, and especially after the death of his deputy, Sardar Patel, in 1950, Nehru – as a contemporary observer recorded – 'wielded an authority usually reserved to dictators'.[4] In these 'unassailable years',[5] a pax-Nehruana, so to speak, when he was referred to as India's 'thaumaturgic personality',[6] his ideas moulded the imagination of two entire generations, defining the political contours of India and leaving an imprint so deep that they continue to be debated furiously by academics, intellectuals, commentators, journalists and politicians alike. 'The story of Jawaharlal Nehru,' as his obituary in the *New York Times* noted, 'is the story of contemporary India, which he in large part has shaped.'[7]

Nearly six decades after his passing, Nehru continues to make the newspapers with surprising regularity, not only in the context of the past but also in the context of the present. Deified and vilified in equal measure, he retains his centrality to political discourse, often cast as a player in current-day debates. In May 2021, for example, as India reeled from a ferocious second wave of Covid-19, furious commentators invoked Nehru to fulminate against the government's response. 'How Jawaharlal Nehru would have dealt with the Covid-19 pandemic in India,' ran one scathing headline in the newspaper *Gulf News*.[8] Writing soon after Nehru's death, the Australian diplomat (and Nehru biographer) Walter Crocker observed: 'Whatever the verdict of history on Nehru may be, either as a leader or as a man, he will remain one of those rare personages who form an inseparable part of their age.'[9] With the benefit of hindsight, we might add a postscript: in India, Nehru forms an inseparable part of any age. Even today, Nehru's ideas constitute the centre ground in Indian politics and the ideological spectrum is defined by degrees of divergence from them.

Before he came to enjoy this hegemonic power,[10] however, this was not the case; and before his ideas enjoyed the status of received wisdom, they were fiercely contested. Sharing the stage with political and intellectual figures who considered themselves his equals and peers, if not competitors, Nehru had to pit himself vigorously against them in the public realm. In this marketplace of ideas, he had to fend off not only political opponents like Mohammad Ali Jinnah of the All-India Muslim League and Syama Prasad Mookerjee of the Hindu Mahasabha, but also colleagues like the Congress leader Sardar Patel, with whom he often disagreed.

This was a challenge that Nehru took up with gusto. Engaging with them, arguing with them, debating with them and attempting to manipulate them, Nehru fought for his corner, clarifying and structuring his own ideas in the process. In this intellectual combat, he did not even spare Mahatma Gandhi, although he shied away from open confrontation with his mentor. As Gandhi once described to the Viceroy, Lord Linlithgow, after debating his protégé over the Quit India Movement, Nehru had the capacity to argue for days together 'with a passion that I [Gandhi] have no words to describe'.[11]

Some of the most profound questions in South Asian history were debated this way, many of which continue to remain unresolved, bedevilling the contemporary world as intensely as they did Nehru's – for example, questions about Muslim representation, about the role of religion in public life, the sanctity and inviolability of Fundamental Rights, or India's relations with Pakistan and China. Through such sparring – often conducted directly and openly via speeches, correspondence and articles – ideological disagreements were voiced, political allegiances were forged and public opinion was moulded. These hugely consequential debates decisively influenced political events, generating enduring repercussions.

'Nehru's contests were always over ideas, never any personal interests of his own,' argued Crocker (and other biographers), 'though he waged them without quarter and provoked a good deal of personal enmity.'[12] This is, of course, not strictly true, because there was often more than a tinge of instrumental rationality about many of these contests – especially when Nehru contested the views of his peers. The ways he waged these conflicts, the tools that he deployed and the reasoning he provided marked each such contest as a part of Nehru's manoeuvring for short-term gain and acquiring and consolidating political power; they expressed his tactical and strategic side as much as they did the visionary and the ideational. Engaging in these contests, Nehru and his contemporaries delineated their ideological positions, offered competing visions and configurations for the future, and staked out the political terrain – with consequences that reverberate to this day.

This book shines a spotlight on four such consequential debates that Nehru engaged in: with the poet-philosopher Muhammad Iqbal, with the Muslim League leader and the founder of Pakistan Mohammad Ali Jinnah, with his colleague and deputy Sardar Vallabhbhai Patel and with his first counterfoil in Parliament, Syama Prasad Mookerjee. With Jinnah, Nehru exchanged rancorous letters on Hindu-Muslim relations and the demands of the Muslim League. With Iqbal, he contested the meaning of Muslim solidarity, and the role of religion and religious orthodoxy in public life. Patel and Nehru crossed swords over India's policy towards China and Tibet. And with Mookerjee, Nehru clashed in Parliament over civil liberties and the First Amendment to the Constitution. All four debates represent critical junctures in South Asian history, moments that decided which way the pendulum of events would swing. Each debate is thus a crucial part of the events that followed: unbeknownst to them, for example, Nehru and Jinnah's arguments were the opening act of Partition, in the same way as Patel's confrontation with Nehru contained the seeds of 1962.

'Nehru's political career was rooted in a vision of a new India,' stated Judith Brown, one of Nehru's biographers, '... [and] appreciating the origins and power of this vision is essential for an understanding of the man.'[13] This is indeed true, as almost all his biographers have noted. Nevertheless, it is also true that translating this vision into policy meant leaving the world of visions and interacting with the more mundane world of politics, where arguments and alternatives put forward by his contemporaries had to be disarmed (or often dismissed), opponents confronted and outmanoeuvred, compromises struck, choices made, events responded to and, more importantly, Nehru's own grip on political power enhanced.

It is equally true that Nehru's personality, complex and contradictory in equal measure, heavily influenced his politics. Combining hard work, charm, idealism and ruthlessness with vanity, petulance and frequent (and famous) outbursts of temper,[14] Nehru's predilections and prejudices, his likes and dislikes, had a great bearing on his relationships with his contemporaries, and his engagement with their ideas. Nehru's political career was rooted not only in his vision, but also in the exigencies of practical politics and the personal relationships he shared – an aspect of his politics that admirers tend to play down as much as detractors like to play up.

In this setting, engagement with other political actors was as instrumental as it was ideational, and as personal as it was public. If Nehru the visionary was an idealist, then Nehru the political actor was as much a hard-nosed realist. Nehru's vision is part of the story; so is the intersection of his vision with the wider political world he operated in. Nehru's writings and public utterances accordingly have to be seen in this light – as tools of both intellectual and strategic engagement with other political actors, and as a method of positioning himself in and navigating through the fraught politics of the pre-Nehruana years. Appreciating the origins and power of Nehru's vision of India – which, as Brown contends, is essential for an understanding of the man – thus must be complemented by an appreciation for, and an understanding of, how that vision emerged at the intersection of Nehru's ideas, the ideas of his contemporaries, the vagaries of practical politics and the foibles of Nehru's own personality. Examining his debates enables us to do this.

Reproduced here in their original form, along with introductions that provide the historical contextualization and intellectual scaffolding needed to understand them in their entirety, the four debates between Nehru and his contemporaries together provide an intimate insight into the man and his ideas – as they took shape in the crucible of politics, squared up to the ideas of opponents and colleagues alike, and demarcated their position in the public realm. They give us a first-hand glimpse of Nehru in action, giving us an incisive view into the process through which his ideas came to triumph over those of his contemporaries and allowing a more composite picture of Nehru to emerge.

As many of the foundational questions Nehru was debating – the sanctity of the Constitution and the freedom of speech, the role of religion in public life, Muslim representation, the dynamic with China – have been resurrected as matters of raging dispute in India, and Nehru's legacy (and Nehruvian shibboleths) have come to be questioned like never before, revisiting these debates has become both pertinent and timely. It is instructive to note in this context how commentators and analysts, when making sense of present-day situations, frequently turn to Nehru and to the debates with his contemporaries. In June 2020, for example, as a new Sino-India dispute erupted in the Himalayas, the Quint ran an article headlined, 'Would China Have Won in 1962 if Nehru Had Listened to Patel?'[15], testifying to the long afterlives of these debates and their ability to impinge on the present in multitudinous ways.

Today, Nehru may no longer be alive to answer his critics, but his ideas nonetheless remain locked in ideological combat, reviving debates that many had thought settled by history. In the heat of battle, they are frequently misrepresented or misinterpreted by all sides, not only because of partisan politics but also because Nehru, mediated through interlocutors, was many things to many people. As one of his biographers, B.R. Nanda, remarked, 'To the conservatives he was an extremist, to the Marxists a renegade, to the Gandhians a non-Gandhian, and to Big Business a dangerous radical.'[16] Nowadays, the list would be considerably longer. Stranded amid all these labels, who was the real Nehru? By bringing both Nehru's ideas and those of his contemporaries to the fore, the following chapters cut straight through to the chase – letting Nehru speak for himself and providing a ring side view to the debates that defined India.

1

'I fear the Pandit's articles reveal practically no acquaintance with Islam'

Muhammad Iqbal and Jawaharlal Nehru debate Islamic solidarity and religious orthodoxy

TOWARDS THE END of his life, in 1938, when he had gone almost entirely blind and was dependent on the help of an assistant even for the most moderate of tasks, Muhammad Iqbal, the great Muslim philosopher, sent for Jawaharlal Nehru upon hearing that the latter was in Lahore. Nehru remembered this meeting fondly in his autobiography, framing his visit to Iqbal's modest two-storey house in a leafy neighbourhood as a reunification of two old friends bonding over their shared socialist convictions.

As calling Iqbal a socialist was as controversial then as it is now, Nehru went on to justify his belief in Iqbal's ideological persuasion in some detail. He speculated that it might have been 'the great progress that Soviet Russia had made' in the 1930s that had moved Iqbal to abandon Sufi mysticism and embrace plain materialism.[1] Nehru insisted that Iqbal's shift to socialism was visible in his later poetry and prose, at least for the careful reader. He further claimed that Iqbal had realized that a separate Muslim state on Indian soil was not a viable solution to counter Muslim backwardness. Iqbal was aware of 'its inherent danger and absurdity'.[2] However, the most infamous lines of this interaction are the final words that Iqbal uttered just before Nehru left. 'What is there in common between Jinnah and you? He is a politician, you are a patriot.'[3] Nehru understood this comparison as a double-edged compliment. In his self-deprecating manner, he readily acknowledged that he had never been 'much of a politician'. Being a patriot alone, Nehru continued, would fall way short of his lifelong yearning to solve the problems 'of the world as a whole'.[4]

Whether or not Iqbal truly shared Nehru's passion for socialism or at any stage stopped advocating a separate Muslim homeland, he possessed a string of similarities with the Pandit. Both men had a refined taste for Indian and Western literature and philosophy. They were both of Kashmiri descent and never failed to portray the mountainous region in India's north in the most glowing of terms in their writings and speeches.

Iqbal and Nehru were gifted orators and could keep large crowds enraptured for hours. While both liked to portray themselves as reluctant or even failed politicians, they were remarkably successful in their missions. Both men commanded the respect of their political cadres and were valued negotiators for their parties. When it was still uncommon for Indians to study abroad, Nehru and Iqbal attended the University of Cambridge and trained as barristers in London. They also shared a deep sense of empathy with the impoverished and backward sections of colonized people in India, and devoted their entire lives to stirring change in the material conditions of the poor.

They also saw eye to eye on several pressing questions in the international arena. For instance, both vehemently opposed '[t]he idea of a national home for the Jews in Palestine'. Iqbal saw the partition of Palestine as a 'dangerous experiment' and a sovereign state for Jewish people as a way for British imperialism to entrench itself 'in the religious home of the Muslims'.[5] Nehru, ever the internationalist, regarded the Palestine question as a 'gross betrayal of the Arabs' and stood in solidarity with Arab nationalism's 'heroic fights for attaining independence' from British imperialism.[6]

Yet, the list of things that sets them apart runs equally long. Their first difference was their upbringing. Iqbal was raised in the household of a poor hat maker in the hinterland of Lahore. His early education took place in Indian mission schools and the Government College in Lahore. Nehru's father, Motilal, had risen to be one of India's most accomplished and wealthy lawyers and sent young Nehru to Harrow, a boarding school in England. While both attended Trinity College in Cambridge in the first decade of the twentieth century, Nehru did so as an undergraduate to read for the natural sciences tripos, entirely aloof from any financial burdens. Iqbal was a non-degree student who had taken leave from his work as an untenured college lecturer in Lahore, funding his stay through a sparse monthly stipend he received from his older brother and leaving his young son and wife behind in Lahore.

On more doctrinal points, Nehru promoted an inclusive nationalism and a democratic future with joint electorates. In contrast, Iqbal squarely focused on Muslim rights and their place in India's political and cultural landscape, which led him to endorse separate electorates and reserved seats for Muslims.[7] Iqbal also received and never returned a knighthood. Even at the height of anti-British sentiments among Indians, he preferred to be addressed as Sir Muhammad. As president of the Muslim League in 1930, Iqbal also proposed grouping Muslim majority provinces in India's north-west together, an idea that was later spun forward, albeit in very different shape and form, by proponents of the Pakistan movement.

In 1933, during their first brief spat, Iqbal had sharply criticized Nehru in a public statement for ascribing the failure of the Round Table Conferences, where India's constitutional future was discussed, to the conservative political outlook of the Muslim delegation and their lack of nationalism. Partly embracing this criticism, Iqbal retorted that 'if by "nationalism" he [Nehru] means a fusion of the communities in a biological sense, I should personally plead guilty to the charge of anti-nationalism'.[8] In Iqbal's understanding of nationalism, rejecting the fusion of communities into a single nation was not anti-national. Nationalism in India had to be reimagined as something different than the mere blending of divergent communities into a singular whole.

The best path to make India hospitable for all religious groups would therefore require 'Indian leaders of political thought [to] get rid of the idea of a unitary Indian nation based on something like a biological fusion of the communities'.[9] Iqbal further corrected Nehru that it was not democracy that Indian Muslims feared, as the latter had insinuated in an earlier speech. What Muslims feared was 'communal [Hindu] oligarchy in the garb of democracy'.[10] Iqbal grimly predicted that if Nehru continued to prop up nationalism as the catch-all solution for India's communal and constitutional woes, 'the country will have to be redistributed on the basis of religious, historical and cultural affinities'.[11]

Iqbal would have also accepted Nehru's socialist brotherhood only on the condition of divorcing classical Marxist theory from atheism and making the entire redistributive justice argument more amiable to religion.[12] Only 'Bolshevism plus God', Iqbal wrote to a British admirer, would come close to the Islamic notions of justice he cherished.[13] Perhaps consequentially, this 'plus God' part brought Iqbal into a heated exchange with Nehru in 1935.

IQBAL FIRST ENTERED the national limelight in 1905. During a lecture for the Young Men's Indian Association, a student group loosely modelled on the Young Men's Christian Association (YMCA), Iqbal had skipped his formal speech and decided to sing a hymn he had recently written instead. A few years later, those words would be chanted loudly at anti-colonial rallies all over British India: '*Saare jahaan se acche, yeh Hindustan hamaara* [...] *Hindi hain ham, watan hai Hindustan hamara* [Better than the entire world, is our Hindustan (...) We are of Hind, our homeland is Hindustan].'[14] More than any of his rather abstract philosophical writings or his politically charged poetry, it was this hymn that turned Iqbal into a known entity on India's cultural scene.

Already in 1899, as a young graduate student, Iqbal had caught the attention of the historian Sir Thomas Arnold, who was teaching at Government College, Lahore, at the time. Iqbal had received a gold medal in philosophy for reaching the highest grade in the final examination. In fairness, he was the only student taking the philosophy paper that year. Immediately after graduating, Iqbal was hired as a lecturer in economics. A recent graduate of Arabic and philosophy, Iqbal was an unusual appointment. But he made up for his lack of econometrics by writing an undergraduate textbook that approached the discipline from the broad lens of political economy, the *Ilm-ul-Iqtisad* – his first scholarly publication, and the first modern economics textbook in Urdu.[15] In this work, Iqbal keenly distinguished between the logic behind normative moral sciences, 'good and bad' and the logic of the marketplace, 'profitable and non-profitable'. He offered a balanced view of prevalent economic models at the turn of the century. After Arnold took up a fellowship at Trinity College, Cambridge, Iqbal swapped faculties and taught Arabic in Arnold's place for three years, a role for which he was much more suited.

A few years later, Arnold invited Iqbal to pursue further studies at Cambridge. Iqbal applied for leave from Punjab University and, aged twenty-eight, ventured on a steamship to Dover, where he docked in 1905. As an advanced student, Iqbal was not required to go through the rigours of tripos examinations. Instead, the academic labour of his stay was a short thesis on Persian metaphysics. Since Cambridge did not award doctorate degrees in 1907, Arnold advised Iqbal to hand in the same dissertation at Munich University to secure a PhD. Iqbal's first choice, Heidelberg University, had refused to accept a thesis written in English as they held the language unsuitable for academic pursuits and worried that it might dilute examination standards.

Had Iqbal returned to Trinity College in 1907 and not sailed back to Lahore after his brief stay in Germany, his relationship with Nehru may have turned out very differently. From mere distant but polite observers of each other's political gestures, the two may well have developed a friendship, whether over complaining about the unseasoned food in Trinity's dining hall, sharpening their rhetorical skills at Cambridge Majlis, a debating club for Indian students, or listening to the speeches of Indian freedom fighters on their visits to London. Yet, it took almost three decades for their first real intellectual encounter to happen.

In the summer of 1935, Nehru and Iqbal debated over the constitutional exclusion of Ahmadis, a fringe Messianic sect founded by Mirza Ghulam Ahmad in the 1890s in a remote village in Punjab called Qadian.[16] Mirza Ghulam Ahmad saw his mission in cleansing Islam and preparing it for the modern age. Judging purely by his outward ritualistic behaviour, he seemed to follow his puritanical vision faithfully. However, troubles ensued over his eclectic theological claims. Mirza Ghulam Ahmad claimed that he was the reincarnation of Jesus and an avatar of Vishnu, a claim that upset many orthodox scholars.

Around the turn of the century, until he died in 1908, his movement, the Ahmadiyya of Qadian, grew considerably in size when north India was repeatedly hit by the plague. Hard-pressed for options to survive the ravaging black death, thousands of Muslims adopted Mirza as their saviour. He promised that none of his followers would fall victim to the plague. He also asserted that God spoke to him directly and that He had asked him to take on the mantle of a *zilli* (shadowy) prophet. This unique relationship with God, Mirza claimed, gave him glimpses into the near future that often entailed prophecies about the sudden death of his opponents.[17]

In his youth, Iqbal was mighty impressed with the boldness of such overtly prophetic claims. He even called Mirza Ghulam Ahmad 'the profound theologian among modern Indian Muhammadans' in his earliest scholarly writings.[18] Towards the mid-1930s, his views on the Ahmadiyya community had cooled considerably. Where Iqbal had once invited the members of the Ahmadiyya community to participate in the political struggle for securing the constitutional rights of Kashmiri Muslims, he now abandoned the very organization he had helped set up for this cause, with the argument that Ahmadi influence had turned it into an 'an instrument of a specific [Ahmadiyya] propaganda even though it seeks to cover itself with a thin veneer of non-sectarianism'.[19] Iqbal expanded his criticism in a short pamphlet with the title *Qadianis and Orthodox Muslims*, where he developed the idea that claims to prophethood were severe threats to Islam's solidarity. Modern liberalism had given free rein to such 'religious adventurers' as Mirza Ghulam Ahmad, Iqbal moaned. If this liberalism would continue to force Muslims to tolerate such false prophets, '[t]he Indian mind will then seek some other substitute for religion, which is likely to be nothing less than a form of atheistic materialism which has appeared in Russia'.[20]

It was, however, not just atheism going mainstream as a consequence of liberal toleration that worried Iqbal but the dissolution of Islam itself. For Iqbal, Islam had come directly under threat from Mirza's claims of Divine revelation, as this claim entailed constructing a new spiritual authority. In Iqbal's reading of Islam, the revelation-authority nexus had conclusively come to an end with the revelations the Prophet Muhammad received. Iqbal saw this theological principle firmly established in Islamic doctrine, in what he found to be 'perhaps the most original idea in the cultural history of mankind', the finality of prophethood.[21]

Invoking the authority of the Leiden-based Orientalist Arent Jan Wensinck, Iqbal also sought to establish that the very concept of a returning Messiah had no backing in the earliest sources of Islam. Instead, its origins could be found 'in the pre-Islamic Magian outlook'.[22] Much of the backlash against the Ahmadiyya from groups like the Ahrar was justified in Iqbal's eyes. Such Muslim groups were merely following their 'instinct of self-preservation'.[23] But as their emotionally driven responses could not furnish a permanent solution to the 'Qadiani problem', Iqbal lobbied the British Government to constitutionally 'declare the Qadianis a separate community' as their theological convictions had put them outside the pale of the Muslim fold.

When Nehru received a copy of Iqbal's pamphlet on the Qadianis in Almora jail, where the colonial state had locked him away for seditious activities throughout much of 1935, his primary association with the Ahmadiyya must have been their participation at the All Parties National Convention in 1928. An Ahmadiyya delegation participated in the proceedings as one of two Muslim social reform organizations and wholeheartedly supported Mohammad Ali Jinnah. It would not have escaped Nehru's notice that only Ahmadiyya delegates stood by Jinnah's proposals to bolster constitutional safeguards for Indian Muslims in the Nehru Report.[24]

Several theological and political moves in Iqbal's blistering deconstruction of the Ahmadiyya movement must have struck Nehru as unusual. From Nehru's perspective, the Ahmadiyya support for Jinnah's proposals seemed to align them well within the reactionary spectrum of Muslim political opinion. Iqbal was also departing from conventional political practice with his call for the British Government to step in and ban Ahmadis from labelling themselves as Muslims. This step would violate the principles of non-interference in religious matters that Indians had fought hard for to allow for a sphere of unregulated cultural activity, a sphere that conservatives and liberals cherished.[25] In Nehru's view, Iqbal's invitation for the colonial state to step in to ban a religious reform movement would disadvantage the progressive and moderate sections of each community. Orthodox Hindus, or Sanatanists, as Nehru used to call them interchangeably, for instance, would undoubtedly rely on such a measure to throttle much-needed social-reform efforts in their community, bringing them startlingly close to conservative Muslim opinion.

An inkling of such a pan-orthodox resistance against progressive legislative reform had already become visible with the implementation of the Child Marriage Restraint Act, 1929, also known as the Sarda Act, where fixing the age of marriage for girls to fourteen caused a storm of outrage in conservative quarters across religious communities.[26] Nehru was also baffled that Iqbal would willingly risk losing the thin Muslim-majority margin by excluding the small but critical Ahmadiyya population in the district of Gurdaspur, where many of them resided. Especially after the Government of India Act, 1935, which underlined the importance of numerical strength for voting purposes, Iqbal's proposal for Ahmadiyya exclusion seemed to weaken Muslim chances for electoral success.

Above all, however, Nehru questioned the political wisdom of establishing unity within Islam by excluding groups on theological grounds. For lifting economically backward Muslims out of abject poverty, Iqbal's exclusionary measures to cement Islamic solidarity seemed of little to no relief. According to Nehru, Iqbal's arguments could also easily be levelled against several other Islamic sects. Applying the principles of the finality of revelations strictly to all Muslim denominations, for instance, would undoubtedly lead to the exclusion of other groups as well. If connecting revelation to spiritual authority was to be taken as a guideline to restrict the fold of Islam, Nehru presciently analysed, the Aga Khan and his followers, the Ismailis, would have to suffer the same fate that Iqbal had meted out to the Ahmadis.

Nehru found that the Ismaili concept of a perpetual imamate, which entailed the idea of continuous revelation, and their excessive venerating practices of the Aga Khan, made them appear to follow the same Magian thinking Iqbal had identified in the Ahmadis. While teasing the Aga Khan for possessing the curious quality of bridging

'Mecca and Newmarket, this world and the next, spirituality and racing, politics and pleasure', Nehru's main criticism returned to the fact that Muslim solidarity of the Iqbalian variety meshed seamlessly with 'Anglo-Moslem unity'.[27] Despite Iqbal's repeated vows that he wanted to see British imperialism fade, Nehru pointed out that Iqbal was equally comfortable occupying a seat at the 'Council of Peers and Moslem Leaders' that cooperated directly with the British government.[28]

In June 1936, a year after they had engaged in their public spat on the pages of Indian magazines and newspapers, Iqbal wrote a conciliatory note to Nehru in which he assured him that his responses were 'written with the best of intentions for Islam and India'. Had it not been for the Ahmadi press and their jubilation over the unexpected support that they received from Nehru's writings, their encounter would have remained much more civil. Yet, Iqbal remained firm in his belief that Ahmadis were 'traitors both to Islam and to India'.[29]

Nehru's sober prediction that the exclusion of a group on theological grounds would lead to stagnation in the social and political sphere turned out prescient. Materializing Iqbal's vision would entail a perpetual cycle of 'heresy hunts, excommunication, punishment for apostasy, and a general suppression of so-called "enlightened" Muslims'.[30] For much of its history, Pakistan has been plagued by many of these issues. The question if Ahmadis could legitimately call themselves Muslims tossed the state into its first state of emergency in 1953, led to the constitutional exclusion of Ahmadis to count as Muslims in 1974 and brought about more stringent criminalization against them under the martial rule of

Zia-ul-Haq. On the other hand, Iqbal's prediction that Nehru's egalitarian nationalism would ultimately fail to satisfy the Muslim minority proved accurate as well and culminated in the violent Partition of India along religious lines in 1947.

ARTICLES BY NEHRU AND IQBAL

1. Muhammad Iqbal: Qadianis and Orthodox Muslims

(As reprinted in Shamloo [ed.], *Speeches and Statements of Iqbal*, Lahore: Al Manar Academy, 1944, pp. 93–100.)

THE ISSUE CREATED by the controversy between the Qadianis and the orthodox Muslims is extremely important. The Indian Muslims have only recently begun to realize its importance. I intended to address an open letter to the British people explaining the social and political implications of the issue. But unfortunately my health prevented me from doing so. I am, however, glad to say a few words for the present on the matter, which, to my mind, affects the entire collective life of the Indian Muslims. It must, however, be pointed out at the outset that I have no intention to enter into any theological argument. Nor do I mean to undertake a psychological analysis of the mind of the founder of the Qadiani movement; the former will not interest those for whom this statement is meant and the time for the latter has not yet arrived in India. My point of view is that of a student of general history and comparative religion.

India is a land of many religious communities; and Islam is a religious community in a much deeper sense than those communities whose structure is determined partly by the religious and partly by the race idea. Islam repudiates the race idea altogether and founds itself on the religious idea alone. Since Islam bases itself on the religious idea alone, a basis which is wholly spiritual and consequently far more ethereal than [any] blood-relationship, Muslim society is naturally much more sensitive to forces which it considers harmful to its integrity. Any religious society historically arising from the bosom of Islam, which claims a new prophethood for its basis, and declares all Muslims who do not recognize the truth of its alleged revelation as kafirs, must, therefore, be regarded by every Muslim as a serious danger to the solidarity of Islam. This must necessarily be so, since the integrity of Muslim society is secured by the idea of the Finality of Prophethood alone.

This idea of Finality is perhaps the most original idea in the cultural history of mankind; its true significance can be understood only by those who carefully study the history of pre-Islamic Magian culture in western and Middle Asia. The concept of Magian culture, according to modern research, includes cultures associated with Zoroastrianism, Judaism, Jewish Christianity, and the Chaldean and Sabaean religions. To these creed-communities the idea of the continuity of prophethood was essential, and consequently they lived in a state of constant expectation. It is probable that the Magian man psychologically enjoyed this state of expectation. The modern man is spiritually far more emancipated than the Magian man. The result of the Magian attitude was the disintegration of old communities and the constant formation of new ones by all sorts of religious adventurers. In the modern world of Islam, ambitious and ignorant Mullaism taking advantage of the modern Press, has shamelessly attempted to hurl the old pre-Islamic Magian outlook in the face of the twentieth century. It is obvious that Islam, which claims to weld all the various communities of the world into one single community, cannot reconcile itself to a movement which threatens its present solidarity and holds the promise of further rifts in human society.

Of the two forms which the modern revival of pre-Islamic Magianism has assumed, Bahaism appears to me to be far more honest than Qadianism, for the former openly departs from Islam, whereas the latter apparently retains some of the more important externals of Islam with an inwardness wholly inimical to the spirit and aspirations of Islam. Its idea of a jealous God with an inexhaustible store of earthquakes and plagues for its opponents; its conception of the prophet as a soothsayer; its idea of the continuity of the spirit of the Messiah, are so absolutely Jewish that the movement can easily be regarded as a return to early Judasim. The idea of the continuity of the spirit of the Messiah belongs more to Jewish mysticism than to positive Judaism. Professor Buber, who has given an account of the movement initiated by the Polish messiah Baalshem, tells us that 'it was thought that the spirit of the Messiah descended upon the earth through the prophets and even through a long line of holy men stretching into the present time – the Zaddiks (Sadiqs)'. Heretical movements in Muslim Iran under the pressure of pre-Islamic Magian ideas invented the words 'buruz', 'hulul', 'zill', to cover this idea of a perpetual reincarnation. It was necessary to invent new expressions for a Magian idea in order to make it less shocking to Muslim conscience. Even the phrase 'promised Messiah' is not a product of Muslim religious consciousness. It is a bastard expression and has its origin in the pre-Islamic Magian outlook.

We do not find it in early Islamic religious and historical literature. This remarkable fact is revealed by Professor Wensinck's *Concordance of the Traditions of the Holy Prophet*, which covers no less than eleven collections of the traditions and three of the earliest historical documents of Islam. One can very well understand the reasons why early Muslims never used this expression. The expression did not appeal to them probably because they thought that it implied a false conception of the historical process. The Magian mind regarded time as a circular movement; the glory of elucidation, the true nature of the historical process as a perpetually creative movement was reserved for the great Muslim thinker and historian, Ibn Khaldun.

The intensity of feeling which the Indian Muslims have manifested in opposition to the Qadiani movement is, therefore, perfectly intelligible to the student of modern sociology. The average Muslim, who was the other day, described as '*Mulla*-ridden' by a writer in *The Civil and Military Gazette* is inspired in his opposition to the movement more by his instinct of self-preservation than by a fuller grasp of the meaning of the idea of Finality in his faith. The so-called 'enlightened' Muslim has seldom made an attempt to understand the real cultural significance of the idea of Finality in Islam, and a process of slow and imperceptible Westernization has farther deprived him even of the instinct of self-preservation. Some of these so-called enlightened Muslims have gone to the extent of preaching 'tolerance' to their brethren-in-faith. I can easily excuse Sir Herbert Emerson for preaching toleration to Muslims; for a modern European who is born and brought up in an entirely different culture does not, and perhaps cannot, develop the insight which makes it possible for one to understand an issue vital to the very structure of a community with an entirely different cultural outlook.

In India circumstances are much more peculiar. This country of religious communities, where the future of each community rests entirely upon its solidarity, is ruled by a Western people who cannot but adopt a policy of non-interference in religion. This liberal and indispensable policy in a country like India has led to most unfortunate results. Insofar as Islam is concerned, it is no exaggeration to say that the solidarity of the Muslim community in India under the British is far less safe than the solidarity of the

Jewish community was in the days of Jesus under the Romans. Any religious adventurer in India can set up any claim and carve out a new community for his own exploitation. This liberal state of ours does not care a fig for the integrity of a parent community, provided the adventurer assures it of his loyalty and his followers are regular in the payment of taxes due to the state. The meaning of this policy for Islam was quite accurately seen by our great poet Akbar, who in his usual humorous strain, says:

گورنمنٹ کی خیربارومناؤ اناالحق کہو اور پھانسی نہ پاؤ

'O friend! pray for the glory of the Briton's name:
Say, "I am God" *sans* chain, *sans* cross, *sans* shame.'

I very much appreciate the orthodox Hindus' demand for protection against religious reformers in the new constitution. Indeed, the demand ought to have been first made by the Muslims who, unlike Hindus, entirely eliminate the race idea from their social structure. The government must seriously consider the present situation and try, if possible, to understand the mentality of the average Muslim in regard to this issue which he regards as absolutely vital to the integrity of his community. After all, if the integrity of a community is threatened, the only course open to that community is to defend itself against the forces of disintegration.

And what are the ways of self-defence?

Controversial writings and refutations of the claims of the man who is regarded by the parent community as a religious adventurer. Is it then fair to preach toleration to the parent community whose integrity is threatened and to allow the rebellious group to carry on its propaganda with impunity, even when the propaganda is highly abusive?

If a group, rebellious from the point of view of the parent community, happens to be of some special service to [the] Government, the latter are at liberty to reward their services as best as they can. Other communities will not grudge it. But it is too much to expect that a community should calmly ignore the forces which tend seriously to affect its collective life. Collective life is as sensitive to the danger of dissolution as individual life. It is hardly necessary to add in this connection that the mutual theological bickerings of Muslim sects do not affect vital principles on which all these sects agree with all their differences in spite of their mutual accusations of heresy.

There is one further point which demands [the] Government's special consideration. The encouragement in India of religious adventurers on the ground of modern liberalism tends to make people more and more indifferent to religion and will eventually completely eliminate the important factor of religion from the life of Indian communities. The Indian mind will then seek some other substitute for religion, which is likely to be nothing less than the form of atheistic materialism which has appeared in Russia.

But the religious issue is not the only issue which is at present agitating the minds of the Punjab Muslims. There are other quarrels of a political nature to which, according to my reading, Sir Herbert Emerson [Governor of the Punjab] hinted in his speech at the Anjuman's [Anjuman Himayat-i-Islam, Lahore] anniversary. These are, no doubt, of a purely political nature, but they affect the unity of Punjab Muslims as seriously as the religious issue. While thanking the Government for their anxiety to see the Punjab Muslims united, I venture to suggest a little self-examination to the Government themselves. Who is responsible, I ask, for the distinction of rural and urban Muslims – a distinction which has cut up the Muslim community into two groups and the rural group into several subgroups constantly at war with one another?

Sir Herbert Emerson deplores the lack of proper leadership among the Punjab Muslims. But I wish Sir Herbert Emerson realized that the rural-urban distinction created by the Government and maintained by them through ambitious political adventurers whose eyes are fixed on their own personal interests and not on the unity of Islam in the Punjab has already made the community incapable of producing a real leader. It appears to me that this device probably originated in a desire rather to make it impossible for real leadership to grow. Sir Herbert Emerson deplores the lack of leadership in Muslims; I deplore the continuation by the Government of a system which has crushed out all hope of a real leader appearing in the province.

Postscript

I understand that this statement has caused some misunderstanding in some quarters. It is thought that I have made a subtle suggestion to the Government to suppress the Qadiani movement by force. Nothing of the kind. I have made it clear that the policy of non-interference in religion is the only policy which can be adopted by the rulers of India. No other policy is possible. I confess, however, that to my mind this policy is harmful to the interests of religious communities; but there is no escape from it and those who suffer will have to safeguard their interests by suitable means. The best course for the rulers of India is, in my opinion, to declare the Qadianis a separate community. This will be perfectly consistent with the policy of the Qadianis themselves, and the Indian Muslim will tolerate them just as he tolerates other religions.

2. Jawaharlal Nehru: 'The Solidarity of Islam'

(*The Modern Review* [1935], Vol. 58, No. 5, pp. 504–05.)

SOME TIME BACK I read with great interest an article by Sir Mohamad Iqbal on the Solidarity of Islam. Sir Mohamad's writings always attract me, for they give me some insight into a world which I find difficult to understand. So far as religion and the religious outlook are concerned, I live in the outer darkness, but, in spite of this deficiency in me, I am sufficiently interested in the historical, cultural and even the philosophical aspects of religion.

In his article Sir Mohamad dealt with the issue created between the Qadianis and the orthodox Muslims and considered this as 'extremely important' and affecting the integrity of the parent community. The Qadianis, according to him, had discarded the basic idea of Islam – the Finality of Prophethood – and had reverted to some extent to early Judaism and the pre-Islamic Magian culture. He was, therefore, of opinion that this 'rebellious group' should not be allowed to carry on its subversive propaganda, and, in any event, should not be permitted to masquerade as Muslims. Qadiani leaders did not accept Sir Mohamad's argument and vigorously repelled some of his statements.

Sir Mohamad's article raises a host of issues and makes one furiously to think in many directions. I hope that he will develop some of his points in future writings, for they deserve a full discussion. For the moment I am concerned with one aspect of his argument only. It would be impertinent of me to discuss the validity or otherwise of this argument from the point of view of Islam. That is a matter for erudite Muslims. For me Sir Mohamad is an authority on Islam worthy of respect and I must assume that he represents the orthodox viewpoint correctly.

If that is so, I presume that Turkey under the Ataturk Kemal has certainly ceased to be an Islamic country in any sense of the word. Egypt has been powerfully influenced by religious reformers who have tried to put on new garments on the ancient truths, and, I imagine, that Sir Mohamad does not approve of this modernist tendency. The Arabs of Syria and Palestine more or less follow Egyptian thought-currents and are partly influenced by Turkey's example. Iran is definitely looking for its cultural inspiration to pre-Islamic Magian days. In all these countries, indeed in every country of western and Middle Asia, nationalist ideas are rapidly growing, usually at the expense of the pure and orthodox religious outlook. Islam, as Sir Mohamad tells us, repudiates the race idea (and of course the geographical idea) and founds itself on the religious idea alone. But in the Islamic countries of western Asia we find today the race and geographical ideas all-powerful. The Turk takes pride in the Turanian race; the Iranian in his own ancient racial traditions; the Egyptian and Syrian (as well as the people of Palestine, Trans-Jordan and Iraq) dream of Arab unity in which the Muslim and Christian Arabs will share.

All this clearly shows that these nations have fallen away from the ideal of Islamic solidarity which Sir Mohamad lays down. Where then does this solidarity exist at present? Not in Central Asia, for in the Soviet parts the breakaway from orthodoxy is far greater; in the Chinese parts the predominant currents are probably nationalist (Turanian) and Soviet. Afghanistan and Arabia proper remain in Asia, and then there are a number of Islamic countries in north Africa, apart from Egypt. How far this orthodox outlook of religious solidarity is prevalent there I do not know, but reports indicate that nationalistic ideas have penetrated even there. And nationalism and the solidarity of Islam do not fit in side by side. Each weakens the other.

From Sir Mohamad's viewpoint this situation in the Islamic world must be a deplorable one. The question of the Qadianis, important as he considers it, sinks into relative insignificance before these world happenings. He stresses the need of a real leader to rise in the Punjab apparently to combat the 'Qadiani menace'. But what lead does he give in regard to the wider menace? The Aga Khan, we are told, is the leader of Indian Muslims. Does he stand for this solidarity of Islam as defined by Sir Mohamad Iqbal?

These questions are relevant even for a non-Muslim; for on the answer to them depends the political, social and economic orientation of Indian Muslims and their reactions to modern ideas and thought-currents, in which some of us are interested. Islam being a world community, its policy must also be a world policy if it is to preserve that sense of solidarity. Sir Mohamad should give us some hint of this policy to meet the nationalist, social and economic problems that confront each country and group.

The only hint he gives in the article is a negative one: that religious reformers should be put down. In this, he tells us, he cordially agrees with the orthodox Hindus, and religions reform is supposed to include all social reform. He makes a provincial suggestion also that the distinction of rural and urban Muslims be abolished, as this interferes with the unity of Islam in the Punjab. Presumably the fact that some Muslims cultivate the fields, some are big landlords and live on rent, some are professional people living in cities, or bankers, or artisans or captains of industry, or labourers, some have an abundance of good things in life while most others starve, will still remain and will not interfere with Islamic unity.

Perhaps it is the object of the recently reformed 'Council of Peers and Moslem Leaders', of which Sir Mohamad Iqbal is a member, to further this unity and the solidarity of Islam. To an outsider it seems a little odd that Christian members of the British House of Lords should be so interested in the progress and solidarity of Islam. But at the lunch at Claridge's in London that followed the formation of this Council, the Aga Khan, we are told, 'developed the theme of Anglo-Moslem unity'. Perhaps the two unities lead into one another, and build up a wider and more embracing unity. It is all very confusing. I wish Sir Mohamad would explain and enlighten us.

Almora District Jail
20 August 1935

3. Jawaharlal Nehru, 'His Highness the Aga Khan'

(*The Modern Review* [1935], Vol. 58, No. 5, pp. 505–07.)

Sir Mohamad Iqbal's earnest plea for the solidarity of Islam and his protest against fissiparous tendencies led me to wonder as to where the line should be drawn. His Highness the Aga Khan is today considered the outstanding leader of the Indian Muslims. The Government treats him and honours him as such, orthodox Muslim leaders, whenever in trouble or faced with difficulty, seek refuge under his sheltering wings. Even Sir Mohamad might, so to speak, be said to march under his political banner. From the point of view of orthodox Islam and its unity of conception, politics, sociology and economics can hardly be separate from religion. One would think, therefore, that the Aga Khan was the ideal representative of this unity and solidarity of religious belief.

Whether this is so I do not know and I should welcome wiser people to inform me. I have long had a vague kind of idea, however, that he hardly belongs to the inner orthodox fold, and I have admired him for the truly wonderful way in which he manages to combine, and gracefully carry in his own person, the most contradictory qualities, and to take part in multifarious activities which appear to be mutually antagonistic and irreconcilable. He is the head and spiritual leader of a widespread and wealthy sect and, I am told, that almost divine attributes are assigned to him by his devoted followers. He is said to derive a vast ecclesiastical revenue from the faithful, and one of his sources of income is supposed to be the granting of spiritual favours and indulgences. It is interesting to find these old-world practices being continued today in an intensive form. But the really remarkable fact is that the spiritual head who supports and encourages these practices is a modern of moderns, highly cultured in Western ways, a prince of the turf, most at home in London and Paris. Only a remarkable personality could successfully carry this double burden. The Aga Khan not only does so with supreme ease, but he adds to it many public and political activities as well as the leadership of the Indian Muslims. That is an astonishing feat which, even though one may disagree with the Aga Khan, fills one with admiration for him.

But the question that is troubling me, as a result of reading Sir Mohamad Iqbal's statement on the solidarity of Islam, is how all this fits in with that solidarity. It may be perfectly justifiable to spend the money of the faithful on racing; that after all is a minor matter. But is the Aga Khan's sect a partner in that Islamic solidarity or not? I remember reading long ago Mark Twain's account of a visit paid by the Aga Khan to him in Bombay. Mark Twain's Indian servant burst into his hotel room one day in a state of extreme excitement and announced that God had come to pay a call on him. Many pray to God daily – and Mark Twain was a religious type of man – and each one of us, according to his early teaching or mental and spiritual development, has his own conception of God. But the best of us are apt to be taken aback by a sudden visitation of the Almighty. Mark Twain, after he had recovered from his initial surprise, discovered that God had come to him in the handsome and corporeal shape of the Aga Khan.

This characterization of the Aga Khan as God was no doubt a foolish error of Mark Twain's servant and the Aga Khan cannot be held responsible for it. So far as I know, he does not claim divinity. But there seem to be a large number of foolish persons about, who ascribe certain divine or semi-divine attributes to him. Some of the propagandists of the sect describe him as an avatar or incarnation of the divinity. They have every right to do so if they believe in it. I have absolutely no complaint. But how does this all fit in with the solidarity of Islam? A story that has long fascinated me is the account of the Aga Khan giving chits or notes of introduction for the Archangel Gabriel to his followers, or some of them. This, so the tale runs, is to ensure their comfort and happiness in the next world. I cannot vouch for the truth of this story, but I do hope that it is based on fact. There is little of romance left in this drab and dreary world, and to correspond with an archangel is a captivating idea. It seems to bring heaven nearer, and even our life here down below assumes a rosier hue.

Then there is another story, not so attractive, but nevertheless extraordinary enough. I had heard of it previously and lately I read an account in a book by an American traveller. Colonel E. Alexander Powell in his *The Last Home of Mystery* referring to the Aga Khan says:

> His sanctity is so great, indeed, in the eyes of his followers that the water in which he bathes is carefully conserved and sold annually to the representatives of the various Mohammedan sects at a ceremony held once each year at Aga Hall in Bombay.

> The price paid for this holy water is the Aga Khan's weight in gold, the scales used for the weighing ceremony being adjusted to the fraction of an ounce troy. As the Aga Khan is a plump little man, the price paid for his used bath water is a high one.

Colonel Powell has probably added some journalistic and fancy touches of his own to this account. But the story is an old and oft-repeated one and, to my knowledge, has never been contradicted. If the Aga Khan can find a profitable use for his bath water and at the same time serve and exalt faith, surely it is no one's business to object. Tastes differ and it takes all sorts to make this world of ours. But again I am led to wonder if all this further the solidarity and 'democracy of Islam'.

Another incident comes to my mind. It was after the War when Kemal Pasha had driven out the Greeks and established himself firmly in power in Turkey. His casual treatment of the new Caliph, appointed by him, drew forth a protest – a very polite protest – from the Aga Khan and Mr Amir Ali. Kemal Pasha scented an English conspiracy and suddenly started a fierce attack on England, the Aga Khan, the Caliph and some Constantinople journalists.[31] He was not very polite to the Aga Khan and drew all manner of unjust inferences from his long and intimate associate with the British Government and ruling classes. He pointed out that the Aga Khan had not been keen on following the previous Caliph's religious mandate when war had broken out between Turkey and England. He even stressed that the Aga Khan was no true Muslim, or at any rate not an orthodox one, for did he not belong to a heretical sect? All this and much more he said, keen on gaining his end, which was to discredit the Aga Khan and make him out to be an accomplice of British foreign policy. And making the Aga Khan's move a pretext, the Ataturk put an end to the ancient Khilafat.

Kemal Pasha can hardly be said to be an authority on Islam, for he has deliberately broken away from many of its tenets. His motives were purely political, but his criticisms were not wholly without apparent force.

As I write this, another aspect of the Aga Khan's many-sided personality comes up before me. It is given in an intimate, everyday account and is thus all the more valuable and revealing. It appears in the London *Bystander* and I have come across it in a quotation in the *New Statesman*. This tells us that,

> Although the Aga Khan loves the good things of life, he is a great gourmet and has his own cook, there is a very considerable spiritual side to his life. It is hard to pin him down exactly on this point. But he will admit to a strong feeling of the battle between good and evil. At any rate, he is a wonderfully good sportsman, and when Jack Joel offered him a blank cheque the other day for Bahram he refused because he said he wanted in his decrepit old age to be wheeled alongside his Derby winner and say, 'Well, that was a jolly day!'

Much to my regret I have never met the Aga Khan. Only once have I seen him. This was in the early non-co-operation days at a Khilafat meeting in Bombay, where I sat not far from him on the platform. But this glimpse of an attractive and remarkable personality was hardly satisfying, and I have often wanted to find out what curious quality he possesses which enables him to fill with distinction so many and such varied roles, combining the thirteenth century with the twentieth, Mecca and Newmarket, this world and the next, spirituality and racing, politics and pleasure. Wide indeed must be the range of Islam to include all this in its unity and solidarity.

But looking at Sir Mohamad Iqbal's statement I am again led to doubt, for Sir Mohamad seems to have little love for the non-conformists. He believes in the straight and narrow path of true orthodoxy and those who stray from this must forthwith remove themselves from his ken. How then am I to remove this doubt and difficulty? Will Sir Mohamad help in solving the riddle?

Almora District Jail
21 August 1935

4. Jawaharlal Nehru, 'Orthodox of All Religions, Unite!'

(*The Modern Review* [1935], Vol. 58, No. 5, pp. 625–31)

SOME YEARS AGO I happened to be in Benares and as I was driving through the narrow city streets, my car was held up by a crowd. A procession was passing through and, apart from the processionists, there were many sightseers and little boys intent on sharing in the fun. Crowds interest me and I got down from the car to find out what was afoot. The procession was certainly an interesting one and it had certain unique features. We saw Brahmans, the most orthodox of their kind, with all manner of caste-marks proudly displayed on their foreheads marching shoulder to shoulder with bearded moulvis, the priests from the ghats fraternized with the mullahs from the mosques, and one of the standards they carried in triumph bore the flaming devise: *Hindu Musalman ekta ki jai* – Victory to Hindu-Muslim Unity! Very gratifying, we thought. But still what was all this about?

We soon found out from the cries and the many other standards they carried. This was a joint protest by the orthodox of both religions against the Sarda Act (or perhaps it was a Bill at the time) which prohibited marriages of girls under fourteen. The pious and the holy of both faiths had joined ranks and bands to declare that they would not submit to this outrage on their deepest convictions and most cherished rights. Were they going to be bullied by the threats of so-called reformers into giving up their right to marry child-wives? Never! Law or no law, they would continue to marry little immature girls – for was not post-puberty marriage a sin? – and thus enhance the glory of religion. Had not a noted Vaidya (physician) of Benares stated that in order to proclaim his adherence to the ancient dharma and his abhorrence of new-fangled notions like the Sarda Act, he, even he, although he was round about sixty years of age, would marry afresh a girl under the prescribed legal age? Faith and religion had built up their great structure on the sacrifice of their votaries. Surely the movement against the Sarda Act would not lack its martyrs.

We moved with the crowd and marched along for some distance by the side of the procession. Devadas Gandhi was with me and some Benares friends and soon we were recognized by the processionists. They did not welcome us or shower greetings on us from the ranks of the faithful – we had neither beards nor caste marks – and we carried on an irreverent and somewhat aggressive commentary on the procession and its sponsors. Offensive slogans were hurled at us and there was some jostling about. Just then the procession arrived at the Town Hall and for some reason or other started stone-throwing. A bright young person thereupon pulled some crackers and this had an extraordinary effect on the serried ranks of the orthodox. Evidently thinking that the police and the military had opened fire, they dispersed and vanished with exceeding rapidity.

A few crackers were enough to put the procession to flight, but not even a cracker was required to make the British Government in India surrender on this issue. A little shouting, in which oddly enough the Muslims took the leading share, was enough to kill and bury the Sarda Act. It was feeble enough at birth with all manner of provisions which hindered its enforcement, and then it gave six months' grace which resulted in a very spate of child marriages. And then, after the six months were over? Nothing happened; child marriages continued as before and the Government and magistrates looked the other way while the Sarda Act was torn to shreds and cast to the dogs. In some instances the person who ventured to bring a breach to a court, himself got into trouble for his pains and was fined. True, in one instance a Punjab villager who had given his ten-year[-old] daughter in marriage and deliberately broken the provisions of the Sarda Act despite warning was sentenced to one month's imprisonment. But this error on the part of the magistrate was soon rectified by the Punjab Government who hastened to send a telegram ordering the release of the offender against the Act (This case has been taken from Miss E.F. Rathbone's interesting little book *Child Marriage*.)

What were we doing all this time? We were in prison. For six years now we have been mostly in prison, sometimes as many as sixty or seventy thousand at a time. Outside, a strict censorship prevailed, meetings were forbidden and an attempt to enter a rural area was almost certain to lead to prison, if not worse. The various emergency laws and denial of civil liberties were certainly not aimed at preventing support of the Sarda Act. But in effect they left the field clear to the opponents of that measure. And the Government in its distress at having to combat a great political movement directed against it, sought allies in the most reactionary of religious and social bigots. To obtain their goodwill the Sarda Act was sat upon, extinguished. *Hindu Musalman ekta ki jai* – Victory to Hindu-Muslim Unity!

The Muslims deserve their full share in this victory. Most of us had thought that the child-wife evil was largely confined to Hindus. But whatever the early disproportion might have been, Muslims were evidently determined not to be outdistanced in this matter as in others, by Hindus. So while on the one hand they claimed more seats in the council, more jobs as policemen, deputy collectors, tahsildars, chaprasis and the like, they hurried on with the work of increasing their child-wives. From the most noted taluqadars in Oudh to the humble workers, they all joined in this endeavour, till at last the 1931 census proclaimed that victory had come to them. The report of the Age of Consent Committee had previously prepared us to revise our previous opinion but the census went much further than had been expected.[32] It told us that Muslims had actually surpassed the Hindus in the proportion of their child-wives. In Assam 'Muslims have now far the largest proportion of child-wives in all the early age groups', in Bihar and Orissa [now Odisha], the census tells us that 'Whereas the proportion of Hindu girl wives (including widows) below the age of ten has increased since 1921 from 103 to 160, among Muslims it has increased from 76 to 202.' Truly a triumph for the Sarda Act and the Government that is supposed to enforce it.

Lest it be said that our enlightened Indian states lag behind on this issue the Government of Mysore has recently made its position clear. A venturesome member sought to introduce a Child Marriage Restraint Bill on the lines of the Sarda Act, in the Mysore Council. The motion was stoutly opposed by a Dewan Bahadur on behalf of Muslims. The Government generously permitted the official members to vote as they liked but, oddly enough, the entire official bloc, including two European members, voted against the motion and with their votes helped to defeat it. Religion was again saved.

This instance of the Sarda Act was a revealing one, for it showed that all the shouting about Hindu-Muslim friction and disunity was exaggerated and, in any event misdirected. That there was such friction nobody could deny, but it was the outcome not so much of religious differences as of economic distress, unemployment, and a race for jobs, which put on a sanctified garb and in the name of religion deluded and excited the masses. If the difference had been essentially religious, one would have thought that the orthodox of the two faiths would be the farthest removed from each other and the most hostile to each other's pretensions. As a matter of fact they combine frequently enough to combat any movement of reform, social, economic, political. Both look upon the person who wants to change the existing order in any way as the real enemy; both cling desperately and rather pathetically to the British Government for instinctively they realize that they are in the same boat with it.

Nearly twenty-two years ago before the War, in January 1914 the Aga Khan wrote an article in the *Edinburgh Review* on the Indian situation. He advised the Government to abandon the policy of separating Hindus from Muslims and to rally the moderate of both creeds in a common camp so as to provide a counterpoise to the radical nationalist tendencies of young India, both Hindu and Muslim. In those days extremism was confined to nationalism and did not go beyond the political plane. Even so the Aga Khan sensed that the vital division lay not along religious lines but along political – between those who more or less stood for British domination in India and others who desired to end it. That nationalist issue still dominates the field and is likely to do so as long as India remains politically unfree. But today other issues have also assumed prominence – social and economic. If radical political change was feared by the moderate and socially backward elements much more are they terrified by the prospect of social and economic change. Indeed it is the fear of the latter that has reacted on the political issue and made many a so-called advanced politician retrace his steps. He has in some cases become, frankly, a reactionary in politics, or a camouflaged reactionary like the communalists, or an open champion of his class interest and vested rights, like the big zamindars and taluqadars and industrialists.

I have no doubt that this process will continue and will lead to the toning down of communal and religious animosities, to Hindu-Muslim unity – of a kind. The communalists of various groups, in spite of their mutual hostility, will embrace each other like long-lost brothers and swear fealty in a new joint campaign against those who are out for radical change, politically or socially or economically. The new alignment will be a healthier one and the issues will be clearer. The indications towards some such grouping are already visible, though they will take some time to develop.

Sir Mohamad Iqbal, the champion of the solidarity of Islam, is in cordial agreement with orthodox Hindus in some of their most reactionary demands. He writes: 'I very much appreciate the orthodox Hindus' demands for protection against religious reformers in the new constitution. Indeed this demand ought to have been first made by the Muslims.' He further explains that 'the encouragement in India of religious adventurers on the ground of modern liberalism tends to make people more and more indifferent to religion and will eventually completely eliminate the important factor of religion from the life of the Indian community. The Indian mind will then seek some other substitute for religion which is likely to be nothing less than the form of atheistic materialism which has appeared in Russia.'

This fear of communism has driven many liberals and other middle groups in Europe to fascism and reaction. Even the old enemies, the Jesuits and the Freemasons, have covered up their bitter hostility of two hundred years to face the common enemy. In India communism and socialism are understood by relatively very few persons and most people who shout loudest against them are supremely ignorant about them. But they are influences partly instinctively because of their vested interests and partly because of the propaganda on the part of the Government, which always stresses the religious issue.

Sir Mohamad Iqbal's argument, however, takes us very much further than merely anti-communism or anti-socialism and it is worthwhile examining it in some detail. His position on this issue of suppression of all reformers is, it should be remembered, almost the same as that of the Sanatanist Hindus. And even a party which presumes to call itself democratic or nationalist (or perhaps some other name – it is difficult to keep pace with the periodic transformations of half a dozen worthy gentlemen in western India) declared recently in its programme that it was opposed to all legislative interference with religious rights and customs. In India this covers a wide field and there are few departments of life which cannot be connected to religion. Not to interfere with them legislatively is a mild way of saying that the orthodox may continue in every way as before and no changes will be permitted.

Sir Mohamad would go further, for Islam, according to him, does not believe in tolerance. Its solidarity consists in a certain uniformity which does not permit any heresy or non-conformists within the fold. Hinduism is utterly different because, in spite of a common culture and outlook, it lacks uniformity and for thousands of years has actually encouraged the formation of innumerable sects. It is difficult to define heresy when almost every conceivable variation of the central theme is held by some sect. This outlook of Islam is probably comparable to that of the Roman Catholic Church. Both think in terms of a world community swearing allegiance to one definite doctrine and are not prepared to tolerate any deviation from it. A person belonging to an entirely different religion is preferable to a heretic for a heretic creates confusion in the minds of true believers. Therefore, a heretic must be shown no quarter and his ideas must be suppressed. That essentially has always been and still is the belief of the Catholic Church but its practice has been toned down to meet modern liberal notions. When the practice fitted in with the theory it led to the Spanish Inquisition, the *autos da fe* [act of faith], and various crusades and wars against Christian non-conformists in Europe. The Inquisition has a bad odour now and we shiver to think of its cruelties. Yet it was carried on by high-minded, deeply religious men who never thought of personal gain. They believed with all their intensity of religious conviction that the heretic would go to hell if he persisted in his error and with all their might they sought to save his immortal soul from the eternal pit. What did it matter if in this attempt the body was made to suffer?

Islam is obviously different from the Roman Catholic Church because it has no Pope, no regular priesthood and not so many dogmas. But I imagine that the general exclusive intolerant outlook is the same and it would approve of heresy hunts for the suppression of the evil before it spread. Cardinal Newman denying the nineteenth-century assumption of the progress of our race said that our races progress and perfectibility is a dream because revelation contradicts it.[33] Further, he said that it would be a gain to this country were it vastly more superstitious, more bigoted, more gloomy, more fierce in its religion than at present it shows itself to be. He was referring to England.

I wonder how far Sir Mohamad Iqbal would accept Cardinal Newman's dictum, applying to Islam of course. I imagine that quite a large number of both Hindus and Muslims would agree with the Cardinal, each thinking in terms of his own religion. Indeed, I should say that most truly religious people belonging to almost any organized religion would agree with him. Personally I entirely disagree with him because my outlook is not that of religion. But I think I can dimly understand the religious outlook and to some extent even appreciate it. Granting the supreme importance of certain dogmas and beliefs, the rest seems to follow. If I am absolutely convinced that a thing is evil it is absurd to talk about tolerating it. It must be suppressed, removed, liquidated. If I believe that this world is a snare and a delusion and the only reality is the next world, then the question of progress or change here below hardly arises. Because I have no such absolute convictions and the beliefs I hold in matters of theological and metaphysical religions are negative rather than positive, I can easily pose as a tolerant individual. It costs me nothing in mental suppression or anguish. It is far more difficult for me to be tolerant about other matters relating to this world in regard to which I hold positive opinions. But even then the opinion has not got the intensity of religious belief and so I am not likely to favour inquisitional methods for the suppression of opinions and beliefs I consider harmful. Not being interested in the other world, whatever it may be, I judge largely by the effects I observe in this world. I am unable, therefore, to find a supernatural sanction for inflicting cruelty, physical or mental, here below. Perhaps also, most of us of the modern world (facists and Hitlerites excluded) are far more squeamish in the matter of causing pain or even watching it with unconcern than our stout old ancestors were.

Thus we make a virtue of our interference and call it tolerance just as the British Government takes credit for impartiality and neutrality in matters of religion, when in reality it is supremely indifferent to them so long as its secular interests are not touched. But there is no shadow of toleration when its administration is criticized or condemned. That is sedition to be expiated by long years of prison.

Sir Mohamad Iqbal would thus like to have, so far as Muslims are concerned, a strict uniformity and conformity enforced by the power of the state. But who would lay down the common standard which was to be followed? Would there be a kind of permanent commission of the Jamiat-ul-Ulema advising the secular arm, as the Roman Church used to advise the princes of Europe in the days of its temporal glory? Sir Mohamad, however, does not seem to approve of the present generation of moulvis and ulemas. He says that 'in the modern world of Islam ambitious and ignorant mullaism taking advantage of modern Press, has shamelessly attempted to hurl the old pre-Islamic Magian outlook at the face of the twentieth century'. On the other hand he expresses his sorrowful contempt for the 'so-called "enlightened" Muslims', who 'have gone to the extent of preaching "tolerance" to their brethren in faith'.

The election or nomination of competent authority to interpret the ecclesiastical law under modern conditions will be no easy matter, and it is well known that even the pious and the orthodox often disagree among themselves. Orthodoxy ultimately becomes one's own doxy, and the other person's doxy is heterodoxy.

If such an authority is established it will deal presumably with the Muslims alone. But Islam is a proselytizing religion and questions touching other faiths will frequently arise. Even now doubtful cases arise, especially relating to girls and women who, with little thought of religion, marry a Muslim or elope with him or are abducted by him. If they slide back from the strict path of the faith, are they to be subjected to the terrible punishment for apostasy?

In the purely religious sphere then we might have, if Sir Mohamad's suggestions were carried out, 'the institution of a kind of Inquisition with heresy hunts, excommunication, punishment for apostasy, and a general suppression of so-called "enlightened Muslims" and a prohibition of the practice or teaching of "tolerance"'. Other spheres of life would be equally affected for Islam and Hinduism do not believe in confining themselves to Sunday observance. They are weekday religions invading every department of life.

The next step is obviously one of full application of the personal law in strict accordance with the ancient texts. In theory, this personal law is still applied both to Hindus and Muslims in the British courts, but in practice many changes have crept in. The criminal law at present prevailing in the country has very little or perhaps nothing to do with the old Muslim or Hindu codes. In civil law, the divergence is not marked and inheritance, marriage, divorce, adoption, etc., are supposed to be according to the old directions. But even here some changes have crept in and attempts are constantly being made to widen their range (civil marriage, divorce among Hindus, Sarda Act, etc.). In regard to inheritance, there is a very curious Oudh Estate Act affecting the Oudh taluqadars, which lays down a peculiar and unique rule which is applied equally to Hindu, Muslim or Christian taluqadars.

This tendency to drift away from the old personal law will have to be stopped if the orthodox have their way. An attempt to do so is now being made by the Frontier Province Council where a 'Moslem Personal law (Shariat) Application Bill' was recently referred to a Select Committee for report. I have no idea what happened to this Bill afterwards. In the course of a debate in the Council on this Bill, a speaker 'analysing the fundamental principles of Islam' said that 'if the Bill were passed they would have to see the law was carried out strictly in accordance with the Shariat'. He was opposed to the partial enforcement of the Shariat and wanted its full enforcement.

The demand that only a Muslim should administer the Shariat seems reasonable, for non-Moslims can hardly enter into its spirit. If the Moslims have their separate courts with their *qazi*s, there is no valid ground for refusing the same privilege to the Hindus or any other religious group. We shall thus have a number of courts of law functioning independently in each geographical area for each separate group. It will be something like the capitulation of semi-colonial countries but in a greatly exaggerated form, for the whole population will be divided up and not merely by some foreigners. Perhaps that will be a logical development of our communal separate electorates.

Each group of these separate courts will have its own laws and methods of procedure. Some difficulties will no doubt arise when the parties involved belong to different religious groups. Which court are they to go to and which law to follow? Perhaps mixed courts will grow up to deal with such cases and some kind of amalgam of laws and procedure be adopted by these courts. Criminal cases are likely to prove especially troublesome. If a Hindu steals a Muslim's property, whose law is to be applied? Or in the case of adultery where the persons profess different religions. The choice between the two codes might have serious consequences for the punishments might vary greatly between them. I am not sure what punishment Manu has laid down for theft or adultery, but I have an idea (I write subject to correction) that according to the old Islamic law, following Mosaic parallels, the thief has his hand cut off and the adulterers must be stoned to death.

It seems to me that all this will produce a certain confusion in our administration of justice, there will be considerable overlapping and friction. But it may lead indirectly to one good result. For more lawyers will be needed to unravel, or at any rate to profit by, the tangled web of laws and procedures, and thus perhaps we might lessen to some extent the widespread unemployment among our middle classes.

Other far-reaching consequences would follow the adoption and application of the joint views of Sir Mohamad Iqbal and the *sanatanist* Hindus. The ideals aimed at will largely be (subject to some inevitable adjustment with modern conditions) the reproduction of the social conditions prevailing in Arabia in the seventh century (in the case of the Muslims) or those of India two thousand or more years ago (in the case of Hindus). With all the goodwill in the world, a complete return to the golden ages of the past will not be possible, but at any rate all avoidable deviations will be prevented and an attempt will be made to stereotype our social and economic structure and make it incapable of change. So-called reform movements will, of course, be frowned upon or suppressed. The long tentacles of the law of sedition may grow longer still and new crimes may be created. Thus to advocate the abolition of the purdah (veil) by women might (from the Muslim side) be made into an offence, to preach the loosening of caste restrictions or inter-dining might (from the *sanatanist* side) be also made criminal. Beards may become de rigueur for Muslims, caste-marks and top knots for Hindus. And, of course, all the orthodox of all shapes and hues would join in the worship and service of Property, especially the extensive and wealthy properties and endowments belonging to religious or semi-religious bodies.

Perhaps all this is a somewhat exaggerated picture of what might happen under the joint regime of the *sanatanists* and the ulemas, but it is by no means a fanciful picture as anyone who has followed their recent activities can demonstrate. Only two months ago (in June 1935) a Sanatan Dharma Conference was held in Bezwada [Vijayawada]. The holy and learned Swami who opened the Conference told us that 'co-education, divorce and post-puberty marriages would mean the annihilation of Hinduism'. I had not realized till then that these three or rather the absence of them, were the main props of Hinduism – this is rather involved but I suppose my meaning is clear. The chairman of the Reception Committee of that Conference further told us that he 'viewed with grave concern the growth of the Indian women's movement and asserted that the women who were fighting for equal rights with men did not represent the real women of India. They are merely agitators who have thrown modesty – the outstanding quality of Indian women – to the winds.'

I am afraid I cannot bring myself to agree with Sir Mohamad Iqbal and the *sanatanists.* Partly, the reason perhaps is a personal and selfish one. I do not think I shall get on at all under their joint regime, I may even land myself in prison. I have spent a long enough period of my life in prison under the British Government and I see no particular reason why I should add to it under the new dispensation. But my personal fate is of little account, what matters is the larger theme of India and her millions. It is an astonishing thing to me that while our millions starve and live like beasts of the field, we ignore their lot and talk of vague metaphysical ideas and the good of their souls; that we shirk the problems of today in futile debate about yesterday and the day before yesterday; that when thoughtful men and women all over the world are considering problems of human welfare and how to lessen human misery and stupidity, we, who need betterment and raising most, should think complacently of what our ancestors did thousands of years ago and for ourselves should continue to grovel on the ground. It astonishes me that a poet like Sir Mohamad Iqbal should be insensitive to the suffering that surrounds him, that a scholar and thinker like Sir Mohamad should put forward fantastic schemes of states within states, and advocate a social structure which may have suited a past age but is a hopeless anachronism today. Does his reading of history not tell him that nations fell because they could not adapt themselves to changing conditions and because they stuck too long to that very structure which he wants to introduce in a measure in India today? We were not wise enough in India and the other countries of the East in the past, and we have suffered for our folly. Are we to be so singularly foolish as not even to profit by our and others' experience?

Bertrand Russell says somewhere: 'If existing knowledge were used and tested methods applied, we could in a generation produce a population almost wholly free from disease, malevolence and stupidity. In one generation, if we chose, we could bring in the millennium.'[34] It is the supreme tragedy of our lives that this millennium should be within our reach, so tantalizingly near us and yet so far as almost to seem unattainable. I do not know what the future has in store for India and her unhappy people, what further agonies, what greater humiliation and torture of the soul. But I am confident of this that whatever happens, we cannot go back inside the shell out of which we have emerged.

Almora District Jail
23 August 1935

5. Muhammad Iqbal's Reply to Questions Raised by Pandit J.L. Nehru

(As reprinted in Shamloo [ed.], *Speeches and Statements of Iqbal*, Lahore: Al Manar Academy, 1944, pp. 111–44.)

On the appearance of Pandit Jawahar Lal Nehru's three articles in *The Modern Review* of Calcutta I received a number of letters from Muslims of different shades of religious and political opinion. Some writers of these letters want me to further elucidate and justify the attitude of the Indian Muslims towards the Ahmadis. Others ask me what exactly I regard as the issue involved in Ahmadism. In this statement I propose first to meet these demands which I regard as perfectly legitimate, and then to answer the questions raised by Pandit Jawahar Lal Nehru. I fear, however, that parts of this statement may not interest the Pandit, and to save his time I suggest that he may skip over such parts.

It is hardly necessary for me to say that I welcome the Pandit's interest in what I regard as one of the greatest problems of the East and perhaps of the whole world. He is, I believe, the first nationalist Indian leader who has expressed a desire to understand the present spiritual unrest in the world of Islam. In view of the many aspects and possible reactions of this unrest, it is highly desirable that thoughtful Indian political leaders should open their mind to the real meaning of what is, at the present moment, agitating the heart of Islam.

I do not wish, however, to conceal the fact either from the Pandit or from any other reader of this statement that the Pandit's articles have for the moment given my mind rather a painful conflict of feelings. Knowing him to be a man of wide cultural sympathies my mind cannot but incline to the view that his desire to understand the questions he has raised is perfectly genuine; yet the way in which he has expressed himself betrays a psychology which I find difficult to attribute to him. I am inclined to think that my statement on Qadianism – no more than a mere exposition of a religious doctrine on modern lines – has embarrassed both the Pandit and the Qadianis, perhaps because both inwardly resent, for different reasons, the prospects of Muslim political and religious solidarity particularly in India. It is obvious that the Indian nationalist whose political idealism has practically killed his sense for fact, is intolerant of the birth of a desire for self-determination in the heart of north-west Indian Islam. He thinks, wrongly in my opinion, that the only way to Indian nationalism lies in a total suppression of the cultural entities of the country through the interaction of which alone India can evolve a rich and enduring culture. A nationalism achieved by such methods can mean nothing but mutual bitterness and even oppression. It is equally obvious that the Qadianis, too, feel nervous by the political awakening of the Indian Muslims, because they feel that the rise in political prestige of the Indian Muslims is sure to defeat their designs to carve out from the *Ummat* of the Arabian Prophet a new *Ummat* for the Indian prophet. It is no small surprise to me that my effort to impress on the Indian Muslims the extreme necessity of internal cohesion in the present critical moment of their history in India, and my warning them against the forces of disintegration, masquerading as Reformist movements, should have given the Pandit an occasion to sympathize with such forces.

However, I do not wish to pursue the unpleasant task of analysing the Pandit's motives. For the benefit of those who want further elucidation of the general Muslim attitude towards the Qadianis, I would quote a passage from Durant's *Story of Philosophy* which I hope will give the reader a clearer idea of the issue involved in Qadianism. Durant has in a few sentences summed up the Jewish point of view in the excommunication of the great philosopher, Spinoza. The reader must not think that in quoting this passage I mean to insinuate some sort of comparison between Spinoza and the founder of Ahmadism. The distance between them, both in point of intellect and character, is simply tremendous. The 'God-intoxicated' Spinoza never claimed that he was the centre of a new organization and that all the Jews who did not believe in him were outside the pale of Judaism. Durant's passage, therefore, applies with much greater force to the attitude of Muslims towards Qadianism than to the attitude of the Jews towards the excommunication of Spinoza. The passage is as follows:

> Furthermore, religious unanimity seemed to the elders their sole means of preserving the little Jewish group in Amsterdam from disintegration, and almost the last means of preserving the unity, and so, ensuring the survival of the scattered Jews of the world. If they had had their own state, their own civil law, their own establishments of secular force and power, to compel internal cohesion and external respect, they might have been more tolerant; but their religion was to them their patriotism as well as their faith; the synagogue was their centre of social and political life as well as of ritual and worship; and the Bible whose veracity Spinoza had impugned was the 'Portable Fatherland' of their people; under the circumstances they thought heresy was treason, and toleration suicide.

Situated as the Jews were – a minority community in Amsterdam – they were perfectly justified in regarding Spinoza as a disintegrating factor threatening [to dissolve] their community. Similarly, the Indian

Muslims are right in regarding the Qadiani movement, which declares the entire world of Islam as kafir and socially boycotts them, to be far more dangerous to the collective life of Islam in India than the metaphysics of Spinoza to the collective life of the Jews. The Indian Muslim, I believe, instinctively realizes the peculiar nature of the circumstances in which he is placed in India and is naturally much more sensitive to the forces of disintegration than the Muslims of any other country. This instinctive perception of the average Muslim is, in my opinion, absolutely correct and has, I have no doubt, a much deeper foundation in the conscience of Indian Islam. Those who talk of toleration in a matter like this are extremely careless in using the word 'toleration' which I fear they do not understand at all. The spirit of toleration may arise from very different attitudes of the mind of man. As Gibbon would say: 'There is the toleration of the philosopher to whom all religions are equally true; of the historian to whom all are equally false; and of the politician to whom all are equally useful. There is the toleration of the man who tolerates other modes of thought and behaviour because he has himself grown absolutely indifferent to all modes of thought and behaviour. There is the toleration of the weak man who, on account of sheer weakness, must pocket all kinds of insults heaped on things or persons whom he holds dear. It is obvious that these types of tolerance have no ethical value. On the other hand, they unmistakably reveal the spiritual impoverishment of the man who practises them. True toleration is begotten of intellectual breadth and spiritual expansion. It is the toleration of the spiritually powerful than who, while jealous of the frontiers of his own faith, can tolerate and even appreciate all forms of faith other than his own.' Of this type of toleration the true Muslim alone is capable. His own faith is synthetic and for this reason he can easily find grounds of sympathy and appreciation in other faiths. Our great Indian poet, Amir Khusrau, beautifully brings out the essence of this type of toleration in the story of an idol-worshipper. After giving an account of his intense attachment to his idols the poet addresses his Muslim readers as follows:

اے کہ ابت طعنہ بہ ھندوبری

ھم زوے اموز پرستش کری

'O you, who is accusing a Hindu of idolatry,
Go learn the method of worship from him!'

Only a true lover of God can appreciate the value of devotion even though it is directed to gods in which he himself does not believe. The folly of our preachers of toleration consists in describing the attitude of the man who is jealous of the boundaries of his own faith as one of intolerance. They wrongly consider this attitude as a sign of moral inferiority. They do not understand that the value of his attitude is essentially biological. Where the members of a group feel, either instinctively or on the basis of rational argument, that the corporate life of the social organism to which they belong is in danger, their defensive attitude must be appraised in reference mainly to a biological criterion. Every thought or deed in this connection must be judged by the life-value that it may possess. The question in this case is not whether the attitude of an individual or community towards the man who is declared to be a heretic is morally good or bad. The question is whether it is life-giving or life-destroying.

Pandit Jawahar Lal Nehru seems to think that a society founded on religious principles necessitates the institution of Inquisition. This is indeed true of the history of Christianity; but the history of Islam, contrary to the Pandit's logic, shows that during the last thirteen hundred years of the life of Islam, the institution of Inquisition has been absolutely unknown in Muslim countries. The Qur'an expressly prohibits such an institution: 'Do not seek out the shortcomings of others and carry not tales against your brethren.' Indeed the Pandit will find from the history of Islam that the Jews and Christians, fleeing from religious persecution in their own lands, always found shelter in the lands of Islam. The two propositions on which the conceptual structure of Islam is based are so simple that it makes heresy in the sense of turning the heretic outside the fold of Islam almost impossible. It is true that when a person declared to be holding heretical doctrines threatens the existing social order, an independent Muslim state will certainly take action; but in such a case the action of the state will be determined more by political considerations than by purely religious ones.

I can very well realize that a man like the Pandit, who is born and brought up in a society which has no well-defined boundaries and consequently no internal cohesion, finds it difficult to conceive that a religious society can live and prosper without state-appointed commissions of inquiry into the beliefs of the people. This is quite clear from the passage which he quotes from Cardinal Newman and wonders how far I would accept the application of the Cardinal's dictum to Islam. Let me tell him that there is a tremendous difference between the inner structure of Islam and Catholicism wherein the complexity, the ultra-rational character and the number of dogmas has, as the history of Christianity shows, always fostered possibilities of fresh heretical interpretations.

The simple faith of Mohammad is based on two propositions – that God is One, and that Mohammad is the last of the line of those holy men who have appeared from time to time in all countries and in all ages to guide mankind to the right ways of living. If, as some Christian writers think, a dogma must be defined as an ultra-rational proposition which, for the purpose of securing religious solidarity, most be assented to without any understanding of its metaphysical import, then these two simple propositions of Islam cannot be described even as dogmas; for both of them are supported by the experience of mankind and are fairly amenable to rational argument. The question of a heresy, which needs the verdict whether the author of it is within or without the fold, can arise, in the case of a religious society founded on such simple propositions, only when the heretic rejects both or either of these propositions.

Such heresy must be and has been rare in the history of Islam which, while jealous of its frontiers, permits freedom of interpretation within these frontiers. And since the phenomenon of the kind of heresy which affects the boundaries of Islam has been rare in the history of Islam, the feeling of the average Muslim is naturally intense when a revolt of this kind arises. That is why the feeling of Muslim Persia was so intense against the Bahais. That is why the feeling of the Indian Muslims is so intense against the Qadianis.

It is true that mutual accusations of heresy for differences in minor points of law and theology among Muslim religious sects have been rather common. In this indiscriminate use of the word *kufr*, both for minor theological points of difference as well as for the extreme cases of heresy which involve the excommunication of the heretic, some present-day educated Muslims, who possess practically no knowledge of the history of Muslim theological disputes, see a sign of social and political disintegration of the Muslim community. This, however, is an entirely wrong notion. The history of Muslim theology shows that mutual accusation of heresy on minor points of difference has, far from working as a disruptive force, actually given an impetus to synthetic theological thought. 'When we read the history of development of Muhammaden Law,' says Professor Hurgronje, 'we find that, on the one hand, the doctors of every age, on the slightest stimulus, condemn one another to the point of mutual accusations of heresy; and, on the other hand, the very same people with greater and greater unity of purpose try to reconcile the similar quarrels of their predecessors.' The student of Muslim theology knows that among Muslim legists this kind of heresy is technically known as 'heresy below heresy', i.e., the kind of heresy which does not involve the excommunication of the culprit. It may be admitted, however, that in the hands of *mullas* whose intellectual laziness takes all oppositions of theological thought as absolute and is consequently blind to the unity in difference, this minor heresy may become a source of great mischief. This mischief can be remedied only by giving to the students of our theological schools a clearer vision of the synthetic spirit of Islam, and by re-initiating them into the function of logical contradiction as a principle of movement in theological dialectic.

The question of what may be called major heresy arises only when the teaching of a thinker or a reformer affects the frontiers of the faith of Islam. Unfortunately, this question does arise in connection with the teachings of Qadianism. It must be pointed out here that the Ahmadi movement is divided into two camps known as the Qadianis and the Lahoris. The former openly declare the founder to be a full prophet; the latter, either by conviction or policy, have found it advisable to preach an apparently toned-down Qadianism. However, the question whether the founder of Ahmadism was a prophet the denial of whose mission entails what I call the 'major heresy' is a matter of dispute between the two sections. It is unnecessary for my purposes to judge the merits of this domestic controversy of the Ahmadis. I believe, for reasons to be explained presently, that the idea of a full prophet whose denial entails the denier's excommunication from Islam is essential to Ahmadism; and that the present head of the Qadianis is far more consistent with the spirit of the movement than the Imam of the Lahoris.

The cultural value of the idea of Finality in Islam I have fully explained elsewhere. Its meaning is simple: No spiritual surrender to any human being after Mohammad who emancipated his followers by giving them a law which is realizable as arising from the very core of human conscience. Theologically, the doctrine is that the socio-political organization called 'Islam' is perfect and eternal. No revelation the denial of which entails heresy is possible after Mohammad. He who claims such a revelation is a traitor to Islam. Since the Qadianis believe the founder of the Ahmadiyyah movement to be the bearer of such a revelation, they declare that the entire world of Islam is infidel. The founder's own argument, quite worthy of a mediaeval theologian, is that the spirituality of the Holy Prophet of Islam must be regarded as imperfect if it is not creative of another prophet. He claims his own prophethood to be an evidence of the prophet-rearing power of the spirituality of the Holy Prophet of Islam. But if you further ask him whether the spirituality of Muhammad is capable of rearing more prophets than one, his answer is 'No'. This virtually amounts to saying: 'Muhammad is not the last Prophet; I am the last.'

Far from understanding the cultural value of the Islamic idea of Finality in the history of mankind generally and of Asia especially, he thinks that finality in the sense that no follower of Mohammad can ever reach the status of prophethood is a mark of imperfection in Mohammad's prophethood. As I read the psychology of his mind, he, in the interest of his own claim to prophethood, avails himself of what he describes as the creative spirituality of the Holy Prophet of Islam and, at the same time, deprives the Holy Prophet of his 'finality' by limiting the creative capacity of his spirituality to the rearing of only one prophet, i.e., the founder of the Ahmadiyyah movement. In this way does the new prophet quietly steal away the 'finality' of one whom he claims to be his spiritual progenitor.

He claims to be a *buruz* (بروز), (spiritual manifestation), of the Holy Prophet of Islam insinuating thereby that, being a *buruz* of him, his 'finality' is virtually the 'finality' of Mohammad; and that this view of the matter, therefore, does not violate the 'finality' of the Holy Prophet. In identifying the two finalities, his own and that of the Holy Prophet, he conveniently loses sight of the temporal meaning of the idea of Finality. It is, however, obvious that the word *buruz*, in the sense even of complete likeness, cannot help him at all; for the *buruz* must always remain the other side of its original. Only in the sense of reincarnation a *buruz* becomes identical with the original. Thus if we take the word *buruz* to mean 'like in spiritual qualities' the argument remains ineffective; if, on the other hand, we take it to mean reincarnation of the original in the Aryan sense of the word, the argument becomes plausible; but its author turns out to be only a Magian in disguise.

It is further claimed on the authority of the great Muslim mystic, Muhyuddin ibn Arabi of Spain, that it is possible for a Muslim saint to attain, in his spiritual evolution, to the kind of experience characteristic of the prophetic consciousness. I personally believe this view of Shaikh Muhyuddin ibn Arabi to be psychologically unsound; but assuming it to be correct the Qadiani argument is based on a complete misunderstanding of his exact position. The Shaikh regards it as a purely private achievement which does not, and in the nature of things cannot, entitle such a saint to declare that all those who do not believe in him are outside the pale of Islam. Indeed, from the Shaikh's point of view, there may be more than one saint, living in the same age or country, who may attain prophetic consciousness. The point to be seized is that, while it is psychologically possible for a saint to attain to prophetic experience, his experience will have no socio-political significance making him the centre of a new organization and entitling him to declare this organization to be the criterion of the faith or disbelief of the followers of Mohammad.

Leaving his mystical psychology aside, I am convinced from a careful study of the relevant passages of the *Futuhat* that the great Spanish mystic is as firm a believer in the Finality of Mohammad as any orthodox Muslim. And if he had seen in his mystical vision that one day in the East some Indian amateurs in Sufism would seek to destroy the Holy Prophet's finality under cover of his mystical psychology, he would have certainly anticipated the Indian *ulama* in warning the Muslims of the world against such traitors to Islam.

Coming now to the essence of Ahmadism. A discussion of its sources and of the way in which pre-Islamic Magian ideas have, through the channels of Islamic mysticism, worked on the mind of its author would be extremely interesting from the standpoint of comparative religion. It is, however, impossible for me to undertake this discussion here. Suffice it to say that the real nature of Ahmadism is hidden behind the mist of mediaeval mysticism and theology. The Indian ulama, therefore, took it to be a purely theological movement and came out with theological weapons to deal with it. I believe, however, that this was not the proper method of dealing with the movement; and that the success of the ulama was, therefore, only partial. A careful psychological analysis of the revelations of the founder would perhaps be an effective method of dissecting the inner life of his personality.

In this connection, I may mention Maulvi Manzur Elahi's collection of the founder's revelations which offers rich and varied material for psychological research. In my opinion, the book provides a key to the character and personality of the founder; and I do hope that one day some young student of modern psychology will take it up for serious study. If he takes the Qur'an for his criterion, as he must for reasons which cannot be explained here, and extends his study to a comparative examination of the experiences of the founder of the Ahmadiyyah movement and contemporary non-Muslim mystics, such as Rama Krishna of Bengal, he is sure to meet more than one surprise as to the essential character of the experience on the basis of which prophethood is claimed for the originator of Ahmadism.

Another equally effective and more fruitful method, from the standpoint of the plain man, is to understand the real content of Ahmadism in the light of the history of Muslim theological thought in India at least from the year 1799. The year 1799 is extremely important in the history of the world of Islam. In this year fell Tippu, and his fall meant the extinguishment of Muslim hopes for political prestige in India. In the same year was fought the battle of Navarneo which saw the destruction of the Turkish fleet. Prophetic were the words of the author of the chronogram of Tippu's fall which visitors of Serangapatam find engraved on the wall of Tippu's mausoleum: 'Gone is the glory of Ind as well as of Roum.' Thus in the year 1799 the political decay of Islam in Asia reached its climax. But just as out of the humiliation of Germany on the day of Jena arose the modern German nation, it may be said with equal truth that out of the political humiliation of Islam in the year 1799 arose modern Islam and her problems. This point I shall explain in the sequel. For the present I want to draw the reader's attention to some of the questions which have arisen in Muslim India since the fall of Tippu and the development of European imperialism in Asia.

Does the idea of Caliphate in Islam embody a religious institution? How are the Indian Muslims, and for the matter of that all Muslims outside the Turkish Empire, related to the Turkish Caliphate? Is India *Dar-ul-Harb* or *Dar-ul-Islam*? What is the real meaning of the doctrine of Jihad in Islam? What is the meaning of the expression 'From amongst you' in the Qur'anic verse: 'Obey God, obey the Prophet and the masters of the affair, i.e., rulers, from amongst you?' What is the character of the Traditions of the Prophet foretelling the advent of Imam Mehdi? These questions and some others which arose subsequently were, for obvious reasons, questions for Indian Muslims only. European imperialism, however, which was then rapidly penetrating the world of Islam, was also intimately interested in them. The controversies which these questions created form a most interesting chapter in the history of Islam in India. The story is a long one and is still waiting for a powerful pen.

Muslim politicians whose eyes were mainly fixed on the realities of the situation succeeded in winning over a section of the ulama to adopt a line of theological argument which, as they thought, suited the situation; but it was not easy to conquer by mere logic the beliefs which had ruled for centuries the conscience of the masses of Islam in India. In such a situation logic can either proceed on the ground of political expediency or on the lines of a fresh orientation of texts and traditions. In either case the argument will fail to appeal to the masses. To the intensely religious masses of Islam, only one thing can make a conclusive appeal, and that is Divine Authority. For an effective eradication of orthodox beliefs it was found necessary to find a revelational basis for a politically suitable orientation of theological doctrines involved in the questions mentioned above. This revelational basis is provided by Ahmadism. And the Ahmadis themselves claim this to be the greatest service rendered by them to British imperialism. The prophetic claim to a revelational basis for theological views of a political significance amounts to declaring that those who do not accept the claimant's views are infidels of the first water and destined for the flames of hell.

As I understand the significance of the movement, the Ahmadi belief that Christ died the death of an ordinary mortal, and that his second advent means only the advent of a person who is spiritually 'like unto him', give the movement some sort of a rational appearance; but they are not really essential to the spirit of the movement. In my opinion, they are only preliminary steps towards the idea of full prophethood which alone can serve the purposes of the movement eventually brought into being by new political forces. In primitive countries it is not logic but authority that appeals. Given a sufficient amount of ignorance, credulity, which strangely enough sometimes coexists with good intelligence, and a person sufficiently audacious to declare himself a recipient of Divine revelation whose denial would entail eternal damnation, it is easy, in a subject Muslim country to invent a political theology and to build a community whose creed is political servility. And in the Punjab even an ill-woven net of vague theological expressions can easily capture the innocent peasant who has been for centuries exposed to all kinds of exploitation.

Pandit Jawahar Lal Nehru advises the orthodox of all religions to unite and thus to delay the coming of what he conceives to be Indian nationalism. This ironical advice assumes that Ahmadism is a reform movement; he does not know that as far as Islam in India is concerned, Ahmadism involves both religious and political issues of the highest importance. As I have explained above, the function of Ahmadism in the history of Muslim religious thought is to furnish a revelational basis for India's present political subjugation. Leaving aside the purely religious issues, on the ground of political issues alone, it does not lie in the mouth of a man like Pandit Jawahar Lal Nehru to accuse Indian Muslims of reactionary conservatism. I have no doubt that if he had grasped the real nature of Ahmadism, he would have very much approbated the attitude of Indian Muslims towards a religious movement which claims Divine authority for the woes of India.

Thus the reader will see that the pallor of Ahmadism which we find on the cheeks of Indian Islam today is not an abrupt phenomenon in the history of Muslim religious thought in India. The ideas which eventually shaped themselves in the form of this movement became prominent in theological discussions long before the founder of Ahmadism was born. Nor do I mean to insinuate that the founder of Ahmadism and his companions deliberately planned their programme. I dare say the founder of the Ahmadiyyah movement did hear a voice; but whether this voice came from the God of Life and Power or arose out of the spiritual impoverishment of the people must depend upon the nature of the movement which it has created and the kind of thought and emotion which it has given to those who have listened to it. The reader must not think that I am using metaphorical language.

The life history of nations shows that when the tide of life in a people begins to ebb, decadence itself becomes a source of inspiration, inspiring their poets, philosophers, saints, statesmen and turning them into a class of apostles whose sole ministry is to glorify, by the force of a seductive art or logic, all that is ignoble and ugly in the life of their people. These apostles unconsciously clothe despair in the glittering garment of hope, undermine the traditional values of conduct and thus destroy the spiritual virility of those who happen to be their victims. One can only imagine the rotten state of a people's will who are, on the basis of Divine authority, made to accept their political environment as final. Thus all the actors who participated in the drama of Ahmadism were, I think, only innocent instruments in the hands of decadence. A similar drama had already been [en]acted in Persia; but it did not lead, and could not have led, to the religious and political issues which Ahmadism has created for Islam in India.

Russia offered tolerance to Babism and allowed the Babis to open their first missionary centre in Ishqabad. England showed Ahmadism the same tolerance in allowing them to open their first missionary centre in Woking. Whether Russia and England showed this tolerance on the ground of imperial expediency or pure broadmindedness is difficult for us to decide. This much is absolutely clear that this tolerance has created difficult problems for Islam in Asia. In view of the structure of Islam, as I understand it, I have not the least doubt in my mind that Islam will emerge purer out of the difficulties thus created for her. Times are changing. Things in India have already taken a new turn. The new spirit of democracy which is coming to India is sure to disillusion the Ahmadis and to convince them of the absolute futility of their theological inventions.

Nor will Islam tolerate any revival of mediaeval mysticism which has already robbed its followers of their healthy instincts and given them only obscure thinking in return. It has, during the course of the past centuries, absorbed the best minds of Islam leaving the affairs of the state to mere mediocrities. Modern Islam cannot afford to repeat the experiment. Nor can it tolerate a repetition of the Punjab experiment of keeping Muslims occupied for half a century in theological problems which had absolutely no bearing on life.

Islam has already passed into the broad daylight of fresh thought and experience; and no saint or prophet can bring it back to the fogs of mediaeval mysticism.

Let me now turn to Pandit Jawahar Lal Nehru's questions. I fear the Pandit's articles reveal practically no acquaintance with Islam or its religious history during the nineteenth century. Nor does he seem to have read what I have already written on the subject of his questions. It is not possible for me to reproduce here all that I have written before. Nor is it possible to write here a religious history of Islam in the nineteenth century without which a thorough understanding of the present situation in the world of Islam is impossible. Hundreds of books and articles have been written on Turkey and modern Islam. I have read most of this literature and probably the Pandit has also read it. I assure him, however, that not one of these writers understands the nature of the effect or of the cause that has brought about that effect. It is, therefore, necessary to briefly indicate the main currents of Muslim thought in Asia during the nineteenth century.

I have said above that in the year 1799 the political decay of Islam reached its climax. There can, however, be no greater testimony to the inner vitality of Islam than the fact that it practically took no time to realize its position in the world. During the nineteenth century were born Sir Syed Ahmad Khan in India, Syed Jamal-ud-Din Afghani in Afghanistan and Mufti Alam Jan in Russia. These men were probably inspired by Muhammad ibn Abdul Wahhab who was born in Najd in 1700, the founder of the so-called Wahhabi movement, which may fitly be described as the first throb of life in modern Islam. The influence of Sir Syed Ahmad Khan remained on the whole confined to India. It is probable, however, that he was the first modern Muslim to catch a glimpse of the positive character of the age which was coming. The remedy for the ills of Islam proposed by him, as by Mufti Alam Jan in Russia, was modern education. But the real greatness of the man insists in the fact that he was the first Indian Muslim who felt the need [for] a fresh orientation of Islam and worked for it. We may differ from his religious views, but there can be no denying the fact that his sensitive soul was the first to react to the modern age.

The extreme conservatism of Indian Muslims, which had lost its hold on the realities of life, failed to see the real meaning of the religious attitude of Syed Ahmad Khan. In the north-west of India, a country more primitive and more saint-ridden than the rest of India, the Syed's movement was soon followed by the reaction of Ahmadism – a strange mixture of Semitic and Aryan mysticism with whom spiritual revival consists not in the purification of the individual's inner life according to the principles of the old Islamic Sufism, but in satisfying the expectant attitude of the masses by providing a 'Promised' Messiah. The function of this 'Promised Messiah' is not to extricate the individual from an enervating present but to make him slavishly surrender his ego to its dictates. This reaction carries within itself a very subtle contradiction. It retains the discipline of Islam, but destroys the will which that discipline was intended to fortify.

Maulana Syed Jamal-ud-Din Afghani was a man of a different stamp. Strange are the ways of Providence! One of the most advanced Muslims of our time, both in religious thought and action, was born in Afghanistan! A perfect master of nearly all the Muslim languages of the world and endowed with the most winning eloquence, his restless soul migrated from one Muslim country to another, influencing some of the most prominent men in Persia, Egypt and Turkey. Some of the greatest theologians of our times such as Mufti Muhammad Abduhu, and some of the men of the younger generation who later became political leaders, such as Zaghlul Pasha of Egypt, were his disciples. He wrote little, spoke much and thereby transformed into miniature Jamal-ud-Dins all those who came into contact with him. He never claimed to be a prophet or a renewer; yet no man in our time has stirred the soul of Islam more deeply than he. His spirit is still working in the world of Islam and nobody knows where it will end.

It may, however, be asked, what exactly was the objective of these great Muslims? The answer is that they found the world of Islam ruled by three main forces and they concentrated their whole energy on creating a revolt against these forces.

(1) *Mullaism* – The ulama have always been a source of great strength to Islam. But during the course of centuries, especially since the destruction of Baghdad, they became extremely conservative and would not allow any freedom of *Ijtihad*, i.e., the forming of independent judgement in matters of law. The Wahhabi movement, which was a source of inspiration to the nineteenth-century Muslim reformers, was really a revolt against this rigidity of the ulama. Thus the first objective of the nineteenth-century Muslim reformers was a fresh orientation of the faith and a freedom to reinterpret the law in the light of advancing experience.

(2) *Mysticism* – The masses of Islam were swayed by the kind of mysticism which blinked actualities, enervated the people and kept them steeped in all kinds of superstition. From its high estate as a force of spiritual education, mysticism had fallen down to a mere means of exploiting the ignorance and the credulity of the people. It gradually and invisibly unnerved

the will of Islam and softened it to the extent of seeking relief from the rigorous discipline of the law of Islam. The nineteenth-century reformers rose in revolt against this mysticism and called Muslims to the broad daylight of the modern world. Not that they were materialists. Their mission was to open the eyes of the Muslims to the spirit of Islam which aimed at the conquest of matter and not flight from it.

(3) *Muslim kings* – The gaze of Muslim kings was solely fixed on their own dynastic interests and who, so long as these were protected, did not hesitate to sell their countries to the highest bidder. To prepare the masses of Muslims for a revolt against such a state of things in the world of Islam was the special mission of Syed Jamal-ud-Din Afghani.

It is not possible here to give a detailed account of the transformation which these reformers brought about in the world of Muslim thought and feeling. One thing, however, is clear. They prepared to a great extent the ground for another set of men, i.e., Zaghlul Pasha, Mustafa Kamal and Raza Shah. The reformers interpreted, argued and explained; but the set of men who came after them, although inferior in academic learning, are men who, relying on their healthy instincts, had the courage to rush into sunlit space and do, even by force, what the new conditions of life demanded. Such men are liable to make mistakes; but the history of nations shows that even their mistakes have sometimes borne good fruit. In them it is not logic but life that struggles restless to solve its own problems.

It may be pointed out here that Syed Ahmad Khan, Syed Jamal-ud-Din Afghani and hundreds of the latter's disciples in Muslim countries were not Westernized Muslims. They were men who had sat on their knees before the *mullas* of the old school and had breathed the very intellectual and spiritual atmosphere which they later sought to reconstruct. Pressure of modern ideas may be admitted; but the history thus briefly indicated above clearly shows that the upheaval which has come to Turkey and which is likely, sooner or later, to come to other Muslim countries, is almost wholly determined by the forces within. It is only the superficial observer of the modern world who thinks that the present crisis in the world of Islam is wholly due to the working of alien forces.

Has, then, the world of Islam outside India, or especially Turkey, abandoned Islam? Pandit Jawahar Lal Nehru thinks that Turkey had ceased to be a Muslim country. He does not seem to realize that the question whether a person or a community has ceased to be a member of Islam is, from the Muslim point of view, a purely legal question and must be decided in view of the structural principles of Islam. As long as a person is loyal to the two basic principles of Islam, i.e., the Unity of God and Finality of the Holy Prophet, not even the strictest *mulla* can turn him outside the pale of Islam even though his interpretations of the law or of the text of the Qur'an are believed to be erroneous.

But perhaps Pandit Jawahar Lal Nehru has in his mind the supposed or real innovations which the Ataturk has introduced. Let us for a moment examine these. Is it the development of a general materialist outlook in Turkey which seems inimical to Islam? Islam has had too much of renunciation; it is time for the Muslims to look to realities. Materialism is a bad weapon against religion; but it is quite an effective one against *mulla*-craft and Sufi-craft which deliberately mystify the people with a view to exploiting their ignorance and credulity. The spirit of Islam is not afraid of its contact with matter. Indeed the Qur'an says: 'Forget not thy share in the world.' It is difficult for a non-Muslim to understand that, considering the history of the Muslim world during the last few centuries, the progress of a materialist outlook is only a form of self-realization. Is it, then, the abolition of the old dress or the introduction of the Latin script? Islam as a religion has no country; as a society it has no specific language, no specific dress. Even the recitation of the Qur'an in Turkish is not without some precedent in Muslim history. Personally, I regard it as a serious error of judgement for the modern student of the Arabic language and literature knows full well that the only non-European language which has a future is Arabic. But the reports are that the Turks have already abandoned the vernacular recitation of the Qur'an. Is it then the abolition of polygamy or the licentiate *ulama*? According to the Law of Islam, the Amir of a Muslim state has the power to revoke the 'permissions' of the law, if he is convinced that they tend to cause social corruption. As to the licentiate *ulama* I would certainly introduce it in Muslim India if I had the power to do so. The inventions of the myth-making *mulla* is largely due to the stupidity of the average Muslim. In excluding him from the religious life of the people, the Ataturk has done what would have delighted the heart of an Ibn Taimiyyah or a Shah Wali Ullah.

There is a tradition of the Holy Prophet reported in the *Mishkat* to the effect that only the Amir of the Muslim state and the person or persons appointed by him are entitled to preach to the people; I do not know whether the Ataturk ever knew of this tradition; yet it is striking how the light of his Islamic conscience has illumined the zone of his action in this important matter. The adoption of the Swiss Code with its rule of inheritance is certainly a serious error which has arisen out of the youthful zeal for reform excusable in a people furiously desiring to go ahead. The joy of emancipation from the fetters of a long-standing priestcraft sometimes drives a people to untried courses of action. But Turkey as well as the rest of the world of Islam have yet to realize the hitherto unrevealed economic aspects of the Islamic law of inheritance which Von Kremer describes as the 'supremely original branch of Muslim law'.

Is it the abolition of the Caliphate or the separation of church and state? In its essence Islam is not imperialism. In the abolition of the Caliphate which, since the days of Umayyads, had practically become a kind of empire, it is only the spirit of Islam that has worked out through the Ataturk. In order to understand the Turkish Ijtihad in the matter of the Caliphate we cannot but seek the guidance of Ibn Khaldun, the great philosophical historian of Islam and the father of modern history. I can do no better than to quote here a passage from my *Reconstruction* [pp. 157–58]:

> Ibn-i-Khaldun, in his famous *Prolegomena*, mentions three distinct views of the idea of Universal Caliphate in Islam: (1) That Universal Imamate is a Divine institution, and is consequently indispensable. (2) That it is merely a matter of expediency. (3) That there is no need of such an institution. The last view was taken by the Khawarij [the early Republicans of Islam]. It seems that modern Turkey has shifted from the first to the second view, i.e., to the view of the Mutazila who regarded Universal Imamate as a matter of expediency only. The Turks argue that in our political thinking we must be guided by our past political experience which points unmistakably to the fact that the idea of Universal Imamate has failed in practice. It was a workable idea when the Empire of Islam was intact. Since the break-up of this empire independent political units have arisen. The idea has ceased to be operative and cannot work as a living factor in the organization of modern Islam.

Nor is the idea of separation of church and state alien to Islam. The doctrine of the Major Occultation of the Imam in a sense effected this separation long ago in Shi'ah Persia. The Islamic idea of the division of the religious and political functions of the state must not be confounded with the European idea of the separation of church and state. The former is only a division of functions as is clear from the gradual creation in the Muslim state of the offices of *Shaikh-ul-Islam* and ministers; the letter is based on the metaphysical dualism of spirit and matter. Christianity began as an order of monks having nothing to do with the affairs of the world; Islam was, from the very beginning, a civil society with laws civil in their nature though believed to be revelational in origin. The metaphysical dualism on which the European idea is based has borne bitter fruit among Western nations. Many years ago a book was written in America called *If Christ Came to Chicago*.[35] In reviewing this book an American author says:

> The lesson to be learned from Mr Stead's book is that the great evils from which humanity is suffering today are evils that can be handled only by religious sentiments; that the handling of those evils has been in the great part surrendered to the state; that the state has itself been delivered over to corrupt political machines; that such machines are not only unwilling, but unable, to deal with those evils; and that nothing but a religious awakening of the citizens to their public duties can save countless millions from misery, and the state itself from degradation.

In the history of Muslim political experience the separation has meant only a separation of functions, not of ideas. It cannot be maintained that in Muslim countries the separation of church and state means the freedom of Muslim legislative activity from the conscience of the people which has for centuries been trained and developed by the spirituality of Islam. Experience alone will show how the idea will work in modern Turkey. We can only hope that it will not be productive of the evils which it has produced in Europe and America.

I have briefly discussed the above innovations more for the sake of the Muslim reader than for Pandit Jawahar Lal Nehru. The innovation specifically mentioned by the Pandit is the adoption by the Turks and Persians of racial and nationalist ideals. He seems to think that the adoption of such ideals means the abandonment of Islam by Turkey and Persia. The student of history knows very well that Islam was born at a time when the old principles of human unification, such as blood-relationship and throne-culture were failing. It, therefore, finds the principle of human unification not in the blood and bones but in the mind of man. Indeed, its social message to mankind is: 'Deracialize yourself or perish by internecine war.' It is no exaggeration to say that Islam looks askance at Nature's race-building plans and creates, by means of its peculiar institutions, an outlook which would counteract race-building forces of Nature. In the direction of human domestication it has done in one thousand years far more important work than Christianity and Buddhism ever did in two thousand years or more. It is no less than a miracle that an Indian Muslim finds himself at home in Morocco in spite of the disparity of race and language. Yet it cannot be said that Islam is totally opposed to race. Its history shows that in social reform it relies mainly on its scheme for gradual deracialization and proceeds on the lines of least resistance. 'Verily,' says the Qur'an, 'we have made you into tribes and sub-tribes so that you may be identified; but the best among you in the eye of God is he who is the purest in life.'

Considering the mightiness of the problem of race and the amount of time which the deracialization of mankind must necessarily take, the attitude of Islam towards the problem of race, i.e., stooping to conquer without itself becoming a race-making factor, is the only rational and workable attitude. There is a remarkable passage in Sir Arthur Keith's little book, *The Problem of Race*, which is worth quoting here:

> And now man is awakening to the fact that Nature's primary end – race-building – is incompatible with the necessities of the modern economic world and is asking himself: What must I do? Bring race-building as practised hitherto by Nature to an end and have eternal peace? Or permit Nature to pursue her old course and have – as a necessary consequence – war? Man has to choose the one course or the other. There is no intermediate course possible.

It is, therefore, clear that if the Ataturk is inspired by Pan-Turanianism he is going not so much against the spirit of Islam as against the spirit of the times. And if he is a believer in the absoluteness of races, he is sure to be defeated by the spirit of modern times which is wholly in keeping with the spirit of Islam. Personally, however, I do not think that the Ataturk is inspired by Pan-Turanianism, as I believe his Pan-Turanianism is only a political retort to Pan-Slavonism, or Pan-Germanism or Pan-Anglo-Saxonism.

If the meaning of the above paragraph is well understood, it is not difficult to see the attitude of Islam towards nationalist ideals. Nationalism in the sense of love of one's country and even readiness to die for its honour is a part of the Muslims' faith: it comes into conflict with Islam only when it begins to play the role of a political concept and claims to be a principle of human solidarity demanding that Islam should recede to the background of a mere private opinion and cease to be a living factor in the national life. In Turkey, Persia, Egypt and other Muslim countries it will never become a problem. In these countries Muslims constitute an overwhelming majority and their minorities, i.e., Jews, Christians and Zoroastrians, according to the law of Islam, are either 'People of the Book' or 'like the People of the Book' with whom the law of Islam allows free social relations including matrimonial alliances. It becomes a problem for Muslims only in countries where they happen to be in a minority, and nationalism demands their complete self-effacement. In majority countries Islam accommodates nationalism; for there Islam and nationalism are practically identical; in minority countries it is justified in seeking self-determination as a cultural unit. In either case, it is thoroughly consistent with itself.

The above paragraphs briefly sum up the exact situation in the world of Islam today. If this is properly understood it will become clear that the fundamentals of Islamic solidarity are not in any way shaken by any external or internal forces. The solidarity of Islam, as I have explained before, consists in a uniform belief in the two structural principles of Islam supplemented by the five well-known 'practices of the faith'. These are the first essentials of Islamic solidarity which has, in this sense, existed ever since the days of the Holy Prophet until it was recently disturbed by the Bahais in Persia and the Qadianis in India. It is a guarantee for a practically uniform spiritual atmosphere in the world of Islam. It facilitates the political combination of Muslim states, which combination may either assume the form of a World-state (ideal) or of a League of Muslim states, or of a number of independent states whose pacts and alliances are determined by purely economic and political considerations.

That is how the conceptual structure of this simple faith is related to the process of time.

The profundity of this relation can be understood only in the light of certain verses of the Qur'an which is not possible to explain here without drifting away from the point immediately before us. Politically, then, the solidarity of Islam is shaken only when Muslim states war on one another; religiously, it is shaken only when Muslims rebel against any of the basic beliefs and practices of the Faith. It is in the interest of this eternal solidarity that Islam cannot tolerate any rebellious group within its fold. Outside the fold such a group is entitled to as much toleration as the followers of any other faith. It appears to me that at the present moment Islam is passing through a period of transition. It is shifting from one form of political solidarity to some other form which the forces of history have yet to determine. Events are so rapidly moving in the modern world that it is almost impossible to make a prediction. As to what will be the attitude towards non-Muslims of a politically united Islam, if such a thing ever comes, is a question which history alone can answer.

All that I can say is that, lying midway between Asia and Europe and being a synthesis of Eastern and Western outlook on life, Islam ought to act as a kind of intermediary between the East and the West. But what if the follies of Europe create an irreconcilable Islam? As things are developing in Europe from day to day they demand a radical transformation of Europe's attitude towards Islam. We can only hope that political vision will not allow itself to be obscured by the dictates of imperial ambition or economic exploitation. Insofar as India is concerned, I can say with perfect confidence that the Muslims of India will not submit to any kind of political idealism which would seek to annihilate their cultural entity. Sure of this they may be trusted to know how to reconcile the claims of religion and patriotism.

One word about His Highness the Aga Khan. What has led Pandit Jawahar Lal Nehru to attack the Aga Khan it is difficult for me to discover. Perhaps he thinks that the Qadianis and the Isma'ilis fall under the same category. He is obviously not aware that however the theological interpretation of the Isma'ilis may err, they believe in the basic principles of Islam. It is true that they believe in a perpetual *Imamat*; but the Imam according to them is not a recipient of Divine revelation. He is only an expounder of the Law. It is only the other day (*vide*, the *Star* of Allahabad, 12 March 1934) that His Highness the Aga Khan addressed his followers as follows:

> Bear witness that Allah is One. Muhammad is the Prophet of Allah. Qur'an is the Book of Allah. Ka'bah is the Qiblah of all. You are Muslims and should live with Muslims. Greet Muslims with *Assalam-o-Alaikum*.
>
> Give your children Islamic names. Pray with Muslim congregations in mosques. Keep fast regularly. Solemnise your marriages according to Islamic rules of *Nikah*. Treat all Muslims as your brothers.

It is for the Pandit now to decide whether the Aga Khan represents the solidarity of Islam or not.

2

'Safeguarding the rights and interests of the Mussalmans'

Mohammad Ali Jinnah and Jawaharlal Nehru discuss Muslim representation and the 'communal question'

AFTER A SERIES of personal tragedies that culminated in the death of his wife Kamala in February 1936, for whose treatment he had travelled to Germany, France and Switzerland, Jawaharlal Nehru returned to India to take up the presidency of the Indian National Congress for the second time.[1] Six months later, amidst heavy August downpours, Jawaharlal Nehru fought his way through the flooded roads of Lucknow to Ganga Prasad Memorial Hall, where he appeared on stage with Mohammad Ali Jinnah. Both men had followed the invitation of the All-India Student Federation, a relatively recent addition to the growing list of outspokenly anti-colonial student unions.

It was the first and last time they would share a podium. Jinnah, the president of the Muslim League, a party founded to voice the interests of Muslims on the national level in colonial India, was presiding and spoke a few introductory words on the future task of students in the freedom struggle against British rule. He praised Nehru for 'his sincerity and genuineness of purpose'. While for the moment they were speaking for different political bodies, their love for their 'motherland was common'. Nehru was less conciliatory and plunged straight into a new set of political ideas that he had tailored for India. After offering a few pleasantries to Jinnah, whom he called a 'distinguished leader', Nehru ran through a long laundry list of issues that differentiated his vision of India from Jinnah's.[2]

Nehru first asserted that he fundamentally disagreed with Jinnah on how to tackle the political problems of the day. According to Nehru, all Indians 'without any difference of caste, religion or political party' were faced with the same political situation of living under colonialism.[3] It was a political situation that they shared with many other oppressed peoples around the world. From 'Palestine, Syria, Egypt, Java, Indo-China and several other countries', Nehru stressed during a string of speeches he gave in the run-up to his Lucknow encounter with Jinnah, the proper response to that situation could only be 'to attaining independence'.[4] As India's struggle was interconnected with a broader global issue around imperialism, local issues could only be solved by approaching them from an international perspective.

In the past, Nehru outlined, Jinnah had often accused him of focusing too much on the international situation and ignoring the immediate issues plaguing Indians. Nehru readily accepted that he was 'always fighting shy of the immediate problem [with which he is faced], whether they are in the domain of politics [...] or in other spheres of national activity'.[5] He disarmingly conceded this was partly 'due to the fact that I am not competent to deal with the immediate problems'.[6] But more importantly, it had to do with his theory of change through which he saw 'the whole of the world' transforming.[7] According to this theory of change, Nehru elaborated at some length, problems of an immediate nature appeared to him as mere placeholders for more significant questions lurking in the background.[8]

In Nehru's unspooling of history, taking the occasional cue from Marx and Hegel, 'the forces of progress' were constantly rubbing against the 'the forces of reaction'. Yet, for most people, it was difficult 'to draw a line between the two because there are so many middle forces'.[9] These middle forces or 'vested interests' muddled the picture by appealing to earthly 'emotions and urges'.[10] Speaking directly to Jinnah, Nehru identified the communal question as a conservative reaction to the progressive forces. Employing religious identities as the primary drivers in politics as Jinnah did with his Muslim League had made him 'petty-minded'. It had also distracted him 'from the real problems of the country'.[11]

These fundamental problems were of an economic kind and related to exploitative capitalism. Over much of the past two centuries, Nehru explained, capitalism had 'helped add to the wealth of the world'. But it had outstayed its welcome after fulfilling its function and as opposed to benefiting society, capitalism had become 'a terror to further progress'. The main reason for this terror that capitalism had brought about was the uneven distribution of wealth. For Nehru, socialism could cure the inequality in wealth that capitalist modernity had ushered in. All the wealth that capitalism had created required fair redistribution. For this to occur, the 'abnormal condition' of British imperialism had to end immediately.[12]

There were two ways that imperialism could end: in an 'orderly way', through a constitutional transfer of power, or a 'chaotic way' that involved some form of revolutionary uprising.[13]

As the transformations capitalism ushered in were global in reach and not limited to a single country alone, any seeker of political wisdom needed to examine the phenomena in an international context. Nehru compared the British occupation of India to the Austria-Hungarian empire of the nineteenth century. Just like Austria's sudden disintegration, British imperialism too would soon shrink to a mere 'page in a big book'.[14]

Nehru also voiced grave concerns regarding the upcoming provincial elections under the newly reformed colonial Constitution, the Government of India Act, 1935. While the Congress would participate in those elections, once elected, it would use the gained power to destroy the system of imperial governance. As Nehru emphasized in several speeches given in Lahore in the early months of 1936, the battle for freedom would not come through occupying seats in an imperial council – it would be won 'in the fields, in the factories, and in the bazaars'.[15]

Nehru saw his and the Congress's allies, in alignment with Gandhi, in the 'dumb semi-starved millions scattered over the length and breadth of the land'.[16] This economic framing of his political constituency stood at odds with the separate electorates that the British had introduced through the Indian Council Act, 1909, which grouped voters according to religious affiliations. Nehru thought that universal franchise would immediately end British rule. It would also 'give effect to the economic urges of the masses'.[17]

In Nehru's view, the Hindu-Muslim problem or communalism was at its core a problem of 'upper middle-class people' who only made up a small fraction of the Indian population. If the 'mass elements take part in the election of the constituent assembly', communal issues would 'recede into the background'.[18] Broadly secular in his political outlook, Nehru never warmed to the idea that religion deserved a place in progressive politics. 'The so-called Hindu-Muslim problem,' Nehru disclosed his position in usual frankness, 'is not a genuine problem concerning the masses, but it is the creation of self-seekers, job-hunters, and timid people, who believe in British rule in India till eternity.'[19]

For Nehru, therefore, it was telling that Muslim politicians preferred to discuss the communal question from a numerical perspective and connect it to reserved seats in the legislature or the colonial administration. Nehru openly raged against the Communal Award of 1932, the chief institution that the British had established to ensure the retention of separate electorates for Indian Muslims. At its core, Nehru saw reservations opposed to the egalitarian principles of nationalism.[20] 'It is absurd to consider this question [of communalism] from the point of view of numbers,' Nehru declared in the presence of Jinnah. 'If there was a question of numbers we thirty five crores [350 million] of people would not have become a slave country [...] being dominated by a small number of people in Britain.'[21]

WHILE HE QUIETLY sat through Nehru's speech that questioned many of the fundamental political assumptions he had held for at least a decade, Jinnah may have pondered over what got him to this point. Long before Jawaharlal had entered the political arena with his radical politics to oust British colonialists from India, Jinnah was widely hailed in Congress corners as the 'best ambassador of Hindu-Muslim Unity'.[22] He received this praise for engineering the

Lucknow Pact of 1916, a joint declaration of the Muslim League and the Indian National Congress to increase Indian representation in the colonial services with a weighted role for Muslims. Jinnah's steady disenchantment with the Congress began in the late 1910s. It peaked in 1920 when Mahatma Gandhi captured control of the Congress with the help of pro-Khilafat Indian Muslims who saw him as an ally in their ambiguous cause to reinstate the Ottoman Caliphate after the First World War. Things came to a showdown at the Congress session of 1920 in Nagpur, where Gandhi proposed a change of the Congress constitution to include 'swaraj', or complete self-rule through the adoption of non-violent methods.[23]

Jinnah was not opposed to India's self-rule, but he considered Gandhi's methods ineffective and unnecessarily limiting in the future quest for independence. In Jinnah's words, adopting such practices that heavily relied on whipping up sentiments of the Congress's younger members was 'neither logical nor politically sound or wise'.[24] After a short speech at Nagpur, in which he contradicted the viewpoints of Gandhi, Jinnah was booed off the stage. An enraged audience accused him of 'weakness', 'slave mentality' and of being a 'political imposer'.[25] Disheartened by this backlash, Jinnah soon resigned his membership of the Congress. Despite the Nagpur incident, this resignation came as a surprise to many observers. They had speculated that Jinnah would have soon been the foremost political leader within the Congress party as an essential voice of the moderate wing to endorse the evolutionary process of demanding constitutional changes rather than immediate freedom from the colonial yoke.

In 1928, the arrival of Sir John Simon and Clement Attlee in Bombay, together with five other British Members of Parliament, tasked by the British Government to evaluate the administrative implementation of the Montagu-Chelmsford Reforms of 1919 and map out a constitutional future for India, brought the prospect of a new lease for Hindu-Muslim unity. This hope was quickly frustrated after their arrival. While both the League and the Congress boycotted the Simon Commission for its lack of native Indian representatives, both parties quarrelled over a constructive counter-proposal on framing an Indian constitution.

Jinnah rejected the Congress-backed Nehru Report, a constitutional draft championed, among others, by Motilal Nehru, Jawaharlal's father. Jinnah rejected it for substantive reasons, like its advice to scrap separate electorates and weightage for minorities or vesting residuary powers at the Centre with weaker provinces. However, Jinnah was also incensed by the tone of the report. Motilal ridiculed the legitimate Muslim angst from being dominated by a Hindu majority in a future democracy as a 'baseless fear', the desire for separate electorates as 'clumsy and objectionable', and the demand for reservations as counterproductive to ensuring the security of minorities.[26]

A young Jawaharlal's contribution to the report consisted in the laborious task to extrapolate the potential Muslim vote share by looking at the Census of 1921 in the two big Muslim-majority provinces, the Punjab and Bengal. Agreeing with the overall analysis of his father, Jawaharlal concluded that 'there is no foundation in fact for the fears entertained by the Muslims in these two provinces, and indeed no occasion for any adventitious aid to secure to them the full benefit of their natural majority'.[27] Motilal's secular constitutional assessment found applause within the Hindu Mahasabha, an influential organization that sought to protect Hindu rights and push back against Muslim influence.[28]

Against the Nehru Report, Jinnah proposed his Fourteen Points, which sought, among other things, a federal constitutional make-up of India with residual power vested in the provinces, a fixed Muslim representation in the Central legislature and the upholding of separate electorates. However, Jinnah signalled that he was willing to consider joint electorates if the Congress met his other demands. Clothed into concrete modifications to the Nehru Report during an 'All Parties Conference' in Calcutta, Jinnah pressed the committee members who were deciding on the merits of the Nehru Report that at least 'one-third of the elected representatives of both the Houses of the Central Legislature should be Mussalamans'.[29]

In a moving speech on the fifth day of the convention, Jinnah clarified that his desire was not to overwhelm the Congress with demands that would make it look soft on Muslims in front of the Hindu Mahasabha. Instead, Jinnah's demands were guided solely by dry constitutional observations from other countries. According to Jinnah, by the 1920s, it had become conventional wisdom that 'majorities are apt to be oppressive and tyrannical and minorities always dread and fear that their interests and rights, unless clearly and definitely safeguarded by statutory provisions, would suffer [...].'[30] Jinnah reasoned that because the Nehru Report predicted that a third of the legislature would consist of Muslim delegates anyway, there would be no harm in implementing this figure as a formal constitutional safeguard. Such a written anchor would also allow Indian Muslims to distribute those seats more evenly and distribute the excess seats that they would receive in the Muslim-majority provinces of Bengal and Punjab to regions where Muslims were numerically weaker.[31]

The delegates roundly rejected Jinnah's proposal. Dissent to his suggestions even emerged from within the ranks of the

Muslim League.[32] Other parties rejoiced over the open split in the Muslim League. M.R. Jayakar of the Hindu Mahasabha, for instance, poked right into this wound. In his response to Jinnah's speech, Jayakar cautioned the audience to 'bear in mind that the demands, as set forth by Mr Jinnah, do not proceed on behalf of the entire Muslim Community, not even a large bulk of it'. With some justification, Jayakar reiterated that the position Jinnah voiced reflected the desires of 'a small minority of Muhammadans'.[33] This speech left a mark on Jinnah. Responding to Jayakar, he moved away from his otherwise carefully measured statements that tended to evoke constitutional principles as an acid test for minority protections. Now Jinnah asserted that lasting harmony between communities could not be established in 'a Court of Law' or through a constitution 'however perfect from a theoretical point of view it may seem'.[34] Instead, it could only turn into a reality through 'the highest order of statesmanship and political wisdom' and the recognition that 'there is no progress for India until the Musalmans and Hindus are united'.[35] The alternative Jinnah presciently predicted was 'a revolution and civil war'.[36]

When Jinnah re-emerged on the political scene in 1934, after an extended hiatus to heal from the humiliation in the aftermath of the Nehru Report, he began to filter politics more squarely through the lens of war and peace. In his earliest engagements to uphold Muslim rights upon his return, Jinnah ventured to arbitrate the Shahidganj dispute. In this dispute, Lahori Muslims demanded that the local Sikh community return a former mosque to them that had since been used as a Sikh shrine.[37] While hearing both sides and establishing a joint Sikh-Muslim committee to investigate this conflict further, Jinnah did not resolve the dispute. But it was the first move away from his earlier politics. He had begun to embrace religious symbolism to further the politics of the Muslim League. Contractual arrangements that he had long championed were in Jinnah's eyes now inherently flimsy and 'always subject to alteration by the nation'.[38] Jinnah was not just referring to the Shahidganj dispute but the broader communal problem in India when he contended that for such issues, the law was insufficient to 'work out an honourable settlement'.[39]

Moving from contractual obligations to honour was reflective of Jinnah's changed perspective. Earlier, he had viewed Indian Muslims primarily as a minority community, constantly vying to petition for rights from the British crown or the Congress party. Now he saw Indian Muslims as a distinct and separate nation capable of ensuring their rights through force. This view clashed severely with the secularist outlook of Jawaharlal Nehru, who could only interpret Jinnah's religious posturing as a profound symptom of political alienation: a desperate attempt to plaster over existential anxieties that ranged from colonial oppression to unemployment and food scarcity. With constitutional reforms bringing more and more Indians into the realm of electoral politics, Jinnah and Nehru's contradictory ideas of India clashed soon after their joint appearance in Lucknow.

IN THE 1937 provincial elections, the Indian National Congress secured a resounding victory. At the polls of India's first large-scale election campaign that departed from the established system of dyarchy and increased the vote to thirty-six million Indians, including some women, the Indian National Congress secured more than 750 of some 1,500 seats. This sweeping success did more than underline the Congress's claim of being a national party. It altogether transformed the Congress from a mass movement to a political party. Congress members now occupied ministries in five provinces outright and constituted coalition governments in another two.

Jinnah suffered a crushing defeat. His All-India Muslim League secured less than 5 per cent of the Muslim vote, although this slim vote share amounted to some 108 seats from 485 reserved for Muslims under the Communal Award. Jinnah had failed to move voters in Punjab and Bengal with his plea that Indian Muslims had to stand under the political flag of a single party and scored seats primarily in Muslim-minority areas. In Bengal, Muslim voters flocked to the local Krishak Praja Party, and in Punjab, they resorted to Sikandar Hayat Khan's Unionist Party in droves. Both the Muslim League and the Congress had failed to make significant inroads to Muslim voters.

With a comfortable electoral majority in tow, Nehru departed from his promised agitational stance towards the 1935 Act and began working with the British Government. He also attempted to liquidate the Muslim League. When League members approached the Congress to constitute a coalition government in the United Provinces, Nehru snubbed their attempts and insisted that they first become members of the Indian National Congress. Nehru also endorsed a large-scale outreach campaign that sought to bring Muslims into the Congress by promising to better their economic conditions. This move ignited further counterefforts from the League to reach out and rally Muslim voters behind their party. It is in this context that Nehru engaged in a brief exchange of letters with Jinnah directly.

In full awareness that the Congress did not require the League to rule, Nehru conducted this communication from a position of strength. Jinnah refused to acknowledge that the election result was an adequate measure of the political value of the Muslim

League. To him, the communal question remained the most critical issue to determine India's future. Jinnah's cold responses were his way to shake Nehru out of this false sense of security that the Hindu-Muslim issue had receded into the background and given way to lofty ideas around socialism and constitutional democracy. Perhaps for this reason, Jinnah refused to lay the Muslim case to Nehru anew.

NEHRU-JINNAH EXCHANGE, 1938

(As reprinted in S.S. Peerzada (ed.), (1944), *Leaders' Correspondence with Mr. Jinnah*, Bombay, India: S.H. Nazir Ahmad, pp. 77–136.)

Nehru to Jinnah – 18 January 1938

Lucknow,
18 January 1938

Dear Mr Jinnah,

I HAVE READ the statement you issued recently to the press with care. I am afraid we approach the question from differing viewpoints and I feel that your approach is not very helpful. But I entirely agree with you that an argument carried on through the medium of the press is not desirable. Indeed I had decided not to issue press statements on the subject, but after your Calcutta speech, in which you mentioned my name and issued some kind of a 'challenge' to me, I felt that a public statement was unavoidable. Hence my statement, in which I tried to avoid unnecessary controversy.

You know perhaps that for some months past I have been in correspondence with Nawab Ismail Khan on this subject and I have been anxious to find out what the points of difference and agreement were. I am afraid I do not know this yet and your last statement does not help. I would feel grateful to you if you could kindly throw some light on this and let me know what exactly are the points in dispute which require consideration. I think this will help us all and lead to an avoidance of needless controversy. We can then come to grips with the subject. As I have said in my last statement, we are eager to do everything in our power to put an end to every misapprehension and to endeavour to solve every problem that comes in the way of our developing our public life along right lines and promoting the unity and progress of the Indian people.

I am leaving for Lahore today. From there I go to the Frontier Province and return to Allahabad in about ten days' time. Kindly address your reply to Allahabad.

Yours sincerely,
Jawaharlal Nehru

Jinnah to Nehru – 25 January 1938

Bombay,
25 January 1938

Dear Pandit Jawaharlal,

I AM IN receipt of your letter of the 18th January 1938.

I must say that it is very difficult for me to understand it. I fail to see what you are driving at. It does not suggest any useful proposal of a concrete character, besides reapproaching me and informing me that 'we approach the question from differing viewpoints', and you further say, 'I feel that your approach is not very helpful.' You further refer to my Calcutta speech and say, '[…] in which you mentioned my name and issued some kind of a "challenge" to me, I felt that the public statement was unavoidable and hence my statement.' But you do not even now give me the purport of my speech, and what was the 'challenge' which compelled you to say what you did in your statement which you considered unavoidable.

I know nothing about your being in correspondence with Nawab Ismail Khan referred to in your letter.

Finally, I note your request that I should let you know 'what exactly are the points in dispute which require consideration'. I am glad that you agree with me that the arguments carried on through the medium of the press are not desirable. But do you now think that this matter can be discussed, much less solved, by and through correspondence? I am afraid that is equally undesirable.

I may state for your information that I received a letter from Mr Gandhi, dated the 19th October 1937, and I replied to him on the 5th November '37, and I am still waiting to hear from him.

I reciprocate the sentiments expressed in the last but one paragraph of your letter at the end of it.

Yours sincerely.
M.A. Jinnah

Nehru to Jinnah – 4 February 1938

Wardha,
4 February 1938

Dear Mr Jinnah,

YOUR LETTER OF the 25th January reached Allahabad on February 1st after I had left. It has been forwarded to me here and reached me yesterday.

I am sorry that my previous letter was difficult to understand. My purpose in writing it was, as I stated, to find out what our points of difference and agreement were. Presumably there are points of difference as you have repeatedly criticized the Congress policy and practice. If these points of difference are noted down and our attention drawn to them it would make their consideration easier. It is possible that some of them may be due to misapprehension and this misapprehension might be removed; it is equally possible that some are more fundamental and then we could try to find a way out or, at any rate, know exactly how and where we stand. When there is a conflict of opinion, a clarification of the opposing opinions is an essential preliminary to their consideration.

I might mention some relatively minor matters which have apparently led to misapprehension. In one of your speeches you referred to being told by someone that a cheque for Rs 5 lakh was recently given to the Congress. I am not aware of this and presumably I ought to know. Indeed, to my knowledge, no one has given even a cheque for Rs 5,000 to the Congress for a considerable time.

In the same, or possibly another, speech you referred to the non-co-operation days and stated that while the Aligarh University was forced to close down and many non-co-operated from it, not a single student non-co-operated from the Benares University. As a matter of fact a very large number of students did in fact non-co-operate from the Benares University. As a result of this a non-official university, the Kashi Vidyapitha, was established in Benares, as also the Gandhi Ashram. Both of these still exist. In the same way, the Jamia Millia came into existence in Aligarh and this now flourishes in Delhi.

You have referred in your speeches to the Congress imposing Hindi-Hindustani and trying to crush Urdu. I presume you were misinformed for I am not aware of any attempt on the part of the Congress to injure Urdu. Some time back I wrote an essay on 'The Question of Language' which represents, I believe, the Congress viewpoint. It was approved by Mr Gandhi and by many people unconnected with the Congress and interested in the advancement of Urdu, including Moulvi Abdul Huque, Secretary, Anju-man-e-Taraqqi-e-Urdu of Hyderabad. I do not know if you have come across this essay. In any event I am asking my office in Allahabad to send you a copy. If you disagree with the argument or conclusions of this essay, I shall be grateful to have your criticisms.

I might mention that the Congress Ministry in Madras is endeavouring to introduce the study of Hindustani in the state schools in the province. They are having primers and text-books prepared especially for the purpose by the Jamia Millia. These primers, etc., are to be in two scripts – Devanagri and Urdu – but in identical language the students having the option of script.

I mention these instances to show how misapprehensions arise. But the real questions at issue are more important and it is in regard to these that clarification is necessary. I presume you are acquainted with the Congress resolutions and statements on minority and fundamental rights and regarding communal questions. If you so wish it, I can have these sent to you. Many of these were collected together in a comprehensive resolution passed by the Working Committee in Calcutta towards the end of October 1937. About the Communal Award the Congress position has been repeatedly made clear.

The Congress policy as laid down in these resolutions may be incomplete or wrong. If so we shall gladly consider suggestions to complete it or rectify it. Personally I do not see what more can be done by the Congress regarding religious or cultural matters. As for political (communal) questions, the Communal Award, unsatisfactory as it is, holds the field for the present and till such time as it may be altered by mutual agreement of the parties concerned.

In considering wider political questions, the Congress has adhered to certain principles and policies for a number of years, though minor variations have taken place from time to time. Our present policy in the legislatures and outside was defined by a comprehensive resolution passed by the Working Committee at Wardha last year. I was very glad to find from Nawab Ismail Khan and Choudhry Khaliquzzaman that the UP Muslim League, or the UP Muslim League Parliamentary Board, accepted this programme. This included our objective of independence, our demand for a constituent assembly, our general attitude to the Constitution Act, and the Federation, and our methods of work inside and outside the legislature. It referred also to our agrarian and labour programmes. Thus there appeared to be a very large measure of agreement between us not only in regard to fundamentals, but even regarding many details.

In view of this agreement it distressed and surprised me to find that there was so much conflict. I have tried, therefore, to find out what this conflict is about. I do not see how I can make any proposal, concrete or vague, when I do not know what the points in issue are. It is true that in reading your speeches I have come across various statements to the effect that the Congress is trying to establish Hindu raj. I am unaware of how this is being done or who is doing it. If any Congress Ministries or the Congress organization have made mistakes, these should be pointed out to us.

A report of your Calcutta speech appeared in the newspaper at the time and is no doubt available to you and for me to give you a purport of it seemed hardly necessary. In this you state that you are fighting the Congress, that you are fighting the Congress leadership which is misleading the Hindus. Further you have said that you want to bring the Congress High Command to its senses. May I suggest that those who are privileged to advise or lead the Congress have no desire to fight anybody expect British imperialism? In any event, if we mislead or misbehave we have a right to enquire from our critics where and how we have done so.

Further in your Calcutta speech you said: 'I have long, long ago, months ago now, thrown out a challenge to Pandit Jawaharlal Nehru and I throw out a challenge now – let him come and sit with us and let us formulate a constructive programme which will give immediate relief to the poor.' It was to this 'challenge' that I referred in my last letter. I do not remember on which previous occasion you had issued a similar challenge to me.

It is always helpful to discuss matters and problems face to face and, as I have said previously, we are always glad to do so. A short while ago you met Maulana Abul Kalam Azad, one of our most respected leaders, than whom there is no one better fitted to explain the Congress viewpoint in regard to the minorities problem or any other matter. Whenever necessity arises every one of us will willingly welcome a talk. But even such a talk is likely to be vague and infructuous if some clarification of ideas does not take place previously. Correspondence helps in this process and sometimes is even preferable as it is more precise than talk. I trust therefore that you will help in clarifying the position by telling us where we differ and how you would like this difference to end. You have also criticized the Congress in vigorous language, as you were no doubt entitled to do. But are we not entitled to ask you to substantiate those criticisms in private at least, if not in public?

I have inquired from Mr Gandhi about your letter to him dated the 5th November 1937. He received it in Calcutta when he was lying ill there and he felt that it needed no answer. Your letter had been in answer to his and the matter seemed to end there for the time being. He was good enough to show me his letter and yours and it seemed to me that no particular reply was called for. I understand that he wrote you yesterday.

I hope to be in Allahabad by the 9th February.

Yours sincerely,
Jawaharlal Nehru

Jinnah to Nehru – 17 February 1938

New Delhi,
17 February 1938

Dear Pandit Jawaharlal,

I AM IN receipt of your letter of the 4th February. You have now flung at me more complaints and grievances of trifling character. Evidently you rely on that section of the press, which is bent on misrepresenting and vilifying me, but I am glad that you say I mention these instances to show how misapprehension arises: '[B]ut the real question at issue is more important and it is in regard to this that clarification is necessary.' Therefore I don't think any useful purpose will be served to carry on correspondence with regard to the various matters mentioned in your letter. You will please not introduce matter which you may have discussed with Nawab Ismail Khan or Choudhry Khaliquzzaman or anybody else. These again will lead to references and cross references and the matter will never end.

As regards my Calcutta speech, the word 'challenge' is obviously due to the imagination of the reporter for the very context shows clearly that it was an invitation. However, the discussion of all these matters in correspondence will lead us nowhere. I do not believe in the doctrine which you lay down 'but are we not entitled to ask you to substantiate all these criticisms in private at least, if not in public': I for my part make no such distinction. I am prepared to substantiate anything that I have said publicly, provided it is correctly reported. The crux of your letter on the real vital point of the Hindu-Muslim unity is a repetition of what you said in your previous letter, namely, that you want me to note down 'the points of difference' and discuss them through and by means of correspondence – a method, which I made it clear in my last letter, is highly undesirable and most inappropriate. I welcome your suggestion when you say, 'whenever necessity arises every one of us would willingly welcome a talk'. If you think that necessity has arisen and any one of you is willing, I shall be glad to see you and equally welcome a talk. The thing is that you prefer talking at each other whereas I prefer talking to each other. Surely you know and you ought to know what are the fundamental points in dispute.

I have received a letter from Mr Gandhi and I have replied to him, a copy of which I am enclosing herewith.

Yours sincerely,
M.A. Jinnah

Nehru to Jinnah - 25 February 1938

Bombay
25 February 1938

Dear Mr Jinnah,

YOUR LETTER OF the 17th February reached me at Haripura. I had no intention of flinging any complaints and grievances at you. In my attempt to find out what your complaints were I read your speeches as reported in the newspapers (usually by a news agency) and noted down some of the points on which you had laid stress. I am glad to know that you have been misreported but you have not pointed out where the misrepresentation comes in nor, so far as I know, have you issued any statement to the press correcting the misrepresentation. May I suggest that it will be worthwhile to correct these errors so that the public might not be misled. A clear and authoritative statement from you will help us also in understanding what you stand for and what you object to.

I note that you do not wish me to introduce in our correspondence any matters which we may have discussed with Nawab Ismail Khan or Choudhry Khaliquzzaman. I did not know that they represented any different viewpoint from yours. I thought it necessary to draw your attention to the repeated attempts I have been making to find out what the political and communal policy of the Muslim League is and wherein it differs from that of the Congress. You will remember saying last year that the Muslim League had an entirely different policy even on political matters from that of the Congress. Since then the League has changed its objective and its economic outlook and has thus approached nearer to the Congress. I am anxious to find out what the real meaning of these changes is. Without this clarification it is difficult for us to understand the present position.

You say that you do not believe in the doctrine that I lay down, namely: '[B]ut are we not entitled to ask you to substantiate all these criticisms in private at least, if not in public.' Further you say that for your part you make no such distinction and are prepared to substantiate anything that you have said publicly, provided it is correctly reported. If you will read my sentence again you will no doubt observe that I have nowhere laid down any such doctrine as you imagine. I would indeed welcome a public treatment by you of the criticisms made by you. But if you yourself were unwilling to write to the press on the subject, as you indicated in your letter, I put it to you that we are at least entitled to request you to substantiate the criticism in private.

If you have made no criticisms of the Congress, and the press reports are entirely wrong, then of course no question of substantiation arises. All that need be done is to contradict the press reports. But if criticisms have been made, as presumably they have been, then I would request you to justify them publicly or privately as you might choose. Personally I would prefer the former method.

I am afraid I must confess that I do not yet know what the fundamental points of dispute are. It is for this reason that I have been requesting you to clarify them. So far I have not received any help in this direction. Of course we shall willingly meet you whenever [the] opportunity arises. Our President, Subhas Chandra Bose, or Maulana Abul Kalam Azad or I or any other member of the Working Committee can meet you at a suitable opportunity.

But when we meet what are we to discuss? Responsible people with organizations behind them can hardly discuss anything in the air. Some clarification of the issues, some clear statement of what is wanted and what is objected to, is always desirable, otherwise we may not come to grips with the subject. You will remember the argument about what transpired at Delhi in 1935 between you and Babu Rajendra Prasad. There has even been difference of opinion about the facts. It would be unfortunate if we repeated this performance and then argued about it later.

It is thus highly desirable for us to define the issues first. This is also necessary as we have always to consult many colleagues in regard to any matter affecting Congress policy. There is surely nothing undesirable or inappropriate about this defining of issues by correspondence. It is the usual method adopted between individuals and organizations. May I therefore beg of you to enlighten me?

Yours sincerely,
Jawaharlal Nehru

Jinnah to Nehru – 3 March 1938

New Delhi
3 March 1938

Dear Pandit Jawaharlal,

I AM IN receipt of your letter of the 25th February. I regret to find the same spirit running through of making insinuations and innuendoes and raising all sorts of matters of trifling character which are not germane to our present subject with which you started, namely, how to find the basis of approach to the most vital and prominent question of Hindu-Muslim unity. You wind up your letter by insisting upon the course that I should formulate the points in dispute and submit to you for your consideration and then carry on correspondence with you. This method, I have already stated in my considered opinion, is undesirable and inappropriate. The method you insist upon may be appropriate between two litigants and that is followed by solicitors on behalf of their clients, but national issues cannot be settled like that.

When you say 'that I am afraid I must confess that I do not know what fundamental points in dispute are' I am only amazed at your ignorance. This matter has been tackled since 1925 right up to 1935 by the most prominent leaders in the country and so far no solution has been found. I would beg to you to study it and do not take up a self-complacent attitude and if you are in earnest I don't think you will find much difficulty in realizing what the main points in dispute are, because they have been constantly mentioned both in the press and public platform even very recently.

Yours sincerely,
M.A. Jinnah

Nehru to Jinnah – 8 March 1938

Allahabad,
8 March 1938

Dear Mr Jinnah,

THANK YOU FOR your letter of March 3rd. I am afraid our letters to each other repeat themselves. I go on requesting you to tell us what exactly are the points in dispute which have to be discussed and you go on insisting that this should not be done by correspondence. At the same time you have pointed out that the main points in dispute have been constantly, and very recently, discussed in the press and public platform. I have carefully followed press statements and your public speeches. In my effort to discover these points of dispute I enumerated some of the criticisms which you were reported to have made in public speeches. In your reply you stated that you were misreported, but you did not say what the correct report should have been. Further you said that these were minor and trifling matters, but again you did not point out what the major matters were. You will perceive my difficulty. I hope I am not making any insinuations or innuendoes, as you suggest in your last letter. Certainly it is not my intention to do so, nor to raise trifling matters which are not germane to the present subject. But what are these matters which are germane? It may be that I am dense or not sufficiently acquainted with the intricacies of the problem. If so I deserve to be enlightened. If you will refer me to any recent statement made in the press or platform which will help me in understanding, I shall be grateful.

It is not my desire, may I repeat, to carry on a controversy by correspondence, only to find out what the main points of discussion and dispute are. It is surely usual for national issues to be formulated and clarified in this way to facilitate discussion. Both in national and international matters we are frequently adopting this course.

You are perfectly right in saying that this matter has been tackled since 1925 repeatedly. Do you not think that this very history warns us not to approach it in a vague manner without clear ideas as to what we object to and what we want? Apart from this, much has happened during these past few years which has altered the position.

For instance, the Communal Award. Do you want this discussed with a view to some settlement arrived at on another basis?

It is obvious that the Congress is exceedingly anxious to remove all causes of misunderstanding and friction. Apart from wider national issues, it would like to do so because such misunderstanding comes in the way of its work. It has frequently considered the problem and passed such resolutions and put forward such proposals as it considered right. I do not wish to discuss as to whether these were right or not. That may be a matter of argument. But according to our lights we tried to do our best. If we did not succeed to the extent we hoped to do that is our misfortune and we shall gladly consider suggestions which might lead to better results.

What are the various aspects of this matter? May I enumerate them?

1. The Communal Award, which includes separate electorates and reservation of seats.
2. Religious guarantees.
3. Cultural protection and guarantees.

Presumably these are the three main heads. There may be some minor matters but I do not refer to them as you wish to concentrate on the main issues.

As regards the Communal Award the position of the Congress has been clarified. If it is your desire to discuss this matter, I should like to know.

As regards religious and cultural guarantees, the Congress has given as full assurances and guarantees as is possible. If, however, any other guarantees are considered necessary, they should be mentioned. About one of the questions which you have referred to in your speeches, the Language question, I have written to you previously and sent you my brochure. I trust that you agreed with its main conclusions.

Are we going to discuss these matters or some others which I have not mentioned above? Then again the background of all such discussions must necessarily be a certain political and economic one – our struggle for independence, our anti-imperialism, our methods of direct action whenever necessary, our anti-war policy, our attempt to remove the exploitation of the masses, agrarian and labour problems, and the like. I take it that with the re-orientation of the Muslim League's policy there will not be any great difference regarding this anti-imperialist background.

You will forgive me for repeating myself in these letters and for saying the same things over and over again. I do so because I am keenly desirous of your appreciating my viewpoint, which I believe is also the viewpoint of my colleagues in the Congress. I have no desire to take up your time and to spend my time in writing long letters. But my mind demands clarity before it can function effectively or think in terms of any action. Vagueness or an avoidance of real issues cannot lead to satisfactory results. It does seem strange to me that in spite of my repeated requests I am not told what issues have to be discussed.

I understand that Gandhiji has already written to you expressing his readiness to have a talk with you. I am not now the Congress President and thus have not the same representative capacity, but if I can be of any help in this matter my services are at the disposal of the Congress and I shall gladly meet you and discuss these matters with you.

Yours sincerely,
Jawaharlal Nehru

Jinnah to Nehru – 17 March 1938

New Delhi,
17 March 1938

Dear Pandit Jawaharlal,

I HAVE RECEIVED your letter of the 8th of March 1938. Your first letter of the 18th of January conveyed to me that you desire to know the points in dispute for the purpose of promoting Hindu-Muslim unity. When in reply I said the subject matter cannot be solved through correspondence and it was equally undesirable as discussing matters in the press you, in your reply of the 4th of February, formulated a catalogue of grievances with regard to my supposed criticism of the Congress and utterances which are hardly relevant to the question for our immediate consideration. You went on persisting on the same line and you are still of opinion that those matters, although not germane to the present subject, should be further discussed, which I do not propose to do as I have already explained to you in my previous letter.

The question with which we started, as I understood, is of safeguarding the rights and the interests of the Mussalmans with regard to their religion, culture, language, personal laws and political rights in the national life, the government and the administration of the country. Various suggestions have been made which will satisfy the Mussalmans and create a sense of security and confidence in the majority community. I am surprised when you say in your letter under reply, 'But what are these matters which are germane? It may be that I am dense or not sufficiently acquainted with the intricacies of the problem. If so, I deserve to be enlightened. If you will refer me to any recent statement made in the press or platform which will help me in understanding, I shall be grateful.' Perhaps you have heard of the Fourteen Points.

Next, as you say, 'Apart from this much has happened during these past few years which has altered the position.' Yes, I agree with you, and various suggestions have appeared in the newspapers recently. For instance, if you will refer to the *Statesman*, dated the 12th of February 1938, there appears an article under the heading 'Through Muslim Eyes' (copy enclosed for your convenience). Next, an article in the *New Times*, dated the 1st of March 1938, dealing with your pronouncement recently made, I believe at Haripura sessions of the Congress, where you are reported to have said: 'I have examined this so-called communal question through the telescope, and if there is nothing what can you see.'

This article in the *New Times* appeared on the 1st of March 1938, making numerous suggestions (copy enclosed for your convenience). Further you must have seen Mr Aney's interview where he warned the Congress mentioning some of the points which the Muslim League would demand.[40]

Now, this is enough to show to you that various suggestions that have been made, or are likely to be made, or are expected to be made, will have to be analysed and ultimately I consider it is the duty of every true nationalist, to whichever party or community he may belong to make it his business and examine the situation and bring about a pact between the Mussalmans and the Hindus and create a real united front and it should be as much your anxiety and duty as it is mine, irrespective of the question of the party or the community to which we belong. But if you desire that I should collect all these suggestions and submit to you as a petitioner for you and your colleagues to consider, I am afraid I can't do it nor can I do it for the purpose of carrying on further correspondence with regard to those various points with you. But if you still insist upon that, as you seem to do so when you say in your letter, 'My mind demands clarity before it can function effectively or think in terms of any action. Vagueness or an avoidance of real issues could not lead to satisfactory results. It does seem strange to me that in spite of my repeated requests I am not told what issues have to be discussed.' This is hardly a correct description or a fair representation, but in that case I would request you to ask the Congress officially to communicate with me to that effect, and I shall place the matter before the Council of the All-India Muslim League; as you yourself say that you are 'not the Congress President and thus have not the same representative capacity but if I can be of any help on this matter my services are at the disposal of the Congress and I shall gladly meet you and discuss these matters with you'. As to meeting you and discussing matters with you, I need hardly say that I shall be pleased to do so.

Yours sincerely,
M.A. Jinnah

[Enclosure I to the above letter]

Through Muslim Eyes

By Ain-el-Mulk

PANDIT JAWAHARLAL NEHRU's Bombay statement of January 2 on the Hindu-Moslem question has produced hopeful reactions and the stage has been set for a talk between the leaders of what, for the sake of convenience, may be described as Hindu India and Moslem India. Whether the Jinnah-Jawaharlal talks will produce in 1938 better results than the Jinnah-Prasad talks did in 1935 is yet to be seen. Too much optimism would not, however, be justified. The Pandit, by way of annotating his Bombay statement while addressing the UP delegates for Haripura at Lucknow, at the end of January, emphatically asserted that in no case would Congress 'give up its principles'. That was not a hopeful statement because any acceptable formula or pact that may be evolved by the leaders of the Congress and the League would, one may guess, involve the acquiescence of the Congress in separate electorates (at least for a certain period), coalition ministries, recognition of the League as the one authoritative and representative organization of Indian Moslems, modification of its attitude on the question of Hindi and its script, scrapping of *Bande Mataram* altogether, and possibly a redesigning of the tricolour flag or at least agreeing to give the flag of the League an equal importance. It is possible that with a little statesmanship on both sides agreement can be reached on all these points without any infringement of the principles of either, but the greatest obstacle to a *satisfactory* solution would still remain, in the shape of the communalists of the Mahasabha, and the irreconcilables of Bengal, all of whom are not of the Mahasabha alone. The right of the Congress to speak in the name of Hindus has been openly challenged and even the Jinnah-Prasad formula which did not satisfy the Moslems – and nothing on the lines of which is now likely to satisfy them – has been vehemently denounced by the Bengal Provincial Conference held at Vishnupur which recently passed an extremely communal resolution, and that the latest utterances of the Congress President-elect on the communal situation generally and the Jinnah-Prasad formula in particular show some restraint. The only thing for Moslems to do in the circumstances is to wait and hope for the best, without relaxing their efforts to add daily to the strength of the League, for it will not do to forget that it is the growing power and representative character of the Muslim League which has compelled Congress leaders to recognize the necessity for an understanding with the Moslem community.

The Statesman, New Delhi Edition, 12 February 1938.

[Enclosure II to the above letter]

The Communal Question

IN ITS LAST session at Haripura, the Indian National Congress passed a resolution for assuring minorities of their religious and cultural rights. The resolution was moved by Pandit Jawaharlal Nehru and was carried. The speech which Pandit Jawaharlal Nehru made on this occasion was as bad as any speech could be. If the resolution has to be judged in the light of that speech, then it comes to this that the resolution has been passed not in any spirit of seriousness, but merely as a meaningless assurance to satisfy the foolish minorities who are clamouring 'for the satisfaction of the communal problem'. Mr Jawaharlal Nehru proceeded on the basis that there was really no communal question. We should like to reproduce the trenchant manner in which he put forward the proposition. He said: 'I have examined the *so-called communal question* through the telescope and, if there is nothing, what can you see.' It appears to us that it is the height of dishonesty to move a resolution with these premises. If there is no minority question, why proceed to pass a resolution? Why not state that there is no minority question? This is not the first time that Pandit Jawaharlal Nehru has expressed his complete inability to understand or see the communal question. When replying to a statement of Mr Jinnah, he reiterated his conviction that in spite of his best endeavour to understand what Mr Jinnah wanted, he could not get at what he wanted. He seems to think that with the Communal Award, which the Congress has opposed, the seats in the Legislature have become assured and now nothing remains to be done. He repeats the offensive statement that the Communal Award is merely a problem created by the middle or upper classes for the sake of few seats in the Legislature or appointments in Government service or for Ministerial positions. We should like to tell Pandit Jawaharlal Nehru that he has completely misunderstood the position of the Muslim minority and it is a matter of intense pain that the President of an All-India organization, which claims to represent the entire population of India, should be so completely ignorant of the demands of the Muslim minority. We shall set forth below some of the demands so that Pandit Jawaharlal Nehru may not have any occasion hereafter to say that he does not know what more the Muslims want. The Muslim demands are:

1. That the Congress shall henceforth withdraw all opposition to the Communal Award and should cease to prate about it as if it were a negation of nationalism. It may be a negation of nationalism but if the Congress has announced in its statement that it is not opposing the Communal Award, the Muslims want that the Congress should at least stop all agitation for the recession of the Communal Award.
2. The Communal Award merely settles the question of the representation of the Muslims and of other minorities in the Legislatures of the country. The further question of the representation of the minorities in the services of the country remains. Muslims demand that they are as much entitled to be represented in the services of their motherland as the Hindus and since the Muslims have come to realize by their bitter experience that it is impossible for any protection to be extended to Muslim rights in the matter of their representation

in the services, it is necessary that the share of the Muslims in the services should be definitely fixed in the constitution and by statutory enactment so that it may not be open to any Hindu head of any department to ride roughshod over Muslim claims in the name of 'Efficiency'. Pandit Jawaharlal Nehru knows that in the name of efficiency and merit, the rights of Indians to man the services of their country was denied by the bureaucracy. Today when Congress is in power in seven Provinces, the Muslims have a right to demand the Congress leaders that they shall unequivocally express themselves in this regard.

3. Muslims demand that the protection of their Personal Law and their culture shall be guaranteed by the statute. And as an acid test of the sincerity of Pandit Jawaharlal Nehru and the Congress in this regard, Muslims demand that the Congress should take in hand the agitation in connection with the Shahidganj Mosque and should use its moral Pressure to ensure that the Shahidganj Mosque is restored to its original position and that the Sikhs desist from profane uses and thereby injuring the religious susceptibilities of the Muslims.
4. Muslims demand that their right to call Azan and perform religious ceremonies shall not be fettered in any way. We should like to tell Pandit Jawaharlal Nehru that in a village, in the Kasur Tehsil, of the Lahore District, known as Raja Jang, the Muslim inhabitants of that place are not allowed by the Sikhs to call out their Azans loudly. With such neighbours it is necessary to have a statutory guarantee that the religious rights of the Muslims shall not be in any way interfered with and on the advent of Congress rule to demand of the Congress that it shall use its powerful organization for the prevention of

such an event. In this connection we should like to tell Pandit Jawaharlal Nehru that the Muslims claim cow slaughter as one of their religious rights and demand that so long as the Sikhs are permitted to carry on Jhatka and to live on Jhatka, the Muslims have every right to insist on their undoubted right to slaughter cows. Pandit Jawaharlal Nehru is not a very great believer in religious injunctions. He claims to be living on the economic plane and we should like Pandit Jawaharlal Nehru to know that for a Muslim the question of cow slaughter is a measure of economic necessity and that therefore it [is] not open to any Hindu to statutorily prohibit the slaughter of cows.

5. Muslims demand that their majorities in the Provinces in which they are at present shall not be affected by any territorial redistributions or adjustments. The Muslims are at present in majority in the provinces of Bengal, Punjab, Sind, North West Frontier Province and Baluchistan. Let the Congress hold out the guarantee and express its readiness to the incorporation of this guarantee in the Statute that the present distribution of the Muslim population in the various provinces shall not be interfered with through the medium of any territorial distribution or re-adjustment.
6. The question of the national anthem is another matter. Pandit Jawaharlal Nehru cannot be unaware that Muslims all over have refused to accept the *Bande Mataram* or any expurgated addition of that anti-Muslim song as a binding national anthem. If Pandit Jawaharlal Nehru cannot succeed in inducing the Hindu majority to drop the use of this song, then let him not talk so tall, and let him realize that the great

Hindu mass does not take him seriously except as a strong force to injure the cause of Muslim solidarity.

7. The question of language and script is another demand of the Muslims. The Muslims insist on Urdu being practically their national language; they want statutory guarantees that the use of [the] Urdu tongue shall not in any wiser manner be curtailed or damaged.
8. The question of the representation of the Muslims in the local bodies is another unsolved question. Muslims demand that the principle underlying the Communal Award, namely, separate electorates and representation according to population strength should apply uniformly in all the various local and other elected bodies from top to bottom.

We can go on multiplying this list but for the present we should like to know the reply of the Congress and Pandit Jawaharlal Nehru to the demands that we have set forth above. We should like Pandit Jawaharlal Nehru fully to understand that the Muslims are more anxious than the Hindus to see complete independence in the real sense of that term established in India. They do not believe in any Muslim Raj for India and will fight a Hindu Raj tooth and nail. They stand for the complete freedom of the country and of all classes inhabiting this country, but they shall oppose the establishment of any majority raj of a kind that will make a clean sweep of the cultural, religious and political guarantees of the various minorities as set forth above. Pandit Jawaharlal Nehru is under the comforting impression that the question set forth above are trivial questions but he should reconsider his position in the light of the emphasis and importance which the minorities which are affected by the programme of the Congress place on these matters. After all it is the minorities which are to judge and not the majorities. It appears to us that with the attitude of mind which Pandit Jawaharlal Nehru betrayed in his speech and which the seconder of that resolution equally exhibited in his speech, namely, that the question of minorities and majorities was an artificial one and created to suit vested interests, it is obvious that nothing can come out of the talks that Pandit Jawaharlal Nehru recently initiated between himself and Mr Jinnah. If the Congress is in the belief that this reiteration of its inane pledge to the minorities will satisfy them and that they will be taken in by mere words, the Congress is badly mistaken.

New Times, Lahore, 1 March 1938

Nehru to Jinnah – 6 April 1938

Calcutta,
6 April 1938

Dear Mr Jinnah,

YOUR LETTER OF the 17th March reached me in the Kumaun hills where I had gone for a brief holiday. From there I have come to Calcutta. I propose to return to Allahabad today and I shall probably be there for the greater part of April. If it is convenient for you to come there we could meet. Or if it suits you better to go to Lucknow I shall try to go there.

I am glad that you have indicated in your last letter a number of points which you have in mind. The enclosures you have sent mention these and I take it that they represent your viewpoint. I was somewhat surprised to see this list as I had no idea that you wanted to discuss many of these matters with us. Some of these are wholly covered by previous decisions of the Congress, some others are hardly capable of discussion.

As far as I can make out from your letter and the enclosures you have sent, you wish to discuss the following matters:

1. The Fourteen Points formulated by the Muslim League in 1929.
2. The Congress should withdraw all opposition to the Communal Award and should not describe it as a negation of nationalism.
3. The share of the Muslims in the state services should be definitely fixed in the Constitution by statutory enactment.
4. Muslim Personal Law and culture should be guaranteed by Statute.
5. The Congress should take in hand the agitation in connection with the Shahidganj Mosque and should use its moral pressure to enable the Muslims to gain possession of the mosque.
6. The Muslim's right to call Azan and perform religious ceremonies should not be fettered in any way.
7. Muslims should have freedom to perform cow-slaughter.
8. Muslim majorities in the Provinces, where such majorities exist at present, must not be affected by any territorial redistribution or adjustments.
9. The *Bande Mataram* song should be given up.
10. Muslims want Urdu to be the national language of India and they desire to have statutory guarantees that the use of Urdu shall not be curtailed or damaged.
11. Muslim representation in the local bodies should be governed by the principles underlying the Communal Award, that is separate electorates and population strength.
12. The tricolour flag should be changed or, alternatively, the flag of the Muslim League should be given equal importance.

13. Recognition of the Muslim League as the one authoritative and representative organization of Indian Muslims.
14. Coalition ministries.

It is further stated that the formula evolved by you and Babu Rajendra Prasad in 1935 does not satisfy the Muslims now and nothing on those lines will satisfy them.

It is added that the list given above is not a complete list and that it can be augmented by the addition of further 'demands'. Not knowing these possible and unlimited additions I can say nothing about them. But I should like to deal with the various matters specifically mentioned and to indicate what the Congress attitude has been in regard to them.

But before considering them, the political and economic background of the free India we are working for has to be kept in mind, for ultimately that is the controlling factor. Some of these matters do not arise in considering an independent India or take a particular shape or have little importance. We can discuss them in terms of Indian independence or in terms of the British dominance of India continuing. The Congress naturally thinks in terms of independence, though it adjusts itself occasionally to the pressure of transitional and temporary phases. It is thus not interested in amendments to the present constitution, but aims at its removal and its substitution by a constitution framed by the people through a Constituent Assembly.

Another matter has assumed an urgent and vital significance and this is the exceedingly critical international situation and the possibility of war. This must concern India greatly and affect her struggle for freedom. This must therefore be considered the governing factor of the situation and almost everything else becomes of secondary importance, for all our efforts and petty arguments will be of little avail if the very foundation is upset. The Congress has clearly and repeatedly laid down its policy in the event of such a crisis and stated that it will be no party to imperialist war. The Congress will very gladly and willingly cooperate with the Muslim League and all other organizations and individuals in the furtherance of this policy.

I have carefully looked through the various matters to which you have drawn attention in your letter and its enclosures and I find that there is nothing in them which refers to or touches the economic demands of the masses or affects the all-important questions of poverty and unemployment. For all of us in India these are the vital issues and unless some solution is found for them, we function in vain. The question of state services, howsoever important and worthy of consideration it might be, affects a very small number of people. The peasantry, industrial workers, artisans and petty shop-keepers form the vast majority of the population and they are not improved in any way by any of the demands listed above. Their interests should be paramount.

Many of the 'demands' involve changes of the constitution which we are not in a position to bring about. Even if some such changes are desirable in themselves, it is not our policy to press for minor constitutional changes. We want to do away completely with the present constitution and replace it by another for a free India.

In the same way, the desire for statutory guarantees involves constitutional changes which we cannot give effect to. All we can do is to state that in a future constitution for a free India we want certain guarantees to be incorporated. We have done this in regard to religious, cultural, linguistic and other rights of minorities in the Karachi resolution on fundamental rights. We would like these fundamental rights to be made a part of the constitution.

I now deal with the various matters listed above.

1. The Fourteen Points, I had thought, were somewhat out of date. Many of their provisions have been given effect to by the Communal Award and in other ways, some others are entirely acceptable to the Congress; yet others require constitutional changes which, as I have mentioned above, are beyond our present competence. Apart from the matters covered by the Communal Award and those involving a change in the constitution, one or two matters remain which give rise to differences of opinion and which are still likely to lead to considerable argument.
2. The Congress has clearly stated its attitude towards the Communal Award, and it comes to this that it seeks alterations only on the basis of mutual consent of the parties concerned. I do not understand how anyone can take objection to this attitude and policy. If we are asked to describe the Award as not being anti-national, that would be patently false. Even apart from what it gives to various groups, its whole basis and structure are anti-national and come in the way of the development of national unity. As you know it gives an overwhelming and wholly underserving weightage to the European elements in certain parts of India. If we think in terms of an independent India, we cannot possibly fit in this Award with it. It is true that under stress of circumstances we have sometimes to accept as a temporary measure something that is on the face of it anti-national. It is also true that in the matters governed by the Communal Award we can only find a satisfactory and abiding solution by the consent and goodwill of the parties concerned. That is the Congress policy.

3. The fixing of the Muslims' share in the state services by statutory enactment necessarily involves the fixing of the shares of other groups and communities similarly. This would mean a rigid and compartmental state structure which will impede progress and development. At the same time it is generally admitted that state appointments should be fairly and adequately distributed and no community should have cause to complain. It is far better to do this by convention and agreement. The Congress is fully alive to this issue and desires to meet the wishes of various groups in the fullest measure so as to give to all minority communities, as stated in No. 11 of the Fourteen Points, 'an adequate share in all the services of the state and in local self-governing bodies having due regard to the requirements of efficiency'. The state today is becoming more and more technical and demands expert knowledge in its various departments. It is right that, if a community is backward in this technical and expert knowledge, special efforts should be made to give it this education to bring it up a to higher level.

   I understand that at the Unity Conference held at Allahabad in 1933 or thereabouts, a mutually satisfactory solution of this question of state services was arrived at.
4. As regards protection of culture, the Congress has declared its willingness to embody this in the fundamental laws of the constitution. It has also declared that it does not wish to interfere in any way with the personal law of any community.
5. I am considerably surprised at the suggestions that the Congress should take in hand the agitation in connection with the Shahidganj Mosque. That is a matter to be decided either legally or by mutual agreement. The Congress prefers in all

such matters the way of mutual agreement and its services can always be utilized for this purpose where there is no opening for them and a desire to this effect on the part of the parties concerned. I am glad that the Premier of the Punjab has suggested that this is the only satisfactory way to a solution of the problem.

6. The right to perform religious ceremonies should certainly be guaranteed to all communities. The Congress resolution about this is quite clear. I know nothing about the particular incident relating to a Punjab village which has been referred to. No doubt many instances can be gathered together from various parts of India where petty interferences take place with Hindu, Muslim or Sikh ceremonies. These have to be tactfully dealt with wherever they arise. But the principle is quite clear and should be agreed to.
7. As regards cow-slaughter there has been a great deal of entirely false and unfounded propaganda against the Congress suggesting that the Congress was going to stop it forcibly by legislation. The Congress does not wish to undertake any legislative action in this matter to restrict the established rights of the Muslims.
8. The question of territorial distribution has not arisen in any way. If and when it arises it must be dealt with on the basis of mutual agreement of the parties concerned.
9. Regarding the *Bande Mataram* song the Working Committee issued a long statement in October last to which I would invite your attention. First of all, it has to be remembered that no formal national anthem has been adopted by the Congress at any time. It is true, however, that the *Bande Mataram* song has been intimately associated with Indian nationalism for more

than thirty years and numerous associations of sentiment and sacrifice have gathered round it. Popular songs are not made to order, nor can they be successfully imposed. They grow out of public sentiment. During all these thirty or more years the *Bande Mataram* song was never considered as having any religious significance and was treated as a national song in praise of India. Nor, to my knowledge, was any objection taken to it except on political grounds by the Government. When, however, some objections were raised, the Working Committee carefully considered the matter and ultimately decided to recommend that certain stanzas, which contained certain allegorical references, might not be used on national platforms or occasions. The two stanzas that have been recommended by the Working Committee for use as a national song have not a word or a phrase which can offend anybody from any point of view and I am surprised that anyone can object to them. They may appeal to some more than to others. Some may prefer another national song. But to compel large numbers of people to give up what they have long valued and grown attached to is to cause needless hurt to them and injure the national movement itself. It would be improper for a national organization to do this.

10. About Urdu and Hindi I have previously written to you and have also sent you my pamphlet on 'The Question of Language'. The Congress has declared in favour of guarantees for languages and culture. I want to encourage all the great provincial languages of India and at the same time to make Hindustani, as written both in the Nagri and Urdu scripts, the national language. Both scripts should be officially recognized

and the choice should be left to the people concerned. In fact this policy is being pursued by the Congress Ministries.

11. The Congress has long been of opinion that joint electorates are preferable to separate electorates from the point of view of national unity and harmonious co-operation between the different communities. But joint electorates, in order to have real value, must not be imposed on unwilling groups. Hence the Congress is quite clear that their introduction should depend on their acceptance by the people concerned. This is the policy that is being pursued by the Congress Ministries in regard to Local bodies. Recently in a Bill dealing with local bodies introduced in the Bombay Assembly, separate electorates were maintained but an option was given to the people concerned to adopt a joint electorate, if they so chose. This principle seems to be in exact accordance with No. 5 of the Fourteen Points, which lays down that 'representation of communal groups shall continue to be by means of separate electorate as at present, provided that it shall be open to any community, at any time, to abandon its separate electorate in favour of joint electorate'. It surprises me that the Muslim League group in the Bombay Assembly should have opposed the Bill with its optional clause although this carried out the very policy of the Muslim League.

May I also point out that in the resolution passed by the Muslim League in 1929, at the time it adopted the Fourteen Points, it was stated that 'the Mussalmans will not consent to join electorates unless Sind is actually constituted into a separate province and reforms in fact are introduced in the NWF Province and Baluchistan on the same footing as in other provinces'. Since then Sind has been separated and the NWF Province has been placed on a level with other provinces. So far as Baluchistan is concerned the Congress is committed to a levelling up of this area in the same way.

12. The national tricolour flag was adopted originally in 1929 by the Congress after full and careful consultation with eminent Muslim, Sikh and other leaders. Obviously a country and national movement must have a national flag representing the nation and all communities in it. No communal flag can represent the nation. If we did not possess a national flag now we would have to evolve one. The present national flag had its colours originally selected in order to represent the various communities, but we did not like to lay stress on this communal aspect of colours. Artistically I think the combination of orange, white and green resulted in a flag which is probably the most beautiful of all national flags. For these many years our flag has been used and it has spread to the remotest village and brought hope and courage and a sense of all India unity to our masses. It has been associated with great sacrifices on the part of our people, including Hindus, Muslims and Sikhs, and many have suffered lathi blows and imprisonment and even death in defending it from insult or injury. Thus a powerful sentiment has grown in its favour. On innumerable occasions Maulana Mohamed Ali, Maulana Shaukat Ali and many leaders of the Muslim League today have associated themselves with this flag and emphasized its virtues and significance as a symbol of Indian unity. It has spread outside the Congress ranks and been generally recognized as the flag of the nation. It is difficult to understand how anyone can reasonably object to it now.

Communal flags cannot obviously take its place for that can only mean a host of flags of various communities being used together and thus emphasizing our disunity and separateness. Communal flags might be used for religious functions but they have no place at any national functions or over any public building meant for various communities.

May I add that during the past few months, on several occasions, the national flag has been insulted by some members or volunteers of the Muslim League. This has pained us greatly but we have deliberately avoided anything in the nature of conflict in order not to add to communal bitterness. We have also issued strict orders, and they have been obeyed, that no interference should take place with the Muslim League flag, even though it might be inappropriately displayed.

13. I do not understand what is meant by our recognition of the Muslim League as the one and only organization of Indian Muslims. Obviously the Muslim League is an important communal organization and we deal with it as such. But we have to deal with all organizations and individuals that come within our ken. We do not determine the measure or importance or distinction they possess. There are a large number, about a hundred thousand, of Muslims on the Congress rolls, many of whom have been our close companions, in prisons and outside, for many years and we value their comradeship highly. There are many organizations which contain Muslims and non-Muslims alike, such as trade unions, peasant unions, kisan sabhas, debt committees, zamindar associations, chambers of commerce, employers' association, etc., and we have contacts with them. There are special Muslim organizations such as the Jamiat-ul-Ulema, the Proja Party, the Ahrars and others, which claim attention. Inevitably the more important the organization, the more the

attention paid to it, but this importance does not come from outside recognition but from inherent strength. And the other organizations, even though they might be younger and smaller, cannot be ignored.

14. I should like to know what is meant by coalition ministries. A ministry must have a definite political and economic programme and policy. Any other kind of ministry would be a disjointed and ineffective body, with no clear mind or direction. Given a common political and economic programme and policy, cooperation is easy. You know probably that some such cooperation was sought for and obtained by the Congress in the Frontier Province. In Bombay also repeated attempts were made on behalf of the Congress to obtain this cooperation on the basis of a common programme. The Congress has gone to the assemblies with a definite programme and in furtherance of clear policy. It will always gladly cooperate with other groups, whether it is a majority or a minority in an assembly, in furtherance of that programme and policy. On that basis I conceive of even coalition ministries being formed. Without that basis the Congress has no interest in a ministry or in an assembly.

I have dealt, I am afraid at exceeding length, with the various points raised in your letter and its enclosures. I am glad that I have had a glimpse into your mind through this correspondence as this enables me to understand a little better the problems that are before you and perhaps others. I agree entirely that it is the duty of every Indian to bring about [a] harmonious joint effort of all of us for the achievement of India's freedom and the ending of the poverty of her people. For me, and I take it for most of us, the Congress has been a means to that end and not an end in itself. It has been a high privilege for us to work through the Congress because it has drawn to itself the love of millions of our countrymen, and through their sacrifice and united effort, taken us a long way to our goal. But much remains to be done and we have all to pull together to that end.

Personally the idea of pacts and the like does not appeal to me, though perhaps they might be necessary occasionally. What seems to me far more important is a more basic understanding of each other, bringing with it the desire and ability to cooperate together. That larger cooperation, if it is to include our millions must necessarily be in the interests of these millions. My mind therefore is continually occupied with the problems of these unhappy masses of this country and I view all other problems in this light. I should live to view the communal problem also in this perspective for otherwise it has no great significance for me.

You seem to imagine that I wanted you to put forward suggestions as a petitioner, and then you propose that the Congress should officially communicate with you. Surely you have misunderstood me and done yourself and me an injustice. There is no question of petitioning either by you or by me, but a desire to understand each other and the problem that we have been discussing. I do not understand the significance of your wanting an official intimation from the Congress. I did not ask you for an official reply on behalf of the Muslim League. Organizations do not function in this way. It is not a question of prestige for the Congress or for any of us, for we are keener on reaching the goal we have set before us, than on small matters of prestige. The Congress is a great enough organization to ignore such petty matters, and if some of us have gained a measure of influence and popularity, we have done so in the shadow of the Congress.

You will remember that I took the initiative in writing to you and requesting you to enlighten me as to what your objections were to the Congress policy and what, according to you, were the points in dispute. I had read many of your speeches, as reported in the press, and I found to my regret that they were full of strong attacks on the Congress which, according to my way of thinking, were not justified. I wanted to remove any misunderstandings, where such existed, and to clear the air.

I have found, chiefly in the Urdu press, the most astounding falsehoods about the Congress. I refer to facts, not to opinions, and to facts within my knowledge. Two days ago, here in Calcutta, I saw a circular letter or notice issued by a secretary of the Muslim League. This contained a list of the so-called misdeeds of the UP Government. I read this with amazement for there was not an atom of truth in most of the charges. I suppose they were garnered from the Urdu press. Through the press and the platform such charges have been repeated on numerous occasions and communal passions have thus been roused and bitterness created. This has grieved me and I have sought by writing to you and to Nawab Ismail Khan to find a way of checking this deplorable deterioration of our public life, as well as a surer basis for cooperation. That problem still faces us and I hope we shall solve it.

I have mentioned earlier in this letter the critical international situation and the terrible sense of impending catastrophe that hangs over the world. My mind is obsessed with this and I want India to realize it and be ready for all consequences, good or ill, that may flow from it. In this period of world crisis all of us, to whatever party or group we might belong and whatever our differences might be, have the primary duty of holding together to protect our people from perils that might encompass them.

Our differences and arguments seem trivial when the future of the world and of India hangs in the balance. It is in the hope that all of us will succeed in building up this larger unity in our country that I have written to you and others repeatedly and at length.

There is one small matter I should like to mention. The report of my speech at Haripura, as given in your letter and the newspaper article, is not correct.

We have been corresponding for some time and many vague rumours float about as to what we have been saying to each other. Anxious inquiries come to me and I have no doubt that similar inquiries are addressed to you also. I think that we might take the public into our confidence now for this is a public matter on which many are interested. I suggest, therefore, that our correspondence might be released to the press. I presume you will have no objection.

Yours sincerely,
Jawaharlal Nehru

Jinnah to Nehru – 12 April 1938

Bombay,
12 April 1938

Dear Pandit Jawaharlal,

I AM IN receipt of your letter of the 6th April 1938. I am extremely obliged to you for informing me that you propose to return to Allahabad and shall probably be there for the greater part of April and suggesting that, if it would be convenient for me to come there, we could meet, or, if it suits me better to go to Lucknow, you will try to go there. I am afraid that it is not possible for me owing to my other engagements, but I shall be in Bombay about the end of April and if it is convenient to you, I shall be very glad to meet you.

As to the rest of your letter, it has been to me a most painful reading. It seems to me that you cannot even accurately interpret my letter, as you very honestly say that your 'mind is obsessed with the international situation and the terrible sense of impending catastrophe that hangs over the world', so you are thinking in terms entirely divorced from realities which face us in India. I can only express my great regret at your turning and twisting what I wrote to you and putting entirely a wrong complexion upon the position I have placed before you at your request. You have formulated certain points in your letter which you father upon me to begin with as my proposals. I sent you extracts from the press which had recently appeared simply because I believed you when you repeatedly asserted and appealed to me that you would be grateful if I would refer you to any recent statements made in the press or platform which would help you in understanding matters. Those are some of the matters which are undoubtedly agitating Muslim India, but the question how to meet them and to what extent and by what means and methods, is the business, as I have said before, of every true nationalist to solve. Whether constitutional changes are necessary, whether we should do it by agreement or conventions and so forth, are matters, I thought, for discussion, but I am extremely sorry to find that you have in your letter already pronounced your judgment and given your decisions on a good many of them with a preamble which negatives any suggestion of discussion which may lead to a settlement, as you start by saying 'I was somewhat surprised to see this list as I had no idea that you wanted to discuss many of these matters with us; some of these are wholly covered by previous decisions of the Congress, some others are hardly capable of discussion', and then you proceed to your conclusions having formulated the points according to your own notions. Your tone and language again display the same arrogance and militant spirit as if the Congress is the sovereign power and, as an indication, you extend your patronage by saying that 'obviously the Muslim League is an important communal organization and we deal with it as such, as we have to deal with all organizations and individuals that come within our ken. We do not determine the measure of importance or distinction they possess,' and then you mention various other organizations. Here I may add that in my opinion, as I have publicly stated so often, that unless the Congress recognizes the Muslim League on a footing of complete equality and is prepared as such to negotiate for a Hindu-Muslim settlement, we shall have to wait and depend upon our inherent strength which will 'determine the measure of importance or distinction it possesses'. Having regard to your mentality it is really difficult for me to make you understand the position any further. Of course, as I have said before, I do not propose to discuss the various matters, referred to by you, by means of and through correspondence, as, in my opinion, that is not the way to tackle this matter.

With regard to your reference to certain falsehoods that have appeared about the Congress in the Urdu press, which, you say, have astounded you, and with regard to the circular letter referred to about the misdeeds of the UP Government, I can express no opinion without investigation, but I can give you [a] number of falsehoods that have appeared in the Congress press and in statements of Congressmen with regard to the All-India Muslim League, some of the leaders and those who are connected with it. Similarly I can give instances of reports appearing in the Congress press and speeches of Congressmen which are daily deliberately misrepresenting and vilifying the Muslim composition of the Bengal, Sind, Punjab and Assam Governments with a view to break those governments, but that is not the subject matter of our correspondence and besides no useful purpose will be served in doing so.

With regard to your request that our correspondence should be released to the press, I have no objection provided the correspondence between me and Mr Gandhi is also published simultaneously, as we both have referred to him and his correspondence with me in ours. You will please therefore obtain the permission of Mr Gandhi to that effect or, if you wish, I will write to him, informing him that you desire to release the correspondence between us to the press and I am willing to agree to it provided he agrees that the correspondence between him and myself is also released.

Yours sincerely,
M.A. Jinnah

Nehru to Jinnah – 16 April 1938

Allahabad,
16 April 1938

Dear Mr Jinnah,

YOUR LETTER OF April 12th has just reached me.

I am exceedingly sorry that anything that I have written to you should have caused you pain. It seems to be true that we approach public problem from different standpoints and inevitably I try to place my viewpoint before you and seek to gain your appreciation of it. To say anything that might pain you would defeat my own purpose, even apart from its impropriety. At the same time I owe it to you and to myself to endeavour to place frankly before you how my mind works and what my views are on the subject matter under discussion. Our viewpoints might differ, but I do believe that the margin of difference can be lessened by a frank approach on either side. I have sought to make this approach in all sincerity and with every desire on my part not to say anything that might come in the way.

In my last letter I dealt with the various points mentioned in the extracts you had sent me as I presumed that, as you had drawn my attention to them, they might to large extent represent what you had in mind. As you know I have been trying to get at these points of difference and when I saw something concrete I wanted to give my reaction to it. I tried to state what the Congress opinion has been in regard to them. There is no finality in day to day politics, although certain principles are supposed to govern policies. It is for the Congress, if it so chooses, to vary any policy. All I can do is to state what the past and present policy is.

I regret that you think that I write in an arrogant and militant spirit and as if I considered the Congress as the sovereign power. I am painfully conscious of the fact that the Congress is not a sovereign power and that it is circumscribed in a hundred ways and further that it may have to go through the wilderness many a time again before it achieves its objective. You have referred to my obsession with the international situation and the sense of impending catastrophe that possesses me. If I feel that way, as I do, I can hardly grow complacent or imagine that the Congress is sovereign. But when I discuss Congress policies as a Congressman I can only repeat what these are and not bring in my own particular view on the subject if these happen to be at variance with Congress resolutions.

You point out to me that the Congress press has contained numerous falsehoods in regard to the Muslim League and some of its leaders, as well as the provincial governments of Bengal, Punjab, Sind and Assam. I entirely agree with you that falsehoods, misrepresentations and insinuations are to be deprecated and countered wherever they might occur, in the Urdu, Hindi or English press, or whatever the political complexion of the newspaper. There is no such thing as the Congress press over which the Congress has control, but it is true that many newspapers generally support the Congress. But whether we can influence them or not, we certainly want to stop all such false and misleading statements and to express our disapproval of them. In this matter I can only beg to you to point out specific instances so that we might take necessary action.

I note what you say about the publication of our correspondence. I have not got with me copies of your correspondence with Mahatma Gandhi. I am therefore writing to him to seek his permission as suggested by you.

I am afraid it will hardly be possible for me to visit Bombay in April or May. Early in June I intend sailing for Europe. In case I go to Bombay earlier I shall inform you so that we might have the opportunity of meeting. I understand that you will be meeting Mahatma Gandhi in the near future.

Yours sincerely,
Jawaharlal Nehru

3

'Communism is no shield against imperialism'

Sardar Patel and Jawaharlal Nehru spar over China and Indian foreign policy

THE CATASTROPHIC MILITARY disaster of 1962 – when Chinese forces overwhelmed the ill-equipped and ill-prepared Indian Army in the Himalaya and nearly swept down to the plains of Assam – has loomed large over the public imagination in India, its ghosts resurrected whenever a crisis erupts on the frigid heights of India's northern frontier. Coming after a decade where the defining objective of Indian foreign policy was friendship with China – immortalized in the oft-quoted slogan 'Hindi Chini Bhai Bhai'[1] – the conflict has also cast a long shadow over the legacy of Jawaharlal Nehru, the man who presided over India's foreign and defence policies throughout the 1950s and had been the architect of the country's policy vis-à-vis China.

In the words of his critic and parliamentary colleague H.V. Kamath, the debacle not only 'shattered Nehru physically and weakened him mentally but, what was more galling to him, eroded his prestige in Asia and the world, dealt a crippling blow to his visions of leadership of the newly emancipated nations'.[2] It was a blow from which he never recovered. Accused of cravenness, vanity and negligence, his foreign policy in a shambles, his illusions of 'Asianism' shattered, his self-appointed mantle of leadership of Asian nationalisms[3] in tatters and his policy of friendship towards China at all costs shown to have been a dangerous misjudgement, the shock of the defeat is said to have precipitated his death in 1964 – though not before he had been forced to jettison his much vaunted 'non-alignment', swallow his pride and beg US President John F. Kennedy for direct military intervention. Kennedy, having just stared down the nuclear abyss during the Cuban Missile Crisis, concluded that Nehru had 'lost both his nerve, and with it, his sense of reason'.[4]

Since then, the defeat – and the supine policy towards China that preceded it – has hung over his reputation. Blinded by his idealism, it is said, Nehru's miscalculations left India diplomatically isolated and militarily unprepared. In his failure to appreciate the Chinese threat, Nehru is juxtaposed with Sardar Patel, his one-time deputy who had warned him of the dangers that China posed and cautioned him against Chinese duplicity in a pointed letter in November 1950. Written shortly after the Chinese occupation of Tibet, Patel's letter has since enjoyed a long afterlife, being regularly reproduced in newspapers, quoted by columnists and celebrated for its prescience. In public discourse it is now used to graphically illustrate Nehru's strategic naivete and disregard of good counsel; and cast Patel as a rare dissenting voice against Nehru's foreign policy prescriptions, whose advice was ignored by the Prime Minister.[5]

Yet, contrary to public perception, Patel's letter was not simply a one-off, sagacious warning to Nehru.[6] It was grounded in, and the culmination of, a long-running disagreement between the two men, and indeed within the Nehru Cabinet, on the direction of India's foreign policy. As the two sets of letters reproduced here demonstrate, this was a critical debate that spanned much of 1950 and is deeply entwined with the story of Indian foreign policy. Nehru responded to Patel's famous letter with a detailed note for his Cabinet, and the resolution of this debate set the terms for Indian diplomacy for the next decade and more.

As early as 1927, when he accepted a position on the executive committee of the League against Imperialism alongside Albert Einstein and the Labour leader George Lansbury,[7] Nehru had emerged as the Congress party's primary spokesperson and thinker on external issues. Given a free hand by his Congress colleagues, he prepared for policymaking two decades before he gained executive power.[8] Many of his worldviews were formed in the crucible of Congress-led nationalist agitations. As one of the few Congress leaders interested in and conversant with world affairs, which he primarily interpreted using a progressive anti-imperialist lens and his own inclination towards socialist internationalism, he developed a deep interest in the broader anti-colonial struggle in Asia – particularly Southeast Asia and China, which he saw 'at once as peer, comrade and soul mate'[9] and of which he seemed to consider himself a patron.[10] Both his interest and his leanings were in full display at the Asian Relations Conference, which he hosted in New Delhi in March 1947 as an assertion of Asian solidarity against European domination, and where he called China 'that great country to which Asia owes so much'.[11]

Little wonder then, that when he finally ascended to the position of Prime Minister, Nehru believed himself to be especially qualified to also occupy the position of minister of external affairs where he proceeded to carve out foreign policy as his exclusive sphere; a turf he guarded jealously from any interference and over which he exercised vast, unchecked power.[12] It was a position that he had greatly coveted right from when the interim government had been proposed in 1946.[13] In this role, from 1947 to his death in 1964, Nehru almost single-handedly demarcated and interpreted India's goals and interests to come up with a foreign policy defined by its moral concerns, a commitment to anti-colonialism and international cooperation, and non-alignment 'on the merits'. These goals and interests were underpinned by many of Nehru's own beliefs and assumptions: an exaggerated sense of India's importance as 'the cultural fountainhead of the new Asia',[14] an instinctive affinity for the notion of 'Asianism' that he axiomatically assumed was shared by China and Southeast Asia, a sentimental and cultural Sinophilia, a sympathetic attitude towards communism and an ambivalence about (if not active distrust of) the United States. These beliefs, in turn, informed Nehru's conception of his own and India's place in the global arena: as the self-appointed leader and spokesperson of Asia (and the Third World more broadly) against European imperial domination with a self-anointed obligation to mitigate conflict on the Asian continent, and as a big brother helping and guiding smaller brothers (i.e., the countries and leaders of Southeast Asia).[15]

To live up to this role, its (and Nehru's) culturally manifest destiny,[16] however, India lacked both the military might and the economic resources.[17] To make up for this shortfall, it relied on the stature and moral authority that Nehru had acquired through his self-sacrifice for the nationalist cause and his position as the first Prime Minister of independent and democratic India. The effectiveness of its diplomacy and its support of Southeast Asian nationalism was thus inextricably tied to Nehru's reputation and personal prestige, as well as the normative power of Nehruvian India's independence and its democratic credentials. In other words, the collective projection of a superior moral standing. Nehru's ideas, then, were as prescriptive as they were descriptive, perhaps even more prescriptive than descriptive.

Conversely, one of the major functions of Indian diplomacy then became the projection and protection of Nehru's image as the champion of the Third World and his self-declared role as the leader of Asian nationalism and anti-colonialism, since doing so allowed it to punch above its weight in global affairs and assume that it would play a significant role in Southeast Asia. This was a role that Nehru himself greatly prized, and refusal to acknowledge it, or even indifference towards it almost always produced a prickly reaction – as, for example, Nehru's reaction to the American invitation to Pakistani Prime Minister Liaquat Ali Khan for a state visit.[18] The demolition of this cherished role and the conceptual plumbing behind it was, in truth, the chief reason that made 1962 such a debilitating blow – described by Shashi Tharoor as 'Nehru's grand international pretensions' being cut down to size.[19]

Inevitably, this fusion of the personal and the political often skewed perceptions, lending credence to the belief in certain quarters that moral grandstanding aside, this stoking of the Prime Minister's vanity was indeed the primary goal of Indian foreign policy – an opinion exemplified by the scathing remarks of the then American vice-president, Richard Nixon, in 1954: 'Mr Nehru does not like the

United States, Great Britain, Communist China or the USSR; he only likes Mr Nehru, and India.'[20]

All of the above-mentioned factors contributed to making Nehru the undisputed czar of India's foreign – and by extension defence – policies. To quote the political commentator Inder Malhotra, he was 'its inventor, interpreter and executor'.[21] These factors also ensured that the moral concerns and presuppositions, in the words of the scholar Paul F. Power, 'of a complex and remarkable man prevailed over a wide spectrum of diplomatic, ideological and strategic considerations'.[22] These concerns and presuppositions, and the policies they engendered – such as the 'Panchsheel' doctrine[23] for example – collectively came to comprise the 'Nehruvian consensus'.

The extraordinary life of this foreign policy consensus, its intellectual and institutional architecture only partially dismantled in 1962 has, however, obscured its heavily contested origins. Three views dominate common perception – first, that Nehru remained unchallenged in the foreign policy domain, allowing no alternative paradigms to be put forward,[24] second that this was due to a paucity of colleagues who could inform foreign policy[25] and third, that the flaws in Nehru's approach and resultant criticism of it only became visible after Sino-Indian clashes first erupted in the bleak Himalayan heights in 1959.[26] All are far from the truth.

Much before it became a consensus, Nehruvian foreign policy constituted a decisive fault line within democratic India's first Cabinet, and a vital point of contention between the Prime Minister and his deputy, Sardar Patel. Few realize how perilously close the consensus came to falling apart in its earliest years. It split the Cabinet right down the middle, forcing Nehru to mount a strenuous defence of his position against his critics. Despite this, the short life of the provisional parliament (1950–52) saw four high-profile resignations rock the government: those of Rehabilitation Minister K.C. Neogy, Industries Minister Syama Prasad Mookerjee, Finance Minister John Matthai[27] and Law Minister B.R. Ambedkar. Alongside other factors, all four pointed to deep misgivings over the direction and orientation of India's foreign policy as a key reason for their departure from the Cabinet, Ambedkar going as far as calling it a cause 'not merely for dissatisfaction, but for actual anxiety and even worry'.[28]

It is in this context that the Patel-Nehru tussle in 1950 over the direction of India's foreign policy unfolded.

ON 26 MARCH 1950, when Nehru wrote to Patel to complain about the critical comments that he had made to restive Congress MPs about the government's foreign policy, it was already apparent that serious doubts had begun to be expressed within the government about the intellectual foundations of Nehruvianism when it came to India's relationship with its neighbours. The trigger in this case was, of course, Pakistan – but, as the exchange bears out, the background remained the direction Indian policy had been taking when it came to China and Southeast Asia.

January and February 1950 had been particularly bloody months for Bengal. State-sponsored pogroms in East Pakistan – what had once been East Bengal – had pushed thousands upon thousands of Hindu refugees into West Bengal, causing a steady deterioration of the communal situation and heightening tensions between India and Pakistan. Disorder spread through much of the province, and the police were frequently called out, often resorting to firing to bring the situation under control. Nehru had been proposing confidence-building measures, joint commissions and joint tours to affected areas to a reluctant Liaquat Ali Khan, his Pakistani counterpart.

By March, he came under intense pressure from all quarters – including his own party – to respond firmly to the situation, even if it meant a forced exchange of populations or military action against Pakistan.

Such views were particularly popular in Bengal, where the leaders like the minister of industries and supplies Syama Prasad Mookerjee, supported by the Bengali press, had been scathing in their criticism of Nehru's attitude to Pakistan. Nehru, on the other hand, was determined to avoid any military action and considered the rousing of popular passions as an attempt to bully him into war. It was in this volatile situation that Sardar Patel spoke to Congress MPs, and apparently undermined Nehru's position as Prime Minister by expressing strong disapproval of the direction of his foreign policy.[29]

While Nehru laid out his case for not taking any precipitate action – the intimate connection between Indo-Pak issues and domestic communal problems where protection of minorities was closely tied to avoidance of military action against Pakistan – and expressed his displeasure at his deputy pulling in a different direction, it is Patel's reply, where he discussed his comments, that provides tantalizing hints about the workings of the Cabinet and the scale of disagreement over foreign policy.

As Patel described, he was almost hustled into having a meeting by restive Congress MPs unhappy with the Prime Minister's policy vis-à-vis Pakistan, where he mostly attempted to pacify their anger, advised them against raising the issue in any public fora and to wait for a resolution of the concerned issue without creating any bitterness. He made it a point to reiterate that he had always worked to strengthen Nehru's hand and given him loyal support, even subjecting himself to 'considerable self-restraint' in the process. He could not recall a single instance when he had asserted himself against any determined course of policy that Nehru had outlined –

nor could he remember a single instance where his difference of opinion had led him to oppose Nehru in the Cabinet with regard to any action that Nehru had deemed proper. In his own words: 'As regards Pakistan in general and East Bengal in particular, there is undoubtedly a difference in our approach … While expressing my view in favour of a firm policy and a more determined stand, I have submitted to any action that you eventually decided.'[30]

Nevertheless, despite his protestations that Nehru had never met any obstruction or opposition from any of his Cabinet colleagues in the making of foreign policy, Patel did take the opportunity – both at the meeting and in his letter – to obliquely, but also incisively, critique its broader framework. In explaining away the dismal performance of India's diplomatic outreach abroad, when compared to Pakistan, as an inevitable outcome of explaining their moral position to an opportunistic world, he subtly but firmly challenged the intellectual foundations of Nehruvian internationalism. He illustrated this by pointing at concrete instances: the recognition of the People's Republic of China (the haste of which Patel had cautioned against) had alienated Nationalist China, Indian antipathy to the recognition of the Bao Dai regime in Vietnam was bound to alienate the West, and the delay in the recognition of Israel was bound to cost them the goodwill of Israel and the countries interested in it.

Many of these points were echoed by Ambedkar in his resignation speech on 10 October 1951, when he contended that India was ploughing a lonely furrow in the world, and its foreign policy, the policy of trying to do the impossible and be too good, had left it friendless and isolated – unable to get food for its starving millions, aid for its industrial development or military support in the face of threats to its security.[31]

Patel's riposte to Nehru on 28 March demonstrates that foreign policy was a major bone of contention and disharmony within the Cabinet, even if Patel himself deliberately shied away from confrontation and allowed Nehru a free hand. Furthermore, it outlined the conceptual challenge to the Nehruvian worldview that was taking shape in the minds of Patel and many other detractors as they came to recognize its pitfalls. Patel's recognition that the failure of India's diplomatic outreach was closely related to the broader thrust of India's foreign policy and constrained its ability to counter Pakistan marked a significant milestone within the Indian establishment. And finally, the exchange of letters in March provides crucial contextual information with which to make sense of the ominous warning on 7 November 1950, the events around it and their true importance.

CHINA HAD BEEN a source of intense fascination for Nehru since his youth,[32] his writings littered with references to it, and the pairing of India and China as akin and alike, comrade and soulmate, imprinted firmly in his mind.[33] This cultural Sinophilia, combined with idealistic visions of Asian unity and the feeling of anti-colonial solidarity, was one of the reasons that India became the first non-communist country after Burma (now Myanmar) to recognize the newly established People's Republic of China on 30 December 1949. It did so without reference to India's rights in Tibet or the principle of Tibetan autonomy. In this, he was also influenced by K.M. Panikkar, the Indian ambassador to China, who was greatly impressed by the new regime and Mao Zedong's 'powerful and analytical mind', which he contrasted with the 'self-centred and cruel' Chiang Kai-Shek.[34]

In full rhetorical flow, Panikkar claimed – or fantasized rather – both Nehru and Mao to be 'men of action with dreamy idealistic temperaments … humanists in the broadest sense of the term'.[35] Patel's advice against any precipitate unilateral recognition, especially without any reciprocal recognition of India's rights in Tibet, was peremptorily brushed aside.

Following the establishment of the People's Republic in October 1949, which both Nehru and his ambassador Panikkar saw as a Chinese victory against Western imperialism, friendship with China became India's foremost foreign policy objective, and India's Prime Minister became China's foremost advocate on the world stage, leading the demand for its inclusion in the United Nations and for a seat in the Security Council. 'Jawaharlal,' states Shashi Tharoor, 'saw it as India's duty to sponsor China's arrival on the world scene.'[36] Borne out of Nehru's Sinophilia and his role as the leader of Asian nationalism against Western domination; and grounded in his belief in 'Asianism' and commitment to anti-colonial solidarity, the diplomatic scaffolding for this duty was often provided by Ambassador Panikkar from his post in Beijing.

Convinced that China and India shared the common ground of Asian identity, Panikkar's impressions of Mao's humanism and China's receptivity to India's friendship provided the subtext for regular reports to Nehru confirming the warm state of Sino-Indian relations and China's continuing goodwill towards India – as evidence of which he often cited trivialities such as Premier Zhou Enlai and other dignitaries attending parties at his house or important members of the Foreign Office being courteous to him at public events.[37] Panikkar's reports, often a lesson in vacuity, deftly propagated the idea that the People's Republic 'demonstrated the resilience of Asian civilization, its ability to incorporate Western knowledge and develop a sense of nationhood that could defeat colonialism in Southeast Asia.'[38]

The other force that shaped India's foreign policy outlook was Nehru's profound ambivalence, even distrust, towards the United States and the West in general. His state visit to the United States in October 1949 had been a disappointment, despite the warm reception from President Truman (who sent his personal aircraft to ferry him) and constructive talks with Secretary of State Dean Acheson. American hopes that India might consider becoming a part of collective security arrangements in Asia had been dashed, in spite of Nehru's proclamations of 'natural friendship'. Indian hopes of getting a million tonnes of wheat as food aid had been belied, notwithstanding private assurances from Truman and Acheson. To top it all, Nehru and his hosts had disagreed on the question of the recognition of the People's Republic of China, and the Indian Prime Minister had expressed his hope that the United States would not mind if he publicly criticized its approach to China.[39]

This distrust was exacerbated by the state visit of Liaquat Ali Khan in May 1950, which Nehru read as a sign of American indifference to his international role and a deliberate attempt to accord prestige to Pakistan.[40] Concurrently, China had continued to carry out 'a vigorous campaign of denunciation of Indian freedom and called Nehru a hireling of Anglo-American imperialism'.[41] Attempting to prevent Chinese criticism from undermining his (and India's) position as the self-declared leader of Asian nationalism, Nehru became determined to demonstrably distance India from the United States 'to disprove Mao's view, congruent with that of the Soviets, that India was still subordinate to Great Britain and the United States'.[42]

Indian diplomacy was thus placed in the curious position of subverting US-India relations, ignoring its own strategic considerations and becoming China's foremost supporter on the world stage for the singular purpose of negating communist propaganda. In doing so, not only did India barter away the legal rights it had inherited in Tibet[43] and champion China's position at the United Nations, it also sought to actively obstruct American efforts to support the Tibetan cause materially and diplomatically (more on that to follow) – all in an attempt to demonstrate its friendship for the People's Republic and its distance from the United States. In the process, it also sought to burnish Nehru's anti-colonial credentials and showcase Asianism in action.

Matters came to a head during the Korean war, when Nehru's attempt at mediation – against the advice of Patel and Secretary-General Girija Shankar Bajpai of the Ministry of External Affairs – was rebuffed by the United States.[44] Conversely, Nehru continued to advocate the Chinese position, criticizing the American move to cross the 38th parallel and pushing the Truman administration to accept Chinese demands for a seat in the UN Security Council and the vacation of Formosa. The policy of 'non-alignment on its merits' was given a quiet burial, and stripped of its moral qualities, redefined as neutrality, as the Indian government avoided criticism of China even after it entered the war on the North Korean side.

During the Korean conflict Indian policy effectively shifted 'to a posture of deference to international communism'[45] – heightening American distrust and leading US policymakers to conclude that Nehru was either a supporter of communist expansion or dangerously naïve in his assessment. So much did the Indian position harden vis-à-vis the United States that when the Truman administration suggested in August 1950 that Nationalist China

(Formosa) be unseated from the Security Council and India put in its place rather than the People's Republic, Nehru rejected the suggestion with great vehemence and declared: '[W]e are not going in at the cost of China … we are not going to countenance it … We shall go on pressing for China's admission to the UN and the Security Council.'[46]

India's determination to prove its friendship to China and disprove Sino-Soviet charges of being the running dog of imperialism made it 'virtually impossible for Nehru to carry out his declared policy of non-alignment on merits'[47] – costing India the goodwill of the United States without any corresponding benefit from the Communist Bloc.

THE ESTABLISHMENT OF the People's Republic, with its irredentist claims on Tibet – till then acknowledged as an autonomous country subject to Chinese suzerainty – profoundly changed the security situation on India's northern frontier. This was a fact that Nehru, despite his Sinophilia and his desire for friendship with China, was acutely aware of, having been warned by Ambassador Panikkar as early as in November 1949 about the prospect of a Chinese invasion of Tibet by June 1950.[48] As the legal successor to British India, India had (in theory at least) inherited all the rights and obligations from treaties between British India and Tibet. These included, among others, the delineation of the McMahon line in the Simla Convention of 1914.[49] This was a position that Nehru himself reiterated when he rejected a Chinese request to renegotiate and revise the Tibet Trade Regulations in 1948.[50] Chinese occupation of Tibet threatened to place all of these inherited rights, including the recognition of the McMahon Line, in jeopardy – a fact that Nehru himself appreciated.

In fact, as early as 1948 itself, the assumption that a strong Chinese government would attempt to seize Tibet, repudiate the McMahon Line and advance claims on Indian territories was already widely shared in the halls of Indian officialdom.[51] The communists announced their intention to 'liberate' Tibet almost as soon as they won power in October 1949. Nevertheless, precious little was done to thwart Chinese designs. When Tibet turned to India for help, 'requesting formal recognition of its independence as the basis of bringing before the United Nations any attack as international aggression',[52] its request was turned down. Anglo-American requests for cooperation in transferring military aid to Lhasa were similarly denied.[53] In January 1950, for example, when Secretary of State Dean Acheson considered inviting a Tibetan mission to Washington and inquired whether the Indian government would be willing to cooperate with the United States in helping strengthen Tibet's military capacity, he received a negative reply from Foreign Secretary K.P.S. Menon.[54]

Hugh Richardson, the representative of the Indian government in Tibet, recommended that in the interests of its own security, India respond positively to Tibetan demands and reiterate that its recognition of Chinese suzerainty was predicated on Chinese acceptance of Tibetan autonomy: both flowed from the 1914 convention, and India could not claim one and repudiate the other. India's disregard of the convention, he warned, would expose it to renewed territorial claims by China. Patel gave similar counsel, reminding Nehru that India had maintained bilateral relations with Tibet on the same basis that the British had.[55] Both pieces of advice were ignored; in fact, Hugh Richardson was painted as violently anti-Chinese and working to incite Tibetans.[56] Long-established policy was jettisoned as Nehru refused to challenge the legitimacy of Chinese claims to sovereignty.

Being the sole country to have inherited legal rights and obligations rooted in Anglo-Tibetan treaties, both the West and Tibet itself thus looked to India to take moral leadership on the Tibetan question. Instead, not only did India fail to openly confront China's aggressive claims, it also facilitated the manifestly unequal and coerced negotiations between the People's Republic and the Tibetan government, with the Indian government telling the Tibetan mission that there was no hope for them but to negotiate with the Chinese – even as the threat of invasion hung over the entire process.

Having spurned American overtures to supply military aid, Nehru and India's foreign policy establishment concluded that India had no effective method to check a potential Chinese advance, beyond diplomatic outreach. Rather than assert their own counterclaims, Indian diplomacy set out to demonstrate its friendly disposition by obstructing American efforts to arm Tibet, discouraging any attempt to raise the issue at the United Nations, acquiescing to Chinese claims of sovereignty and their takeover of Tibet, encouraging the Tibetan mission to accept defeat and continuing to espouse China's cause before the world. Instead of opposing China's claims because they threatened its security and its legal rights, India continually pointed out the difficulties that a Chinese invasion of Tibet would create for its worldwide advocacy of the Chinese cause. The political scientist Dawa Norbu summed up the situation: '[T]he essential functions of Nehruvian India in the communist scheme of things were not only to prevent external intervention in Tibet but also to seek India's legitimation of the communist takeover.'[57]

In the attempt to distance India from the US and demonstrate friendship with China – negating Chinese propaganda of Nehru being a Western stooge – Tibet was an early casualty. The fate of the ongoing negotiations were sealed when the People's Liberation Army marched into Tibet in October 1950. Even after the invasion,

Nehru continued to reject American offers of help to 'avoid giving credence to Peking's charges that great powers had been intriguing in Tibet and had been exercising influence over India's Tibet policies'.[58] By then, so far had Indian diplomacy drifted that when Nehru instructed Ambassador Panikkar to make a forceful argument to the Chinese to stop their invasion – though only because they were making it difficult for him to continue to champion their cause – Panikkar refused and promptly sent a reply justifying Mao's actions and blaming the Tibetans for bringing the invasion on themselves.[59]

THE INVASION OF Tibet and the policy of deference towards China that had preceded it, finally galvanized into action those members of Nehru's Cabinet who had misgivings about the direction of India's foreign policy and the threat it represented to India's security. On 1 November, there was a furious exchange of notes on Tibet and China between C. Rajagopalachari and Nehru.[60] At the Cabinet meeting on 2 November 1950, there was again a sharp and heated exchange between the two. Patel, who had attended at fifteen minutes' notice and been unable to read his papers beforehand, sat silently, preferring to bide his time and build his case.[61] The next day he received a detailed briefing on the subject from Bajpai and a paper on the situation from the Intelligence Bureau – based on which his letter to Nehru was prepared. Bajpai argued that while India was unprepared for war, it should cease its advocacy of China's claim to be admitted to the UN and prepare to defend the McMahon line.[62]

In his celebrated letter of 7 November 1950, Patel deprecated the pathetic state of Indian diplomacy and called for a comprehensive review of Sino-Indian relations: a military and intelligence evaluation of the Chinese threat, a long-term reconsideration of India's defence needs in terms of supplies and infrastructure and the twin threats from China and Pakistan, examination and redisposition of forces to guard important areas that may be subject to dispute, improvement of communications in these areas, political and administrative steps to strengthen frontier governance and an end to India's advocacy of China's entry into the UN. 'Recent and bitter history also tells us,' Patel observed, 'that communism is no shield against imperialism.'

'It is possible,' he continued, 'that a consideration of these matters may lead us into wider questions of our relationship with China, Russia, America, Britain and Burma.' Patel thus hinted that his concerns were not limited to China – and held out the tantalizing possibility that a fundamental reset of the general orientation of India's foreign policy and its position in the Cold War was on the cards. He did not elaborate, making it impossible to determine with certainty how far he was willing to go to demand such a reset. But there are clues to show that a major showdown in the Cabinet was in the offing – for which the letter was only an opening act.

On 10 November, US Ambassador Loy Henderson cabled Secretary of State Dean Acheson, noting that he had reliable and authoritative information that events in Tibet had resulted in increasing dissatisfaction within the government with the direction of India's foreign policy – and that even Nehru's supporters had recognized the threat posed by international communism and the need for a shift in policy.[63] 'Patel has been stating privately,' he continued, 'that within the next few days he will insist in [the] Cabinet meeting that India not only change policy in direction of closer cooperation with Western powers, particularly US, but that it make an announcement to that effect.'[64] Patel was reported to have said privately that he had been willing to defer to Nehru in matters of foreign policy so long as India's security was not at stake; but could not remain passive when the continuation of Nehru's policy would endanger the nation's security.

As Henderson relayed, the deputy prime minister 'felt so strongly in the matter that he would prefer to resign from Cabinet and to break openly with Nehru than to allow matters to drift'.[65] In a showdown with the Prime Minister, Patel believed he could count on the strong support of Rajagopalachari, K.M. Munshi, Baldev Singh, Jagjivan Ram and Sri Prakasa while he expected Nehru to be backed by Maulana Azad, Gopalswami Ayyangar and Rafi Ahmed Kidwai.[66] It is likely that Ambedkar, given his views, would also have lined up behind Patel. In fact, Ambassador Henderson believed Nehru to be almost the only person in the government who still believed in friendship with communist China and argued that India should make no move that might endanger that friendship.[67] Patel also had the option of challenging Nehru in the Congress Working Committee,[68] where his supporters enjoyed a clear preponderance.

An embattled Prime Minister had a note prepared for the Cabinet on 18 November as a response to his critics, where he laid out his case for continuing friendship with China: India lacked the capacity to help Tibet, it should not sponsor a Tibetan appeal in the United Nations because it would embarrass China, there was practically no chance of a major attack on India and only those who lacked perspective thought otherwise, the idea that communism inevitably meant expansion and war was naïve, Tibetan autonomy was inevitable due to the geography, terrain and climate of Tibet, and making provisions for a Chinese attack on India would cast an intolerable burden on government finances. Nehru blithely ruled out the possibility of an attack from China based on his view that such an invasion would undoubtedly lead to a world war. A face-off between the two giants of Indian politics seemed imminent. India stood at the cusp of a 180-degree foreign policy turn. Henderson himself believed that a change in direction was on the anvil.

But at the penultimate moment, fate intervened. Already ailing and often confined to his bed, Patel's health took a drastic turn for the worse. Prone to coughing up blood and frequently losing consciousness, he was too ill to attend the fateful Cabinet meeting on 21 November where Nehru's note came up for discussion. With the heavyweight deputy prime minister absent and debilitated, none of the other ministers challenged Nehru. The anticipated showdown failed to materialize. The sole intervention came from Rajagopalachari, to little consequence – although he did visit Patel later to brief him about what had transpired.[69] Nehru's arguments triumphed – the Nehruvian consensus was born.

The aborted showdown was to be Patel's last major political act. Within weeks, he was dead – his death removing from the scene the only man capable of forcing a course correction vis-à-vis China. With Patel gone, the challenge to Nehruvianism evaporated. Tibet was abandoned at the altar of friendship with China and vapid, ineffectual slogans of anti-imperialism and world peace. India's inherited rights – the trade agencies at Yatung and Gyantse, a permanent representative in Lhasa, military escorts, telegraph lines, rest houses on the road from Sikkim – a legacy of the British empire, were surrendered for the dubious benefit of proving Nehru's (and India's) anti-colonial credentials to China and the world. The People's Republic was assiduously courted. The journey to 1962 began.

PATEL–NEHRU CORRESPONDENCE

(Reproduced from Durga Das [ed.], *Sardar Patel's Correspondence*, Vol. X, pp. 9–22, 335–47.)

1. Jawaharlal Nehru to Sardar Patel, 26 March 1950

My dear Vallabhbhai,

I AM WRITING to you after a great deal of thought, as I feel that I owe it to you and to myself to do so. We have been close friends and colleagues, in spite of differences of opinion, for thirty years or so, and we have passed through numerous crises together. I suppose we have got to know each other fairly well because of this long companionship and working together in all kinds of weather, fair and foul. We have a good deal of affection and respect for each other and this has helped us a great deal in the past to face problems together.

You will remember that some months ago before Gandhiji's death, certain differences of opinion between us were repeatedly discussed before Bapu. In fact, this went on almost to the day of his death. At that time we were faced by a difficult problem. Temperamental differences and differences in viewpoints and approach to certain problems made it a little difficult occasionally for us to pull together. Therefore, the question arose whether it was desirable from the public point of view for those differences of approach to lead to certain consequences which were not good. On the other hand, it was manifest that conditions, as they were in India, demanded that we should pull together and subordinate, to some extent, our personal viewpoints in the interests of the larger good. The problem was a difficult one for us and we took Bapu's advice separately and jointly. Bapu was of opinion for some time that perhaps it was the right course for one of us to retire from Government, leaving the other a free hand. I offered to do so, and so did you. Neither of us, of course, wanted any office or wished any personal equation to affect either our personal relations or public policy. Nevertheless, after repeated discussion we felt, and Bapu appeared to be of this opinion just before his death, that, taking it all in all, it was our duty to pull together. We have tried to do so to the best of our ability for these past two years and more. Difficulties have often arisen, but both of us have this overriding sense that we could not endanger the larger interests of the country by imperilling this joint working.

Lately, however, new developments have taken place which have made me doubt seriously whether this attempt at joint working serves a useful purpose or whether it merely hinders the proper functioning of Government. Your remarks at a Cabinet meeting some days ago hurt me. But apart from the personal reaction, I was made to think, even more than before, that our approaches to certain vital problems were very different. A day or two later I made a statement, at the next meeting of the Cabinet, which you will remember. I made no personal reference then but I stated that I was deeply troubled in my mind and felt that the ideals we had stood for [for] a generation or more were fading away and no longer guided our policy. It was true that circumstances had changed and new problems had arisen which could not easily be dealt with by our old methods. Nevertheless, an ideal or objective or a basic policy could not be made the play thing of circumstances, however immediate policies might vary.

That statement of mine was not due to a reaction to any particular event but rather to an accumulation of many things that had happened previously.

At that time I did not know that you had invited a large number of members of Parliament and spoken to them about various matters. I heard about this later from some of those present and I confess that I was deeply perturbed by what I heard. I was told that you expressed your strong disapproval about many of our policies for which I was responsible and you disclaimed any responsibility. This referred generally to the Bengal situation and what I had said about it, and also to our foreign policy. Other matters were mentioned to me also, but I need not go into them.

For you to refer to all these important matters in the way you were reported to have done, before a large number of members of Parliament, seemed to me very unfortunate and very extraordinary. It was clear that you did so under stress of strong opinions and feelings. The personal aspect of it might be ignored, but the public aspect became important, and indeed a number of members who were present in your house were disturbed by this wider aspect of the problem. The lobbies were full of talk.

A day or two later, a meeting of the party took place where reference was made by several members to whispering campaigns. No names were mentioned but it was clear what was hinted at. I heard also that Government officials were themselves taking part in this whispering business and had encouraged the writing of editorials in newspapers criticizing me or what I had said.

This was an extraordinary state of affairs and I felt that I could hardly continue as Prime Minister if this kind of thing was taking place. Hence the feeling I showed in my speech to the party.

I have narrated some of these past events just to give the background of my own thought. We are facing today a crisis of the deepest magnitude and vital decisions have to be taken from time to time. Those decisions may be right or wrong, but they must be clear. If there is no clear objective or approach guiding them, they will tend to be confusing and contradictory. Hence it has become necessary that we should be perfectly clear about our official aims and policies. Naturally, existing circumstances and the succession of events force our hands.

But even so, we cannot ignore any basic policy that we may pursue.

The whole Bengal problem and the Indo-Pakistan issue have many facets – political, economic, communal, national and international. Of these, the communal aspect has great importance. Indeed the whole problem is in the nature of a communal problem. We have long stood for discouraging and putting an end to communalism. That has been the Congress policy and it has been repeated and affirmed by Parliament. We talk of a secular state. That of course simply means any normal state today, leaving out the abnormality of Pakistan's Islamic state. We adopted our policy regardless of what the Muslim League or Pakistan might say or do, because we thought that was the only policy, both from the idealistic and the practical and opportunist points of view. Any other policy could only lead to disruption and disaster. Certain organizations, notably the Hindu Mahasabha, adopted an exactly contrary policy, that is contrary to ours, though exactly similar, in reverse, to Pakistan's. I find that progressively we are being driven to adopt what is essentially the Pakistan or the Hindu Mahasabha policy in this respect. It may be that the circumstances were too strong for us. I do not think any circumstance can be strong enough to upset a long-term policy which we consider essential. I am quite convinced that that old policy of ours was the only right one and is the only right one in present circumstances. That was the Gandhian approach to the communal problem. It meant an attempt not only to protect the minorities but to win them over and thus demonstrate the rightness of our policy. If we do not adhere to that policy, then inevitably other consequences follow. It is no good at all for us to follow two contradictory policies at one and the same time. That is the worst way out of a difficulty.

The position today is that while Pakistan has followed and is following an intensely communal policy, we are tending to do the same and thus completely playing into the hands of Pakistan. Hindus in Pakistan are terrified and want to come away. There is no doubt that Muslims in India are also full of fear. There is hardly a Muslim in West Bengal or even in Delhi and many other places in India who has a sense of safety. Certainly they have no sense of future well-being and progress. That is no doubt partly due to circumstances beyond our control. But partly also it is due to our own wavering policy and to the thought in the minds of many of us that Muslims are aliens in India, not to be trusted, and to be got rid of as soon and as tactfully as possible.

In West Bengal conditions have become very bad. The murder of Cameron, presumably while defending his Muslim chauffeur, is of high significance, not because he was a prominent Englishman but because it shows up the state of Calcutta today. How can we blame Pakistan for the misdeeds of any individuals or groups in Pakistan when we are totally unable to give security to our own people? There is little doubt that our reputation, whatever it was, is going to pieces and even our bona fides are challenged.

I think we have taken up far too lenient an attitude towards those in India who encourage this communal feeling of hatred and violence. The Hindu Mahasabha talks about Akhand Bharat, which is a direct incentive to conflict. War is openly talked about. As a Government we seem to be fading out of the picture and people publicly say that our Government has contradictory policies and, as a result, no policy at all. The belief that retaliation is a suitable method to deal with Pakistan, or what happens in Pakistan, is growing.

That is the surest way to ruin for India and Pakistan and for vast numbers of human beings in these two countries. That surely is not a way to protect minorities.

Whatever Pakistan may do, we have a certain responsibility for Indian nationals, whether they are Hindu or Muslim. We are progressively unable to discharge that responsibility. The question of foreign policy also comes up and has to be cleared. So also many other matters.

In these circumstances, the fact that you and I pull in different directions, and in any event the belief that we do so, is exceedingly harmful. Our Governmental machinery is suffering because of this and senior Government officers have the temerity to criticize ministers of Government in private and even to some extent in semi-public. It is clear that such a situation must be ended as rapidly as possible.

The matter is far too important for a decision by individuals. It involves national policy. The party, of course, must have a say in the matter. But ultimately it is for the Congress organization to decide, whether it is the Working Committee or the AICC. The Working Committee is meeting soon. Personally I think the matter is important enough for the AICC to have an emergency meeting. I wish we could have a full session of the Congress, but that is not possible for some months. A clear line must be laid down and followed rigorously and loyally.

There should be no doubt in the minds of the people and the party and Government officials what our policy is and how it should be carried out. Any weakness in it on the part of a Government official will have to be sternly met.

I have referred to these larger questions of policy which can be ignored no longer. I remember when the AICC met soon after the Punjab disturbances and Gandhiji was present and guided our deliberations. Personally I feel that that line was correct then and is basically correct now.

The personal equation, as between you and me, has of course importance for both of us and for the country. But I think we should consider this matter primarily, apart from the personal equation. After the decision on principle is taken, other questions can be decided with greater ease. In any event, the present disorderly state of our minds and work should be ended as soon as possible.

Yours,
Jawaharlal

2. Sardar Patel to Jawaharlal Nehru, 28 March 1950

New Delhi
28 March 1950

YOUR LETTER OF 26 March 1950 has surprised and distressed me greatly. From your letter it appears you have carried a weight of mental anguish and a burden and mental worry which, having regard to the relations which have existed between us, I would have expected you to unburden on me not only during the several meetings we have had but also, if necessary, at any special meeting which I would have been only too ready to have had. In fact I feel personally pained and hurt that you should not have thought me to be deserving of such confidence and should have permitted yourself to be upset by what obviously interested and malevolently disposed persons have been telling you or others and propagating with obviously a mischievous design.

What you write about the unfortunate developments which preceded Bapu's death brings vividly to my mind the whole picture.

But one thing in that stands out most prominently and it is the last conversation which I had with him and in which he expressed his considered opinion that both you and I should continue to collaborate in the service of the country since the consequences of any separation would be disastrous to its interests. I have striven to my utmost to execute these last words of Bapu. I have, according to my lights, striven to strengthen your hands as much as I could, while giving expression to my views frankly and sincerely. I have given you my loyal support, often at times subjecting myself to considerable self-restraint. I cannot recall any time during the last two years when I have asserted myself against any determined course of policy which you have adumbrated. We have differed on some matters but have recognized that such differences were natural and have adjusted ourselves in order to evolve an agreed policy. It has, therefore, grieved me greatly to feel that I have been found by you wanting in the execution of Bapu's last message.

This also brings me to the tragic developments which preceded Bapu's death. I warned him and you then of the terrible consequences that I apprehended of the developing serious situation. Unfortunately the tragedy could not be averted and [it] engulfed us. Certain persons even then interested themselves in creating an estrangement between both of us. They tried to poison your ears as well as Bapu's against me. After Bapu's death you wrote to me an affectionate and touching letter which I have prized all along and we resolved to devote ourselves jointly to the cause of our country. It appears that some persons have again found in the present troubled atmosphere and your own troubled state of mind an easy opportunity of creating an atmosphere of doubts, misgivings and conflict. I am really sorry and distressed that you should have listened to their accounts and given credence to them without asking me even once for the authentic version. It is not, however, that aspect which bothers me so much as the parallel with the tragic situation which preceded Bapu's martyrdom. My mind is full of apprehensions about the end and consequence of it all, considering the highly emotional and explosive temperament of the Bengalees and the surcharged atmosphere all over the country, affecting not only the towns but the villages which fortunately had been immune from the pernicious malady. I sometimes have the feeling that we are on the verge of a tragedy which might still be averted if we could act in time.

Now I shall come to the meeting of fifty or sixty persons at my house to which you refer. I had been approached by [Mahavir] Tyagi to meet some members who had some doubts and difficulties about my attitude over various matters and wanted virtually to put me on the defensive. I put him off as I knew that this was likely to be misused. Then came the Home and States ministries' demand on which there were 75 to 100 cut motions. In accordance with the usual arrangements, a meeting of these members was convened in the Council of States room to discuss the cut motions. Subsequently, I was told that members wanted to meet me at the house. Having regard to the view I held of the earlier attempt of Tyagi to have a meeting at my house, I told Satyanarayan [Sinha] Babu of the unwisdom of this step. Then Balkrishna Sharma sent a note to Satyanarayan Babu giving a notice of a cut motion of Rs 100 'to enable Shri Balkrishna Sharma to have tea at the Home Minister's house'. This was obviously done in good humour and I was told that the demand was backed by a large number of members. Even then I told Satyanarayan Babu of the danger in having such a meeting and particularly pointed out that a set of people might try to make capital out of it in their propensity for mischief and might 'carry tales'. However, in view of the pressure I had to yield but it was quite clear even then that the meeting would be devoted to discussing the cut motions and the invitation was restricted to those who had sponsored cut motions.

The tea was accordingly arranged and we all discussed one or two matters arising out of the cut motions in a good-humoured way. It was then that all of them said that they wanted to hear my views about East Bengal. The request was insistent and I had to say something. Even then the line I took was to explain why we could not take any precipitate action; I told them that you were very unhappy about the sufferings which our people were undergoing, that it worried you day and night and that they should not do anything which would irritate you or make you more unhappy. I was then asked about war. I told them that we had to be prepared for all eventualities and were preparing ourselves accordingly but that no action such as war could be taken unless people could speak with one voice. I told them that in Hyderabad also we had long arguments over the pros and cons and a lot of time elapsed. It was only when we all became of one mind that we could take action. Bengal was different. It meant an all-out war between two independent countries and it is all the more necessary that we should have complete unity amongst ourselves. I was then asked that opportunity should be provided to enable the members to express their strong feelings on the subject to you. I told them the time was not appropriate for such a meeting and in the fluid circumstances words might be used which would cause you irritation and unhappiness and therefore I advised [them] against such a move. I also told them that even if there was a difference between what they thought the best course was to wait for time to resolve the differences and not create bitterness. They all seemed to appreciate the position and I was, therefore, surprised when a party meeting was called.

It was at this stage that some persons mentioned our external publicity and its failure to make any impression in foreign countries and amongst foreign correspondence. I then told them the limitations within which our external publicity was functioning and explained that while it had its faults similar to our internal publicity, they had to realize the difficulty of explaining to an opportunistic world the moral standpoint of our foreign policy. I also pointed out to them that they must understand the power and bloc politics of the world and assess the reactions which our moral standpoint must produce on a world used to expediency as against our principles, to intense nationalism as against our internationalism, and to 'group' mentality as against our avoidance of any entanglements. I added that in the process of making our moral standpoint known better and of following our policy we were bound to tread on many corns and make enemies or lose friends. In illustration I cited how having to take the lead in the recognition of China we had to alienate the so-called Nationalist China, whose leader had undoubtedly tried to help us in his own way during our struggle for freedom; similarly our antipathy to the recognition of Bao Dai was bound to be misunderstood by France, the UK, and the USA and the delay in the recognition of Israel because of the feelings of our Muslim citizens on this question would probably cost us some of the goodwill of Israel and countries interested in it. I also pointed out that even some of the Muslim countries had recognized Israel but we had not out of deference for the views of our Muslim brethren. I then referred to the advantage which Pakistan enjoyed over us. In the first place it seemed to arouse the instinctive sympathy of the Europeans. Secondly, it went the whole hog to align itself with the British and Americans and was in the Commonwealth by virtue of common allegiance to the British Crown while we were a republic. There were also British officers in much greater proportion in its [armed] and civil services. All the retired British Civil servants were pro-Pakistanis and the whole of the British Press was practically guided and ruled by them on

Indian affairs. I told them that in these circumstances our external publicity would not achieve everything that they expected it to. You will, therefore, see that it was in a different connection that the question of our foreign policy came up and there was no criticism of it on my part and certainly no disclaimer of my responsibility for it.

It was then that the question was raised about the attitude of the RSS on this issue. I told the meeting that I myself have had some general talks with the RSS leader and have found him generally conforming to my advice of restricting himself to cultural or social matters and advising his followers to support Government. I also told them that my original belief that Bapu's murder was not the result of an RSS conspiracy but that of a section of the Hindu Mahasabha had been confirmed and that I personally regarded the Mahasabha as a greater danger than the RSS. It was at this stage that Balkrishna Sharma said that he had all along felt that the Working Committee's explanation of its earlier decision about the RSS and the Congress was wrong. I replied that I myself felt like that but then the point had been now settled. There were one or two other matters also mentioned namely, Pakistan espionage activities, [Mir] Laik Ali's escape[70] and its consequences, but these are not relevant to your letter and therefore I omit them.

The meeting then terminated. At the end, however, I warned Satyanarayan Sinha that interested persons might misrepresent matters and warned him against their activities. He accordingly went to you and gave you an account of what transpired. I have now given you a fairly detailed account of the genesis of the meeting and what transpired. I can tell you quite frankly that even at this stage I do not see that I have said anything at the meeting which I would not be prepared to repeat in your presence in the same gathering even now and that l do not see how anything that I said can be construed in the manner in which it was apparently represented to you and which upset you so much. In fact I was certain about it that even when I was told after the party meeting which you convened and at which you spoke so vehemently that all that you said was directed at me I discounted the idea and said that I could not believe it.

You have also referred to a Cabinet meeting at which I made remarks which hurt you. I do not know which Cabinet meeting you refer to but if you are referring to the one which you held the day before you made your statement to the Assembly on your return from Calcutta, I might say that I still have the impression shared by many others that we had decided to discuss the matter again after your return from Calcutta and I, therefore, genuinely felt that a statement should have been made only after such discussion in the Cabinet. I am sorry if all this hurt you but I am sure you will agree from the reactions which your statement produced all over India and more especially in Bengal that what I felt was not without substance. As regards Pakistan in general and East Bengal in particular, there is undoubtedly a difference in our approach but I do not think I have at any time allowed that difference to oppose you in regard to any action which you deemed right. While expressing my views in favour of a firm policy and more determined stand, I have submitted to any action that you eventually decided. As regards the differences of our approach, as far as I know there has been none as regard the secular ideals to which we all subscribe and for which we all stand; in fact, I have throughout emphasized the need for full protection of minorities in India and condemned violence. At the same time, I have not ignored the basic cause of such violence, namely, what is happening in Pakistan and the bitterness which it engenders in the country. When we consider stern action to deal with trouble on our side we have to take into account this fact, for to ignore it would mean our depending on coercion and suppression to deal with the psychology of deep-seated grievances and prejudices as regards our neighbours which unfortunately has repercussions on the followers of Islam in this country. You yourself have recognized this in your correspondence with the Pakistan Prime Minister. I have also laid stress on the fact that our secular ideals impose a responsibility on our Muslim citizens in India – a responsibility to remove the doubts and misgivings entertained by a large section of the people about their loyalty founded largely on their past association with the demand for Pakistan and the unfortunate activities of some of them. It is in this light that to my mind some tangible steps to deal with the present situation become urgent and that is why I have been insisting on a well-considered, firm and determined line of approach. I do not think that any discussion in the Working Committee or the AICC would be of any help. In fact, I am convinced that the less we discuss these matters in public or semi-public and the more we concentrate on setting a firm line of policy the better; it will avoid public bitterness and exhibition of tempers such as we are witnessing in Bengal and elsewhere today; it will also convince the people that we have a plan to deal with the problems and that we mean business. This would have a much more settling and steadying effect than a public discussion of the different lines of approach which are holding the field in the Press and on the platform. The need of the hour is to rally the country round a settled programme – settled not in the dust, turmoil and passion of public controversy but quietly in the meetings of a small business-like body as we did in the case of Punjab disturbances or Hyderabad. I am sure the country will follow us in a disciplined way once we have come to a decision in a clear-cut manner. I have no doubt things are going out of control in Bengal and may be more so there and elsewhere in India because of a feeling of frustration and the general belief that the Government has no fixed or final policy to deal with this grave situation.

You have also referred to the attitude which we have taken on communal hatred and violence. I do not think it would be correct to call it lenient. I think figures will bear out that we have controlled the communal Press far more drastically than the communist [press] and our action has been circumscribed only by the provisions of the law as interpreted by our legal advisers and the High Courts. We put thousands in jail and adopted a policy of release only after we were continuously attacked on the score of maintaining civil liberties. You will yourself recall the many letters you wrote to me on this subject last year. We are now faced with a Constitution which guarantees fundamental rights – right of association, right of free movement, free expression and personal liberty – which further circumscribe the action that we can take. That means that for every executive action there must be legal sanction and judicial justification. If within these limits you feel that our policy towards communal organizations has been lenient, steps can certainly be taken in the manner you may suggest.

On the question of foreign policy, I do not think I have at any time expressed any difference of approach except in the Cabinet whenever any particular subject has come up before the Cabinet. I have already expressed to you what I said at the meeting and the context in which it was said. I do not think in the pursuit of foreign affairs you have met any obstruction or opposition from me or any of your Cabinet colleagues. In private some of us may have expressed our disagreement with a particular item of that policy but I do not think it can be your intention that we should not express ourselves even in private.

I am in full accord with you that Government officials, high or low, should live themselves up with such policy as we decide but I do not think we can regiment their private views or muzzle them to that extent. We can only insist that in public as well as in official matters they implicitly execute [the] settled policy. We should also not too readily believe any whispers started about their attitude or activities which interested parties such as those which try to create a rift between you and me might launch against them. I myself feel that allowing for our gossip-mongering which seems to have become our natural vice, they have loyally executed our policies. I agree with you that where we find any lapses in this respect we must deal with them strictly and adequately. I think I have now dealt with all the matters which troubled you and which found an expression in your letter. Your letter has afforded me most painful reading. Both age and health have conspired to cheat me of the full enjoyment and pleasure of carrying the heavy burden I have been undertaking in the cause of the country. If I have persisted, it has been only with a desire to strengthen your hands, share your burden, and continue to serve the country in the evening of my life. I have also held to the position because I have felt that our joint efforts are essential to pull the country through one crisis after another which have unfortunately affected the course of its history after Partition. In fact I even now feel that what Bapu said in January 1948 still holds good and it was in this spirit and out of this realization that I appealed to you in our earlier correspondence not to take the step you contemplated of going out of office. I hold that any parting of the ways would spell disaster to the country. Hitherto I have been sustained in my heavy burden by the thought that I had your trust and confidence but I am shaken in the belief by the manner in which you accepted statements made by those interested persons without even verifying from me as to what I had stated and in what context and manner. I have no desire to continue if I cannot fulfil the mission entrusted to me by Bapu in his last moments and strengthen your hands or if you entertain any suspicion about my loyalty to you; or if you think I am an obstacle in the implementation of your policies. Indeed, but for the series of crises which have threatened the country, I would have preferred to spend the time that is left by Providence in constructive work. After all even from outside I could try to strengthen your hands, having failed to do so to your satisfaction from inside. I would not like that on my account we should in any way convert the organization or the country into an arena of controversy particularly at a time when what the nation needs is a united voice and a strength which comes only from unity.

I have expressed myself fully and frankly. I first thought of coming over to you for a discussion rather than write at such length but then I thought that after I had explained myself on the points you have mentioned, it would be easier for us to discuss. I should not like to prolong your agony and it is possible that a personal discussion may help to assuage each other's feelings if written or spoken words have proved inadequate. I am at your disposal whenever you want me to come over.

Yours,
Vallabhbhai Patel

3. Sardar Patel to Jawaharlal Nehru, 7 November 1950

New Delhi
7 November 1950

My dear Jawaharlal,

EVER SINCE MY return from Ahmedabad and after the Cabinet meeting the same day which I had to attend at practically fifteen minutes' notice and for which I regret I was not able to read all papers, I have been anxiously thinking over the problem of Tibet and I thought I should share with you what is passing through my mind.

2. I have carefully gone through the correspondence between the External Affairs Ministry and our Ambassador in Peking and through him the Chinese Government. I have tried to peruse this correspondence as favourably to our Ambassador and the Chinese Government as possible, but I regret to say that neither of them comes out well as a result of this study. The Chinese Government have tried to delude us by professions of peaceful intentions. My own feeling is that at a crucial period they managed to instil into our Ambassador a false sense of confidence in their so-called desire to settle the Tibetan problem by peaceful means. There can be no doubt that during the period covered by this correspondence the Chinese must have been concentrating for an onslaught on Tibet. The final action of the Chinese, in my judgement, is little short of perfidy. The tragedy of it is that the Tibetans put faith in us; they chose to be guided by us; and we have been unable to get them out of the meshes of Chinese diplomacy or Chinese malevolence. From the latest position, it appears that we shall not be able to rescue the Dalai Lama. Our Ambassador has been at great pains to find an explanation or justification for Chinese policy and actions. As the External Affairs Ministry remarked in one of their telegrams, there was a lack of firmness and unnecessary apology in one or two representations that he made to the Chinese Government on our behalf. It is impossible to imagine any sensible person believing in the so-called threat to China from

Anglo-American machinations in Tibet. Therefore, if the Chinese put faith in this, they must have distrusted us so completely as to have taken us as tools or stooges of Anglo-American diplomacy or strategy. This feeling, if genuinely entertained by the Chinese in spite of your direct approaches to them, indicates that even though we regard ourselves as friends of China the Chinese do not regard us as their friends. With the Communist mentality of 'whoever is not with them being against them', this is a significant pointer, of which we have to take due note. During the last several months, outside the Russian camp, we have practically been alone in championing the cause of Chinese entry into the UNO and in securing from the Americans assurances on the question of Formosa. We have done everything we could to assuage Chinese feeling, to allay its apprehensions and to defend its legitimate claims in our discussions and correspondence with America and Britain and in the UNO. In spite of this, China is not convinced about our disinterestedness; it continues to regard us with suspicion and the whole psychology is one, at least outwardly, of scepticism, perhaps mixed with a little hostility. I doubt if we can go any further than we have done already to convince China of our good intentions, friendliness and goodwill. In Peking we have an Ambassador who is eminently suitable for putting across the friendly point of view. Even he seems to have failed to convert the Chinese. Their last telegram to us is an act of gross discourtesy not only in the summary way it disposes of our protest against the entry of Chinese forces into Tibet but also in the wild insinuation that our attitude is determined by foreign influences. It looks as though it is not a friend speaking in that language but a potential enemy.

3. In the background of this, we have to consider what new situation now faces us as a result of the disappearance of Tibet, as we knew it, and the expansion of China almost up to our gates. Throughout history we have seldom been worried about our north-east frontier. The Himalayas have been regarded as an impenetrable barrier against any threat from the north. We had a friendly Tibet which gave us no trouble. The Chinese were divided. They had their own domestic problems and never bothered us about our frontiers. In 1914, we entered into a convention with Tibet which was not endorsed by the Chinese. We seem to have regarded Tibetan autonomy as extending to independent treaty relationship. Presumably, all that we required was [a] Chinese counter-signature. The Chinese interpretation of suzerainty seems to be different. We can, therefore, safely assume that very soon they will disown all the stipulations, which Tibet has entered into with us in the past. That throws into the melting pot all frontier and commercial settlements with Tibet on which we have been functioning and acting during the last half a century. China is no longer divided. It is united and strong. All along the Himalayas in the north and north-east, we have on our side of the frontier a population ethnologically and culturally not different from Tibetans or Mongoloids. The undefined state of the frontier and the existence on our side of a population with its affinities to Tibetans or Chinese have all the elements of potential trouble between China and ourselves. Recent and bitter history also tells us that communism is no shield against imperialism and that the Communists are as good or as bad imperialists as any other. Chinese ambitions in this respect not only cover the Himalayan slopes on our side but also include

important parts of Assam. They have their ambitions in Burma also; Burma has the added difficulty that it has no McMahon Line round which to build up even the semblance of an agreement. Chinese irredentism and Communist imperialism are different from the expansionism or imperialism of the Western Powers. The former has a cloak of ideology which makes it ten times more dangerous. In the guise of ideological expansion lie concealed racial, national or historical claims. The danger from the north and north-east, therefore, becomes both communist and imperialist. While our western and north-western threat to security is still as prominent as before, a new threat has developed from the north and north-east. Thus, for the first time, after centuries, India's defence has to concentrate itself on two fronts simultaneously. Our defence measures have so far been based on the calculations of a superiority over Pakistan. In our calculations we shall now have to reckon with Communist China in the north and in the north-east, a Communist China which has definite ambitions and aims and which does not, in any way, seem friendly disposed towards us.

4. Let us also consider the political conditions on this potentially troublesome frontier. Our northern or north-eastern approaches consist of Nepal, Bhutan, Sikkim, the Darjeeling [area] and tribal areas in Assam. From the point of view of communications, they are weak spots. Continuous defensive lines do not exist. There is almost an unlimited scope for infiltration. Police protection is limited to a very small number of passes. There, too, our outposts do not seem to be fully manned. The contact of these areas with us is by no means close and intimate. The people inhabiting these portions have no establishing loyalty or devotion to India.

Even the Darjeeling and Kalimpong areas are not free from pro-Mongoloid prejudices. During the last three years we have not been able to make any appreciable approaches to the Nagas and other hill tribes in Assam. European missionaries and other visitors had been in touch with them, but their influence was in no way friendly to India or Indians. In Sikkim, there was political ferment some time ago. It is quite possible that discontent is smouldering there. Bhutan is comparatively quiet, but its affinity with Tibetans would be a handicap. Nepal has a weak oligarchic regime based almost entirely on force; it is in conflict with a turbulent element of the population as well as with enlightened ideas of the modern age. In these circumstances, to make people alive to the new danger or to make them defensively strong is a very difficult task indeed and that difficulty can be got over only by enlightened firmness, strength and a clear line of policy. I am sure the Chinese and their sources of inspiration, Soviet Russia, would not miss any opportunity of exploiting these weak spots, partly in support of their ideology and partly in support of their ambitions. In my judgement, therefore, the situation is one in which we cannot afford either to be complacent or to be vacillating. We must have a clear idea of what we wish to achieve and also of the methods by which we should achieve it. Any faltering or lack of decisiveness in formulating our objectives or in pursuing our policy to attain those objectives is bound to weaken us and increase the threats which are so evident.

5. Side by side with these external dangers, we shall now have to face serious internal problems as well. I have already asked [H.V.R.] Iengar to send to the E.A. Ministry a copy of the Intelligence Bureau's appreciation of these matters. Hitherto,

the Communist Party of India has found some difficulty in contacting Communists abroad, or in getting supplies of arms, literature, etc., from them. They had to contend with the difficult Burmese and Pakistan frontiers on the east or with the long seaboard. They shall now have a comparatively easy means of access to Chinese Communists and through them to other foreign Communists. Infiltration of spies, fifth columnists and Communists would now be easier. Instead of having to deal with isolated Communist pockets in Telengana and Warangal we may have to deal with Communist threats to our security along our northern and north-eastern frontiers where, for supplies of arms and ammunition, they can safely depend on Communist arsenals in China. The whole situation thus raises a number of problems on which we must come to an early decision so that we can, as I said earlier, formulate the objectives of our policy and decide the methods by which those objectives are to be attained. It is also clear that the action will have to be fairly comprehensive, involving not only our defence strategy and state of preparations but also problems of internal security to deal with which we have not a moment to lose. We shall also have to deal with administrative and political problems in the weak spots along the frontier to which I have already referred.

6. It is, of course, impossible for me to be exhaustive in setting out all these problems. I am, however, giving below some of the problems which, in my opinion, require early solution and round which we have to build our administrative or military policies and measures to implement them.

   (a) A military and intelligence appreciation of the Chinese threat to India both on the frontier and to internal security.

(b) An examination of our military position and such redisposition of our forces as might be necessary, particularly with the idea of guarding important routes or areas which are likely to be the subject of dispute.
(c) An appraisement of the strength of our forces and, if necessary, reconsideration of our retrenchment plans for the Army in the light of these new threats.
(d) A long-term consideration of our defence needs. My own feeling is that, unless we assure our supplies of arms, ammunition and armour, we should be making our defence position perpetually weak, and we would not be able to stand up to the double threat of difficulties both from the west and north-west and north and north-east.
(e) The question of Chinese entry into UNO. In view of the rebuff which China has given us and the method which it has followed in dealing with Tibet, I am doubtful whether we can advocate its claims any longer. There would probably be a threat in the UNO virtually to outlaw China in view of its active participation in the Korean war. We must determine our attitude on this question also.
(f) The political and administrative steps which we should take to strengthen our northern and north-eastern frontiers. This would include the whole of the border, i.e., Nepal, Bhutan, Sikkim, Darjeeling and the tribal territory in Assam.
(g) Measures of internal security in the border areas as well as the States flanking those areas, such as UP, Bihar, Bengal and Assam.
(h) Improvement of our communications, road, rail, air and wireless, in these areas and with the frontier posts.

(i) Policing and intelligence of frontier posts.

(j) The future of our mission at Lhasa and the trade posts at Gyantse and Yatung and the forces which we have in operation in Tibet to guard the trade routes.

(k) The policy in regard to the McMahon Line.

5. These are some of the questions which occur to my mind. It is possible that a consideration of these matters may lead us into wider questions of our relationship with China, Russia, America, Britain and Burma. This, however, would be of a general nature, though some might be basically very important, e.g., we might have to consider whether we should not enter into closer association with Burma in order to strengthen the latter in its dealing with China. I do not rule out the possibility that, before applying pressure on us, China might apply pressure on Burma. With Burma, the frontier is entirely undefined and the Chinese territorial claims are more substantial. In its present position, Burma might offer an easier problem for China and, therefore, might claim its first attention.

6. I suggest that we meet early to have a general discussion on these problems and decide on such steps as we might think to be immediately necessary and direct quick examination of other problems with a view to taking early measures to deal with them.

Yours,

Vallabhbhai Patel

4. Prime Minister Jawaharlal Nehru's Note on China and Tibet, 18 November 1950[71]

1. THE CHINESE GOVERNMENT having replied to our last note, we have to consider what further steps we should take in this matter. There is no immediate hurry about sending a reply to the Chinese Government. But we have to send immediate instructions to Shri B.N. Rau[72] as to what he should do in the event of Tibet's appeal being brought up before the Security Council of the General Assembly.
2. The content of the Chinese reply is much the same as their previous notes, but there does appear to be a toning down and an attempt at some kind of a friendly approach.
3. It is interesting to note that they have not referred specifically to our mission [at] Lhasa or to our trade agents or military escort at Gyantse, etc. We had mentioned these especially in our last note. There is an indirect reference, however, in China's note. At the end, this note says that, 'As long as our two sides adhere strictly to the principle of mutual respect for territory, sovereignty, equality and mutual benefit, we are convinced that the friendship between China and India should be developed in a normal way and that problems relating to Sino-Indian diplomatic, commercial and cultural relations with respect to Tibet may be solved properly and to our mutual benefit through normal diplomatic channels.' This clearly refers to our trade agents and others in Tibet. We had expected a demand from them for the withdrawal of these agents, etc. The fact that they have not done so has some significance.
4. Stress is laid in China's note on Chinese sovereignty over Tibet, which, we are reminded, we have acknowledged, on

Tibet being an integral part of China's territory and therefore a domestic problem. It is however again repeated that outside influences have been at play obstructing China's mission in Tibet. In fact, it is stated that liberation of Changtu[73] proves that foreign forces and influences were inciting Tibetan troops to resist. It is again repeated that no foreign intervention will be permitted and that the Chinese Army will proceed.

5. All this is much the same as has been said before, but it is said in [a] somewhat different way and there are repeated references in the note to China desiring the friendship of India.

6. It is true that in one of our messages to the Chinese Government we used 'sovereignty' of China in relation to Tibet. In our last message we used the word 'suzerainty'. After receipt of China's last note, we have pointed out to our Ambassador that 'suzerainty' was the right word and that 'sovereignty' had been used by error.

7. It is easy to draft a reply to the Chinese note, pressing our viewpoint and countering some of the arguments raised in the Chinese note. But, before we do so, we should be clear in our own mind as to what we are aiming at, not only in the immediate future but from a long-term view. It is important that we keep both these viewpoints before us. In all probability China, that is, present-day China, is going to be our close neighbour for a long time to come. We are going to have a tremendously long common frontier. It is unlikely, and it would be unwise to expect that the present Chinese Government will collapse, giving place to another. Therefore, it is important to pursue a policy which will be in keeping with this long-term view.

8. I think it may be taken for granted that China will take possession, in a political sense at least, of the whole of Tibet. There is no likelihood whatever of Tibet being able to resist this or stop it. It is equally unlikely that any foreign Power can prevent it. We cannot do so. If so, what can we do to help in the maintenance of Tibetan autonomy and at the same time avoiding continuous tension and apprehension on our frontiers?
9. The Chinese note has repeated that they wish the Tibetan people to have what they call 'regional autonomy and religious freedom'. This autonomy can obviously not be anything like the autonomy verging on independence which Tibet has enjoyed during the last forty years or so. But it is reasonable to assume from the very nature of Tibetan geography, terrain and climate, that a large measure of autonomy is almost inevitable. It may of course be that this autonomous Tibet is controlled by communist elements in Tibet. I imagine however that it is, on the whole, more likely that what will be attempted will be a pro-communist China administration rather than a communist one.
10. If [a] world war comes, then all kinds of difficult and intricate problems arise and each one of these problems will be inter-related with others. Even the question of defence of India assumes a different shape and cannot be isolated from other world factors. I think that it is exceedingly unlikely that we may have to face any real military invasion from the Chinese side, whether in peace or in war, in the foreseeable future. I base this conclusion on a consideration of various world factors. In peace, such an invasion would undoubtedly lead to [a] world war. China, though internally big, is in a way

amorphous and easily capable of being attacked, on its sea coasts and by air. In such a war, China would have its main front in the south and east and it will be fighting for its very existence against powerful enemies. It is inconceivable that it should divert its forces and its strength across the inhospitable terrain of Tibet and undertake a wild adventure across the Himalayas. Any such attempt will greatly weaken its capacity to meet its real enemies on other fronts. Thus, I rule out any major attack on India by China. I think these considerations should be borne in mind, because there is far too much loose talk about China attacking and overrunning India. If we lose our sense of perspective and world strategy and give way to unreasoning fears, then any policy that we might have is likely to fail.

11. While there is, in any opinion, practically no chance of a major attack on India by China, there are certainly chances of gradual infiltration across our border and possibly of entering and taking possession of disputed territory, if there is no obstruction to this happening. We must therefore take all necessary precautions to prevent this. But, again, we must differentiate between these precautions and those that might be necessary to meet a real attack.
12. If we really feared an attack and had to make full provision for it, this would cast an intolerable burden on us, financial and otherwise, and it would weaken our general defence position. There are limits beyond which we cannot go, at least for some years, and a spreading out of our army on distant frontiers would be bad from every military or strategic point of view.
13. In spite of our desire to settle any points at issue between us and Pakistan, and developing peaceful relations with it,

the fact remains that our major possible enemy is Pakistan. This has compelled us to think of our defence mainly in terms of Pakistan's aggression. If we begin to think of, and prepare for, China's aggression in the same way, we would weaken considerably on the Pakistan side. We might well be got in a pincer movement. It is interesting to note that Pakistan is taking a great deal of interest, from this point of view, in developments in Tibet. Indeed, it has been discussed in the Pakistan Press that the new danger from Tibet to India might help them to settle the Kashmir problem according to their wishes. Pakistan has absolutely nothing in common with China or Tibet. But if we fall out completely with China, Pakistan will undoubtedly try to take advantage of this, politically or otherwise. The position of India thus will be bad from a defence point of view. We cannot have all the time two possible enemies on either side of India. This danger will not be got over, even if we increase our defence forces or even if other foreign countries help us in arming. The measure of safety that one gets by increasing the defence apparatus is limited by many factors. But whatever that measure of safety might be, strategically we would be in an unsound position and the burden of this will be very great on us. As it is, we are facing enormous difficulties, financial, economic, etc.

14. The idea that communism inevitably means expansion and war, or, to put it more precisely, that Chinese communism means inevitably an expansion towards India, is rather naive. It may mean that in certain circumstances. Those circumstances would depend upon many factors, which I need not go into here. The danger really is not from military invasion but from infiltration of men and ideas. The ideas are there already –

and can only be countered by other ideas. Communism is an important element in the situation. But, by our attaching too great importance to it in this context, we are likely to misjudge the situation from other and more important angles.

15. In a long-term view, India and China are two of the biggest countries of Asia bordering on each other and both with certain expansive tendencies, because of their vitality. If their relations are bad, this will have a serious effect not only on both of them but on Asia as a whole. It would affect our future for a long time. If a position arises in which China and India are inveterately hostile to each other, like France and Germany, then there will be repeated wars bringing destruction to both. The advantage will go to other countries. It is interesting to note that both the UK and the USA appear to be anxious to add to the unfriendliness of India and China towards each other. It is also interesting to find that the USSR does not view with favour any friendly relations between India and China. These are long-term reactions which one can fully understand, because India and China at peace with each other would make a vast difference to the whole set-up and balance of the world. Much of course depends upon the development of either country and how far communism in China will mould the Chinese people. Even so, these processes are long-range ones and in the long run it is fairly safe to assume that hundreds of millions of people will not change their essential characteristics.

16. These arguments lead to the conclusion that while we should be prepared, to the best of our ability, for all contingencies, the real protection that we should seek is some kind of understanding of China. If we have not got that, then both

our present and our future are imperilled and no distant power can save us. I think on the whole that China desires this too for obvious reasons. If this is so, then we should fashion our present policy accordingly.

17. We cannot save Tibet, as we should have liked to do, and our very attempts to save it might well bring greater trouble to it. It would be unfair to Tibet for us to bring this trouble upon her without having the capacity to help her effectively. It may be possible, however, that we might be able to help Tibet to retain a large measure of her autonomy. That would be good for Tibet and good for India. As far as I can see, this can only be done on the diplomatic level and by avoidance of making the present tension between India and China worse.

18. What then should be our instructions to B.N. Rau? From the messages he has sent us, it appears that no member of the Security Council shows any inclination to sponsor Tibet's appeal and that there is little likelihood of the matter being considered by the Council. We have said that [we] are not going to sponsor this appeal, but if it comes up we shall state our viewpoint. This viewpoint cannot be one of full support of the Tibetan appeal, because that goes far and claims full independence. We may say that whatever might have been acknowledged in the past about China's sovereignty or suzerainty, recent events have deprived China of the right to claim that. There may be some moral basis for this argument. But it will not take us or Tibet very far. It will only hasten the downfall of Tibet. No outsider will be able to help her and China, suspicious and apprehensive of these tactics, will make sure of much speedier and fuller possession of Tibet than she might otherwise have done. We shall thus not only fail in our

endeavour but at the same time have really a hostile China on our doorstep.

19. I think that in no event should we sponsor Tibet's appeal. I would personally think that it would be a good thing if that appeal is not heard in the Security Council or the General Assembly. If it is considered there, there is bound to be a great deal of bitter speaking and accusation, which will worsen the situation as regards Tibet, as well as the possibility of widespread war, without helping it in the least. It must be remembered that neither the UK nor the USA, nor indeed any other power, is particularly interested in Tibet or the future of that country. What they are interested in is embarrassing China. Our interest, on the other hand, is Tibet, and if we cannot serve that interest, we fail.

20. Therefore, it will be better not to discuss Tibet's appeal in the UN. Suppose, however, that it comes up for discussion, in spite of our not wishing this, what then? I would suggest that our representative should state our case as moderately as possible and ask the Security Council or the Assembly to give expression to their desire that the Sino-Tibetan question should be settled peacefully and that Tibet's autonomy should be respected and maintained. Any particular reference to an article of the Charter of the UN might tie us up in difficulties and lead to certain consequences later which may prove highly embarrassing for us. Or a resolution of the UN might just be a dead letter, which also will be bad.

21. If my general argument is approved, then we can frame our reply to China's note accordingly.

J. Nehru

18 November 1950

4

'You are treating this Constitution like a scrap of paper'

Syama Prasad Mookerjee and Jawaharlal Nehru clash over the First Amendment and Fundamental Rights

ON 16 MAY 1951, Prime Minister Nehru moved the Constitution (First Amendment) Bill to be referred to a standing committee in Parliament, ominously declaring that the magnificent Constitution that he and his compatriots in the Constituent Assembly had framed only fifteen months earlier had been kidnapped and purloined by lawyers.[1] Fundamental Rights, civil liberties and individual freedom, ideas that had dominated political discourse in the nineteenth century, were relics of a static age that preserved existing social relationships and social inequalities, he argued. These ideas were now obsolete and outdated. In the middle of the twentieth century, bigger and better ideas were now in fashion, dynamic ideas of social reform and social engineering – ideas embodied in the grand programmes of the Congress party and enshrined in the Constitution as the Directive Principles of State Policy.[2]

Nehru had many reasons to be angry. The shining new schemes of social engineering that he had pioneered and championed – land reform, zamindari abolition, nationalization of industry, reservations for 'backward classes', a pliant press – were supposed to remake the social and political fabric of the new republic. Zamindari abolition and land reform had been a part of the Congress programme for close to twenty years. Nationalization and a planned economy had been the driving force behind the creation of the first National Planning Committee in 1938, presided over by Nehru himself. And yet, by May 1951 almost all these schemes, the bedrock of Nehru's social and economic policy, had been struck down by the judiciary as being violative of constitutional bounds. The feeling that the government was under judicial siege had grown. To top it all, he was facing withering criticism in the press. The First Amendment was Nehru's way of striking back by constraining the fundamental rights that had proved to be a roadblock for his plans for social transformation.

The amendment circumscribed the right to freedom of speech, the right to property and the right to freedom from discrimination. Given that these far-reaching constitutional changes were sought to be enacted by an indirectly elected provisional parliament, it was only to be expected that the amendment became the subject of some of independent India's fiercest parliamentary debates, in which stalwarts like Acharya Kripalani, B.R. Ambedkar, C. Rajagopalachari, H.V. Kamath, H.N. Kunzru and Frank Anthony crossed swords. But even among the sharp wit and incisive repartee of these luminaries, the verbal duel between Jawaharlal Nehru and the unofficial

Leader of the Opposition Syama Prasad Mookerjee – described by Nehru's biographer Walter Crocker as the most effective speaker in Parliament[3] – over the substance and the timing of the amendment unquestionably ranks as one of the finest oratorical battles in Indian parliamentary history.[4]

Reporting on the debate the following day the *Times of India* approvingly noted: 'Mr Nehru's sentiment was more than outmatched by the impassioned logic of Dr Mookerjee.'[5] So rousing was Mookerjee's oratory that the Congress leader N.G. Ranga, who was next to speak, described it as 'one of the most powerful and eloquent speeches' he had ever heard, and called Mookerjee the 'the Indian Burke' after the great Anglo-Irish parliamentarian and conservative philosopher. 'I began to think,' Ranga rhapsodized, 'how the British Parliament must have reacted to that other great man as he was reeling out his great eloquence.'[6] Mookerjee's eloquent defence of a supposedly 'Burkean' conservatism[7] in the face of the rising tide of Nehruvian progressivism is one of the many reasons that this debate is both absorbing and crucial in the context of India's constitutional history.

Nehru and Mookerjee were at opposite ends of the political spectrum in 1951. Both have enjoyed a long afterlife as icons for their respective followers and parties, afterlives that have proved to divide and animate the two central political and ideological poles of Indian politics and left enduring legacies for their successors. Both were debating foundational issues – the extent of the right to free speech, the space for dissent, the use and abuse of sedition, the balance of power between the organs of the state, constitutional propriety – that remain as relevant now as they were in 1951. Mookerjee is now known as the founder of the Bharatiya Jana Sangh, the forerunner of today's Bharatiya Janata Party, described as a religious conservative[8] and closely identified with Hindu nationalism. It is from him that the BJP claims political descent. Nehru, on the other hand, widely credited with laying the foundations of Indian democracy, often embodies liberalism, secularism and progressivism in the popular imagination – an incarnation in which he often finds himself pitted against the incumbent Prime Minister Narendra Modi. Like in 1951, foundational questions are up for renewed contestation, and the ghosts of Nehru and Mookerjee have found themselves once again in the field, reliving a similar debate.

In truth however, these public images with their lazy dichotomies are later creations: the legacies of Nehru and Mookerjee are as complicated as were the men themselves, to which their verbal duel testifies. The debate on the First Amendment upends many of the lax assumptions and easy caricatures to which the public images of both are subject. The position that Nehru articulated – the curbing of civil liberties including free speech in pursuit of a 'progressive' and 'socialist' government agenda – and the language that he deployed belies his current genteel liberal image. Mookerjee's passionate defence of individual liberty and constitutional morality, no less radical in newly independent India, drew from the tenets of classical liberalism of the whiggish variety – a far cry from religious conservatism[9] and an even further cry from the views of his ideological successors. Boundaries between liberal and authoritarian visions of India, between Nehru and Mookerjee, between a repressive colonial past and a democratic post-colonial future are not only more blurred than commonly imagined – they often do not exist at all.

Current strands of historiography often take diametrically opposite views about the Indian Constitution. Some see it as a constitutional revolution that transformed the relationship between the rulers and the ruled with an expansive chapter on Fundamental Rights.[10] Others see violence and authoritarianism – with an overbearing, centralized executive enabled by the Constitution – as foundational to the postcolonial Indian state.[11] Both dominant interpretations are upended by the First Amendment – and the contours of the debate it engendered in Parliament. If the republic's founding moment was transformative, then this transformation was partially cut short and amputated by the First Amendment.[12] If authoritarianism is indeed foundational to the postcolonial Indian state, then such a state of affairs owes much to the First Amendment.

Turning common perceptions on their head, as the Nehru-Mookerjee debate does, the broader story of the First Amendment both challenges popular beliefs about the halcyon days of Indian democracy in its first flush and asks uncomfortable questions about its present predicaments. It is often asserted, for example, that India's draconian public safety laws, such as the law of sedition, are a legacy of its colonial past that is now being misused as a means of silencing dissent.[13] Yet, contrary to popular perception, not only are such laws constitutionally rooted in the First Amendment that (among other freedoms) curbed free speech – they were also championed by Nehru as a core component of his version of modernity. Far from being a remnant of colonialism, they are an outcome of the Nehruvian state's determination to suppress political alternatives; a vital part of India's Nehruvian legacy.

The story of the amendment, India's first great clash of ideas, reveals the Nehruvian vision of India to have eerie convergences with the modern-day privileging of statism, Nehru's arguments mirroring those put forward by his detractors today – as much as it shows Mookerjee's vision of India to be the antithesis to that of his ideological successors.

RIGHT AT THE outset, in 1946, when India's Constituent Assembly took up the arduous task of framing a constitution for the new nation, the idea that Fundamental Rights and individual liberty underpinned the entire enterprise had enjoyed broad support. The Constitution was meant to be a charter of freedom – the intent was affirmed from the moment the new chairman, Rajendra Prasad, declared the assembly's resolve to: '[P]lace before the world a model of a constitution that will satisfy all our people, all groups, all communities, all religions inhabiting this vast land, and which will ensure to everyone freedom of action, freedom of thought, freedom of belief and freedom of worship.'[14]

These provisions for civil liberties and their enforcement were meant to be the dividing line between a repressive colonial past and a liberal new present,[15] the culmination of the efforts of several generations of nationalists and fulfilment of the Congress pledge to achieve freedom for the Indian people. Part III of the Constitution – the chapter on Fundamental Rights – attested to the determination of the new republic to jettison its colonial baggage. It was thus very apt for B.R. Ambedkar, one of the new constitution's key architects, to describe it as the 'heart and soul' of the whole Constitution,[16] or for it to be hailed on 26 January 1950 as 'the most elaborate declaration of human rights yet framed by any state'.[17] The inauguration of the Constitution was, in the words of the noted lawyer C.P. Ramaswamy Iyer, the beginning of 'the most far-reaching and significant experiment in human history'.[18]

By March 1951, however, the experiment was floundering, and the charter of freedom had become a stumbling block. Armed with Part III of the new Constitution – guaranteeing the Fundamental Rights of the citizens – zamindars, businessmen, editors, activists and concerned citizens had repeatedly taken the government to court over its attempts to curtail civil liberties in the determined pursuit of its social and economic goals (pending an election, without the legitimacy of a democratic mandate). For their part, the courts had vigorously upheld the new constitutional provisions.

In Delhi, the government's attempt to censor *The Organiser*, an RSS newspaper, had been countermanded.[19] In Bombay, the government's order banning *Cross Roads*, a left-leaning weekly critical of Nehru and the Congress government, had been quashed.[20] In Punjab, while releasing the Akali leader and Nehru baiter Tara Singh, who had been clapped in jail for sedition, the high court had taken the opportunity for reiterating that Section 124A of the Indian Penal Code[21] was wholly unconstitutional and void.[22] By delineating strict limits to governmental interference with the freedom of speech, the judiciary had come out decisively in favour of individual liberty – the government's powers to control public discourse, muffle critical voices and curtail the freedom of the press were eviscerated. As a frustrated Sardar Patel wrote to Nehru, the bottom had been knocked out from penal laws for control and regulation of the press.[23]

Land reform had been stalled. In Uttar Pradesh, the Allahabad High Court had passed a series of injunctions restraining the government from taking any action under the newly passed Zamindari Abolition and Land Reform Act while it examined its constitutional validity. In Bihar, the Land Reform Act had been declared ultra vires of the Constitution by the Patna High Court, for violating Article 14 (the right to equality) by prescribing differential rates of compensation for different landholders.[24] Delivering its verdict in March 1951, the Patna High Court mounted a searing critique of the Congress party and the Bihar government, calling the Act 'an unconstitutional law enacted in the belief that the right of the plaintiffs to challenge it and ask for relief from its operation has been taken away'.[25] The most essential pillar of Congress policy, an article of faith for Nehru and a vital element of the Congress-directed road to socialism, stood in danger of crumbling.

In Madras, the infamous 'Communal Government Order' granting community-based reservations in educational institutions and stringently limiting the number of upper-caste students had been struck down by the Madras High Court, which pointedly observed that Article 15(1) preventing discrimination on caste, communal, racial and linguistic grounds would become an empty bubble if such orders were held to be legal and constitutional.[26] The decision was upheld by the Supreme Court, which then went on to also strike down communal reservations in government jobs.[27] A storm of protest had erupted, with the Madras government demanding a constitutional amendment.

Over the course of 1950 and 1951, Nehru had frequently given vent to his frustration over the judiciary and the Constitution undermining his plans and his policies. He was unable to censor or suppress critical voices, especially the scathing criticism of his policy towards Pakistan mounted by figures like Mookerjee, supported and encouraged by right-leaning commentariat and sections of public opinion in Bengal.[28] There had also been frequent outbursts against the press, which stood accused of spreading malicious falsehoods and propaganda against his government and undermining the morale of the nation by spreading fake news. Through the year he had frequently inveighed against the law and the Constitution holding up his plans for zamindari abolition and land reform – something that also represented a political problem in light of the looming general election.

The actual stalling of zamindari abolition and land reform then, albeit temporary, and the prospect of going into the inaugural general election without having delivered the most key plank of Congress policy shook the government. It resulted in a furious Prime Minister declaring: 'if the Constitution is interpreted by the courts in a way which comes in the way of the wishes of the legislature in regard to basic social matters, then it is for the legislatures to consider how to amend the Constitution so that the will of the people as represented in the legislature should prevail.'[29] For Nehru, and others who shared his vision, these judicial defeats represented a defeat of the whole purpose of the Constitution, embedded in the chapter on directive principles: the 'social' revolution that would transform India. The First Amendment was Nehru's answer to this conundrum: make the Constitution bend to the government's will, overcome the courts and pre-empt any further judicial challenges. It embodied, to borrow a term from the historian C.A. Bayly, 'Nehru's judgment' and his belief in a conception of 'liberal communitarianism'.[30]

EVENTUALLY PASSED BY Parliament after a stormy session on 2 June 1951, the Constitution (First Amendment) Act had four prongs. Firstly, it introduced new grounds to curb the freedom of speech enumerated in Article 19 – public order, the interests of the security of the state and relations with foreign states. These had previously been limited to libel, slander, defamation, morality or any matter that undermined the security of or tended to overthrow the state. The addition of these new grounds drastically lowered the bar for legislation abridging free speech and provided the constitutional infrastructure to greatly expand the government's legal arsenal to clamp down on dissenting voices. Much against Nehru's wishes, B.R. Ambedkar and other members of the Cabinet insisted on the term 'reasonable restrictions' to ensure that the judiciary retained its ability to adjudicate on any consequent legislation.

Secondly, it enabled community-based reservations by restricting the freedom against discrimination by stating that nothing in the said article would prevent the state from making special provisions for any socially or educationally backward classes of citizens. This proviso allowed the government to privilege group rights based on caste or community over individual rights and substantively evade both the right to freedom from discrimination and the right to equality in the pursuit of social justice. Notably, the proviso excluded any mention of economic backwardness in order to ensure that caste remained the primary criteria for assessing the condition of backwardness. In this way, community-based reservations beyond those granted to Scheduled Castes and Tribes was secured.

Thirdly, the amendment further circumscribed the right to property and vastly expanded the protection provided to zamindari abolition by adding that no land reform law shall be deemed void on the ground that it abridges any of the rights conferred by the Constitution. And finally, to exclude any prospect of judicial scrutiny altogether, it created a special schedule, the infamous Ninth Schedule, as a vault where laws could be placed to make them immune from legal challenge even if they violated Fundamental Rights. By doing so, Nehru sought to foreclose the possibility of judicial review altogether when it came to legislation connected to land reform or nationalization.[31]

In a nutshell, the amendment subordinated Fundamental Rights to government policy, sought to emasculate the courts and provided the constitutional foundation for state repression of civil liberties and press freedom. Indian democracy, described by Ambedkar as 'top dressing on undemocratic soil' even at the moment of its birth, has never been the same again. Its first-order effects were apparent even at the time: the revalidation of sedition, the post-colonial government's reclamation of the coercive powers its colonial predecessor had once had, the decimation of property rights, community-based reservations, and a constitutional mechanism to pass unconstitutional laws. In the longer term, however, as the constitutional historian Granville Austin noted, the amendment was 'consequential far beyond its immediately visible content'.[32]

Foremost among these consequences was the creation of the precedent of retrospectively amending the Constitution to overturn adverse judicial pronouncements and render constitutional those actions that at the time of their commission had been patently unconstitutional. Within months of its enactment, the Constitution became subject to the vagaries of electoral swings. When a constitution ceased to represent the people or came in the way of the spirit of the age, Nehru argued to his chief ministers, then it was time for it to change.[33] These arguments legitimized a view that the Constitution, 'rather than being the foundation of the nation's social contract, was a legal document to be amended whenever it suited the government or came in the way of the supposed urges of the people'.[34]

Furthermore, by using an indirectly elected provisional parliament to amend the 'heart and soul' of the Constitution even before the inaugural general election, disregarding widespread protestations[35] – from the president,[36] the speaker,[37] the leader of opposition down to civil society organizations – Nehru failed to account for the need to maintain constitutional rectitude and form positive conventions for the future; even if he believed this was a fair trade-off for the sake of progress or demanded by the gravity of the issues at hand.[38] Transplanting Westminster-style democracy to India, noted the constitutional historian Harshan Kumarasingham, 'demanded instant conventions as the polity had not had the benefit of centuries of evolution. Therein lay the problem and the opportunity for the local executive.'[39] With the First Amendment, India's constitutional journey began with an unhealthy emphasis on executive supremacy, deprivileging individual rights and treating Fundamental Rights as secondary to more important electoral and ideological considerations.[40] Such open disregard for democratic propriety on the part of independent India's first government, even if not extra-constitutional in itself, helped foster a spirit of authoritarianism and constitutional subversion, as Mookerjee had predicted. Originally conceived as permanent guarantees, Fundamental Rights became – to quote Chief Justice Hidayatullah[41] – 'the plaything of special majorities'.[42]

Much of this was exacerbated by the reasoning Nehru presented in Parliament as justification for the amendment: judicial striking down of legislation as a denial of democracy, Fundamental Rights as obsolete remnants of the French Revolution, the primacy of the government's promises over the Constitution, the Constitution as an impediment to the will of the people, recurring references to unseen dangers that threatened the survival of the country, the need to curb 'unbridled criticism', the duty of the state to champion socio-economic transformation over the protection of individual freedom and finally, the desire to fulfil the promises he had made to the electorate. 'It is not good for us to say,' he argued, '[that] we are helpless before fate and the situation we have to face at present.'[43] In sum, Nehru's reasoning represented almost an inversion of the constitutional order, in the express pursuit of a political agenda.

There were many reasons that Nehru's views (and the amendment itself) were considered problematic – his timing before the inaugural general election, the use of an indirectly elected, unicameral and provisional parliament to amend a constitution barely fifteen months after its creation, the amendment's consequences for civil liberties, the disregard for democratic propriety and the need to set good precedents. An alternative cause for discontent was also the widespread belief outside the government that there was no clear and pressing reason for the amendment in the first place. Mookerjee was the sharpest proponent of this view in Parliament, as his reply amply demonstrates. But it was a view shared widely across the political spectrum, from the socialist leader Jayaprakash Narayan to the liberal stalwart Hriday Nath Kunzru to the executive committee of the Federation of the Indian Chambers of Commerce and Industry, and including the President of the Republic, Rajendra Prasad.

Beyond the government, few thought that there was an imminent threat to the new nation's security. 'Except those in power, no one else in the country seems to be aware of any threat to the security of the state,' stated Jayaprakash Narayan in May 1951, 'and yet these crippling amendments are sought to be made in the name of this danger.'[44] In the case of land reform as well, many doubted the reasons the government trotted out. There was broad and non-partisan consensus in Parliament and outside on the need for land reform. The judiciary had upheld zamindari abolition laws in Uttar Pradesh and Maharashtra, confirming that in principle, land reform was perfectly compatible with the right to property. No less than the President advised Nehru that it would be more prudent to bring the legislation into conformity with the Constitution instead of 'taking the very serious step of amending the Constitution'.[45]

Given these circumstances, many were convinced that far from enabling 'the true purpose of the Constitution' as Nehru believed, the amendment was an executive power grab to expand the government's legal arsenal and augment Nehru's own power as Prime Minister – a part of an 'executive struggle and search for constitutional pre-eminence'[46] conducted in the grey zone before India had its first election and became a functioning democracy. A prominent newspaper noted: 'These [constitutional] changes seem animated more by a desire to conserve and consolidate the power and patronage of the executive vis-à-vis the rights and liberties of the individual.'[47] Others went further – noting that the amendment demonstrated either India's unfitness for democratic rule or the inability of its rulers to govern within constitutional bounds.[48]

In amending something as central as Fundamental Rights, many believed, Nehru was guided by a partisan political agenda and was, wittingly or unwittingly, laying the constitutional groundwork for potential executive despotism[49] – in the process, creating legal tools and political precedents that could one day be wielded by his ideological opponents. It was this fear – that the expansive notion of republican freedom that the courts had delineated over the previous year could be jeopardized for all time – that led Mookerjee to deliver his prophetic warning: 'Maybe you will continue for eternity, in the next generation, for generations unborn; that is quite possible. But supposing some other party comes into authority? What is the precedent you are laying down?'

Seventy years on, Nehru's legal tools, created through the First Amendment and described as his gift to the succeeding generations, have come to be a central focus of political discourse and point of contestation in India. In this renewed contestation over foundational questions, Mookerjee's arguments are being redeployed by his erstwhile opponents – demonstrating the long afterlife of this debate and the eternally shifting sands of Indian politics.

DEBATE ON THE CONSTITUTION (FIRST AMENDMENT) BILL, 16 MAY 1951

(As reported in *Parliamentary Debates*, Part II, Vol. XII, New Delhi: 1951, pp. 8814–81.)

Prime Minister Jawaharlal Nehru: This Bill is not a very complicated one; nor is it a big one. Nevertheless, I need hardly point out that it is of intrinsic and great importance. Anything dealing with the Constitution and change of it is of importance. Anything dealing with Fundamental Rights incorporated in the Constitution is of even greater importance. Therefore, in bringing this Bill forward, I do so and the Government does so in no spirit of light-heartedness, in no haste, but after the most careful thought and scrutiny given to this problem.

I might inform the House that we have been thinking about this matter for several months, consulting people, State Governments, Ministers of Provincial Governments, consulting, when occasion offered itself, a number of Members of this House, referring it to various Committees and the like and taking such advice from competent legal quarters as we could obtain, so that we have proceeded with as great care as we could possibly give to it. We have brought it forward now after that care, in the best form that we could give it, because we thought that the amendments mentioned in this Bill are not only necessary, but desirable, and because we thought that if these changes are not made, perhaps not only would great difficulties arise, as they have arisen in the past few months, but perhaps some of the main purposes of the very Constitution may be defeated or delayed. In a sense this matter, of course, has been mentioned rather vaguely and has been before the public for some time. But in the precise form that it has been raised in this Bill, it came up only when I introduced this Bill in the House a few days ago.

There have been quite a number of criticisms of various kinds. There have been criticisms not only in our own country, as they should be but also in some foreign countries, where some of our friends or those who were our friends have got into the habit of criticizing whatever we might do. If we seek peace it is criticized. If we do something else, they say that we are not peaceful. And so, as I said, there has been a good deal of criticism and we welcome this criticism, because in a matter of this kind, the greater the scrutiny the better. And may I say that it is with no desire to hurry this that I have mentioned an early date for the report of the Select Committee. I do not myself see how a prolongation of this date for a relatively simple Bill, however important, enables us to give greater thought to it. Such thought and experience that we have with regard to the three or four articles, surely, can be brought to bear on the question within a few days; and even if we make the few days into a few weeks, it is not going to increase the amount of concentrated attention or thought that we might give it.

Now, various types of criticisms have been raised. One of them is a rather curious one, namely, that this House having been elected on a narrow franchise, not being really representative of the country and of the organized will of the community, is not justified or it is not proper for it to deal with such amendments. I seem to remember those very people who raise this criticism criticizing the right, not of this particular House, but nevertheless, very much the same House which preceded it, criticizing the Constituent Assembly for daring to draft the Constitution for India, because they were elected on a certain franchise. Now, that Constituent Assembly which has gone into the history of India is no more; but we who sit here, or nearly all of us, still continue that tradition, that link. In fact, it is we after all, who were the Constituent Assembly and who drafted this Constitution. Then we were not supposed to be competent enough to draft the Constitution. But now, the work we did was so perfect that we are not now competent enough to touch it! That is rather an odd argument. We have come up here, naturally because after the experience of a year and a half or so; we have learned much. We have found out some, if I may say so, errors in drafting or in possible interpretations to be put on what we had drafted. That is but natural. And the House will also remember that when this matter of the Constitution was being considered in the Constituent Assembly, a clause or an article was proposed, that within a space of five years any changes in the Constitution should be relatively easy, that the normal procedure laid down need not be followed, but an easy procedure should be followed. Why? Because it was thought – and if I may say so, rightly thought – that after a little while many little things may come to our notice which did not come up in the course of the debate, and we could rectify them after that experience, with relative ease, so that after this preliminary experience, the final shape may be more final and there would be no necessity for extensive amendments. However, that particular clause unfortunately – if I may say so with due respect – was dropped out. Nevertheless, so far as this House is concerned, it can proceed in the manner provided by the Constitution to amend it, if this House so chooses.

Now, there is no doubt that this House has that authority. There is no doubt about that, and here, I am talking not of the legal or constitutional authority, but of moral authority, because it is, roughly speaking, this House that made the Constitution. We are not merely technically, the inheritors of the fathers of the Constitution. We really shaped it and hammered it after years of close debate. Now we come to this House for amendments because we have noticed some lacunae. We have noticed that difficulties arise because of various interpretations. It has been pointed out to us by judicial interpretations that some of these lacunae exist. Now, let me say right at the outset that so far as the interpretation of the Constitution is concerned, it is the right and privilege of the highest courts of the land to do it, and it is not for us as individuals or even as a Government to challenge that right. The judiciary must necessarily stand above, shall I say, political conflicts and the like, or political interpretations. They have to interpret it in the light of the law and with such light as they can give to it. We respect that and we must obey that. But having followed that interpretation, it becomes our business as Parliament to see whether the purpose we aimed at is fulfilled, because if it is not fulfilled, then the will of the community does not take effect. And if the will of the community ultimately does not take effect, then serious difficulties might arise at any time. And more so at a time like this when powerful and dynamic forces are at work, not merely in India, not merely in Asia, but all over the world, when changes take place and when we cannot think in terms of anything being static and unchanging. Therefore, while fully respecting what the courts of the land have laid down and obeying their decisions, nevertheless it becomes our duty to see whether the Constitution so interpreted was rightly framed and whether it is desirable to change it here and there so as to give effect to what really in our opinion was intended or should be intended. Therefore I come up before this House, not with a view to challenge any judicial interpretation, but rather to find out and to take the assistance of this

House in clearing up doubts and in removing certain approaches to this question which have prevented us sometimes from going ahead with measures of social reform and the like.

This House knows very well that there are many kinds of Constitutions in the world. There is the Constitution, which is not written down, for instance, the Constitution of the United Kingdom where Parliament is absolutely supreme and can do and say what it likes and that is the law of the land, and no court can challenge it, however they may interpret the law. Then there is the written Constitution like the Constitution of that great country – the United States of America – where the Constitution to some extent, limits the authority of the legislature in so far as certain Fundamental Rights or other provisions are given in it. Now, in the United States of America, by a long course of judicial decisions, healthy conventions have been laid down and the power of the legislature has been widened somewhat. Because of the interpretations by high judicial authority and because of those conventions, the extreme rigidity that perhaps the written word might have given it has been made more flexible in the course of generations. I have no doubt that if we live through a static period, gradually those conventions would arise here too, relaxing that extreme rigidity of the written word and that our courts would help relaxing that rigidity. But unfortunately, we have no time. It is barely a little more than a year since we started functioning under this Constitution. And to begin with, therefore, it is only the written word in all its rigid aspects that apparently counts and not the many inner meanings that we sought to give to it. So we are deprived of that slow process of judicial interpretation and development of conventions which the other countries with the written Constitutions have gone through like the United States of America. Therefore, because we live in these rapidly changing times, we cannot wait for that slow process. We have to give a slightly different shape to the written word. In effect we do what in the normal course judicial interpretation might have done and probably would have done and we come up before this House for that purpose.

A great deal has been said about the desire of this Government to put any kind of curb or restraint on the freedom of the citizen or Press or of groups. First of all, may I remind the House that this Bill only perhaps clears up what the authority of Parliament is. We are not putting down any kind of curb or restraint. We are removing certain doubts so as to enable Parliament to function if it so chooses and when it chooses. Nothing else happens when this Bill is passed except to clarify the authority of Parliament. May I also point out to this House that we in this Government and we in this House, have not got a very long life. This session is coming to a close and after this session there is likely to be a brief session again before the General Elections take place in this country. This present Parliament will give place to another – a larger one, perhaps a different one. The Government may give place to another, and whatever changes we may make in the Constitution today, it is highly unlikely that this Government or this Parliament will take advantage of them by passing laws to that effect, unless some very severe crisis, national or international, arises. In effect, therefore, it is not this Government that is trying to seek power or consolidate itself and certainly I do repudiate the suggestion which has been made here and there that any of these amendments are meant to be utilized for political or party purposes. Because nothing could be farther from our thought and indeed, from the practical point of view, the House will observe that that can hardly be done. We do wish, when we walk away from this present scene before the election or after to leave something for the succeeding Parliament and for the younger generation that will come up – something that they can wield and handle with ease for the advancement of India and not something which will come always in their way and deflect them from the set purpose we have in view. Therefore, it is from this point of view that we have put forward this Bill.

The real important provisions which I am putting before the House relate to Articles 19 and 31. There is also Article 15 with which I will deal first. In Article 15 it is sought to add certain words. Perhaps it might appear that these words might almost be considered redundant. Nevertheless it has been considered desirable to add them and I am not quite sure if a slight further addition would not even be better to make it quite clear.

The real difficulty which has come up before us is this. The Constitution lays down certain Directive Principles of State Policy and after long discussion we agreed to them and they point out the way we have got to travel. The Constitution also lays down certain Fundamental Rights. Both are important. The Directive Principles of State Policy is a dynamic move towards a certain objective. The Fundamental Rights represent something static, to preserve certain rights which exist. Both again are right. But somehow and sometimes it might so happen that that dynamic movement and that static standstill do not quite lit into each other.

A dynamic movement towards a certain objective necessarily means certain changes taking place: that is the essence of movement. Now it may be that in the process of dynamic movement certain existing relationships are altered, varied or affected. In fact they are meant to affect those settled relationships and yet if you come back to the Fundamental Rights they are meant to preserve, not indirectly, certain settled relationships. There is a certain conflict in the two approaches, not inherently, because that was not meant,

I am quite sure. But there is that slight difficulty and naturally when the courts of the land have to consider these matters they have to lay stress more on the Fundamental Rights than on the Directive Principles of State Policy. The result is that the whole purpose behind the Constitution, which was meant to be a dynamic Constitution leading to a certain goal step by step, is somewhat hampered and hindered by the static element being emphasized a little more than the dynamic element and we have to find out some way of solving it. The amendment which I seek to move is, to be quite frank with the House, not a solution of the basic problem which will come up before the House in various shapes and forms from time to time. But it does lay stress on one small aspect of it.

May I also point out and try to remove a possible misconception that might be in the minds of some honourable Members. They might think that this is perhaps a devious method to bring in some kind of a communal element in the consideration of this problem. I want to make it perfectly clear that so far as Government are concerned they do not wish to have any truck with communalism in any form. But you have to distinguish between backward classes which are specially mentioned in the Constitution that have to be helped to be made to grow and not think of them in terms of this community or that. Only if you think of them in terms of the community you bring in communalism. But if you deal with backward classes as such, whatever religion or anything else they may happen to belong to, then it becomes our duty to help them towards educational, social and economic advance. Naturally that advance is not meant to be, if I may say so, at the expense of the others. We want to pull people up and not pull them down. But sometimes in this intervening period difficulties arose because we have not got enough provision, let us say, for giving a certain type of education, technical or other. The question arose whether we should give some reasonable encouragement and opportunity for that education to be given to members of the backward classes, which otherwise, without that encouragement and opportunity, they may not get at all, so that they remain where they are and we cannot pull them up. Therefore the object of this amendment is to lay stress on this.

The House may remember Article 29 (2) which says that no one by reason of his religion, etc., etc., should be kept out of an educational institution. That is a fundamental thing by which this Constitution stands and we must stand by it. There is no question of going behind that. What I submit is, respecting that we have also to respect that fundamental directive of this Constitution and the fundamental aims of our policy, that we must encourage and help those who are backward to come up and give them proper training and proper opportunities of social and economic advance.

The essential difficulty is this. The whole conception of the Fundamental Rights is the protection of individual liberty and freedom. That is a basic conception and to know wherefrom it was derived you have to go back to European history from the latter days of the eighteenth century; roughly speaking, you may say from the days of the French Revolution which spread on to the nineteenth century. That might be said to be the dominating idea of the nineteenth century and it has continued and it is a matter of fundamental importance. Nevertheless, as the nineteenth century marched into the twentieth century and as the twentieth century went ahead, other additional ideas came into the field which are represented by our Directive Principles of State Policy. If in the protection of individual liberty you protect also individual or group inequality, then you come into conflict with that Directive Principle which wants, according to your own Constitution, a gradual advance, or let us put it another way, not so gradual but more rapid advance, wherever possible to a State where there is less and less inequality and more and more equality. If any kind of an appeal to individual liberty and freedom is construed to mean as an appeal to the continuation of the existing inequality, then you get into difficulties. Then you become static, un-progressive and cannot change and you cannot realize that ideal of an egalitarian society which I hope most of us aim at. These problems arise and I have mentioned them to the House, not because they arise out of the little amendment that I propose but at the back of these problems they are there and we have to come to grips with them. If this particular amendment can be somewhat varied I should welcome it. In the Select Committee or elsewhere some few words may perhaps make the meaning clearer which I have sought to put before the House and I would personally welcome it.

Then we come to the two main articles which have to be dealt with in this Bill. Article 19 deals with the Fundamental Rights regarding freedom of speech, etc. It has been said that this Government seeks to curb and restrict the freedom of the Press. Honourable Members are fully aware of the state of affairs today. I do not think there is any country in the world at the present moment where there is so much freedom – if I may use that word for the moment – in regard to Press publications as in India. I have frequently given expression to my appreciation of the way responsible journals in this country are conducted. I should like to say so again. But I have also drawn attention to the way the less responsible news-sheets are conducted, and it has become a matter of the deepest distress to me to see from day to day some of these news-sheets which are full of vulgarity and indecency and falsehood, day after day, not injuring me or this House much, but poisoning the mind of the younger generation, degrading their mental integrity and moral standards. (*Hon. Members*: Shame, shame.) It is not for me a political problem but a moral problem. How are we to save our younger generation from this progressive degradation and poisoning of the mind and spirit? From the way untruth is bandied about and falsehood thrown about it has become quite impossible to distinguish what is true and what is false. Imagine our younger generation in the schools and colleges reading this, imagine, I ask this House, our soldiers and our sailors and our airmen reading this from day to day. What kind of impression do they carry?

Yes, we can satisfy ourselves that we have got the completest freedom of the Press. That is true. But freedom like everything else, and more than everything else, carries certain responsibilities and obligations and certain disciplines, and if these responsibilities and obligations and disciplines are lacking then it is no freedom, it is the absence of freedom, whether an individual indulges in it or a group or a newspaper indulges or anyone else.

For my part, as I grow in years I become more and more convinced that one cannot deal with any major problem, whether it is international or national, by simply relying on coercive processes. More and more I have come to realize that. I know of course that essentially, or at any rate a part of the duty of a Government is a duty to coerce the evil doer according to the laws of the land. That is true. And till we rise to higher levels a Government will always have that duty. I know that it is the duty of a Government to protect the freedom of the country from external invasion, by keeping armies and navies and the like. And so, in spite of my deep and almost instinctive belief that this kind of violence does not solve the problem, yet, having responsibility, I have to rely on those coercive processes, on the army and the navy, etc., and keep them in the most effective and efficient way that we can. Therefore, it is not with any idea of trying to improve, if I may say so, the morals of the country by coercive processes that I approach this question. I do not believe that morality is improved by coercive processes whether in the individual or in the group. Nevertheless, when there is a total lack or a great lack of those restraints which make up civilization, which go behind any culture, whether it is of the East or the West, when there is no sense of responsibilities and obligations, what are we to do? How are we to stop that corroding influence, that disintegrating process that goes on?

Now, I am in a difficulty. This particular amendment is not, let me remind the House, a law curbing or restraining anybody. All these amendments are enabling measures merely clarifying the power of Parliament which might be challenged or has been challenged in regard to some matters. Things remain, so far as the law is concerned exactly as they were, so long as this Parliament or a future Parliament does not take some action after due thought. I have never heard of anyone saying that in the United Kingdom there is no freedom of the Press or freedom of anything because Parliament is all-powerful – I have never heard that said. It is only here we seem not to rely on ourselves, not to have faith in ourselves, in our Parliament or our Assemblies, and rely, just as some of us may have relied on external authority like the British power of old days; we rely on some external authority – maybe geographically internal – and not perhaps have faith in this Parliament. After all, the responsibility for the governance of India, for the advancement of India, lies on this and future Parliaments, and if this Parliament or future Parliaments of India do not come up to expectations, fail in their great enterprise then it would not be good for India, and nobody else would preserve India from going towards misfortune. So that you rely on this Parliament for the biggest things, and yet you come and tell us, 'Do not trust this Parliament because it may do something wrong, it may do something against the Constitution.' So, I would beg the House to remember that this Bill does not bring in any offence, any curb, any restraint. It is an enabling measure clarifying the power of Parliament to deal with the matter. To what extent, is another matter and I shall go into it.

As I have said, I have a difficulty in dealing with, let us say, the Press. The Press is one of the vital organs of modern life, more especially in a democracy. The Press has tremendous powers and tremendous responsibilities. The Press has to be respected, the Press has to be co-operated with. In a somewhat varied career I have sometimes considered myself also a bit of a journalist and a Pressman. So I approach this question not as an outsider but to some extent as an insider also, with full sympathy for the difficulties that journalists and newspaper men and editors have to face. But then, what is the Press; those great organs of national opinion, or some two-page news-sheet that comes out overnight from time to time without regularity, full of abuse, sometimes used even for blackmailing persons? What is the Press? Is that news-sheet the Press or the great national organs or the hundreds and thousands of periodicals and newspapers in between? What standard have I to devise? Everything is the Press. Nobody thinks of restraining the freedom of the responsible organs unless some very extraordinary thing occurs. But what are we to do with these little sheets that come out from day to day and poison and vitiate the atmosphere? As I said, it is a difficult thing and a dangerous thing. And power and responsibility do not go together. A Prime Minister of the United Kingdom once, referring to certain types of the Press, said that they had the harlot's privilege of power without responsibility. Well, there it is. One has to face the modern world with its good and bad, and it is better, on the whole, I think, that we give even licence than suppress the normal flow of opinion. That is the democratic method. But having laid that down, still I would beg to say that there is a limit to the licence that one can allow at any time, more so at times of great peril and danger to the State. At the present moment it is our good fortune that in spite of difficult problems in the country, we function normally; we function in this Parliament normally; we function in State Assemblies more or less normally; the machinery of Government goes on: the administration goes on and we try as best we can to face the problems. Yet we live at a time of grave danger in the world, in Asia, in India. No man can say what the next few months may bring, the next few months, or if you like, the next year – I am not thinking of the election, but rather of other happenings that are bigger than elections. Now at this moment when great countries – not to mention smaller ones – even great countries think almost of a struggle for survival when they think that in spite of their greatness and power they are in danger, all of us have to think in terms of survival. And when a country is face to face with grave problems and questions, from the national point of view, of life and death and survival, then there is a certain priority and a certain preference in the way of doing things.

As the House knows, when there is a great war on and your country is involved in it, one has to deal with the situation somewhat differently than otherwise. Today, although there is no great war of that type, although we hope that no great war will come, and even if it comes we hope we shall be out of it; even so, war or no war, we live in a kind of pre-war state of deep crisis and we have to suffer the consequences of it. So, in this critical stage where always there is the question of survival, we cannot function loosely, inefficiently, without discipline, without responsibility, without thinking of our obligations. Therefore, it becomes necessary to give power to this Parliament, or to the future Parliament, which will represent the organized will of the community in India to take in a time of crisis such steps as it chooses. To prevent us from doing so is to deceive yourself and not to have faith in yourself and to be unable to meet a crisis when it arises and thereby perhaps do great injury to the cause we represent.

Now, what are these wonderful amendments which are said to be curbs and restraints on the Press? In the main, the amendment to Article 19, clause (2) that we suggest, contains three new phrases. The three phrases are: friendly relations with foreign States, public order and incitement to an offence. All the rest practically, apart from minor changes in the words, are in the old clause (2). The new clause reads thus:

> (2) Nothing in sub-clause (a) of clause (1) shall affect the operation of any existing law in so far as it imposes, or prevent the State from making any law imposing, in the interests of the security of the State, friendly relations with foreign States, public order, decency or morality, restrictions on the exercise of the right conferred by the said sub-clause, and in particular, nothing in the said sub-clause shall affect the operation of any existing law in so far as it relates to, or prevent the State from making any law relating to, contempt of court, defamation or incitement to an offence.

The three novel words or sets of words, compared to the old phraseology are: friendly relations with foreign States, public order and incitement to an offence. Let us now examine them. For the moment, as I said, it is only an enabling measure giving power to Parliament. But let us go beyond that. Does it involve any radical attack on the basic conception of the Fundamental Rights? Take the first thing – foreign relations. Now if anyone thinks that this is meant to stifle criticism of foreign countries, certainly it is not my intention and I am quite sure not of my Government. Ultimately, of course, if such a matter arises, it will be the subject of legislation that Parliament will frame. We are not framing legislation here. We can only indicate that such a thing can be legislated about. Nobody wants it. At the same time, this House will realize that at this particular moment of a very delicate international situation and tension, we cannot easily take the risk when something said and done, not an odd thing said and done, but something said and done repeatedly and continuously, may lead in regard to foreign countries to the gravest consequences, may lead to our relations with that foreign country deteriorating rapidly. It is a power which every Government possesses and deals with. It is certainly a power which can be used or misused – it is true. But that question has to be examined when that particular power is granted. All that is said here is that the authority to deal with this matter should vest with Parliament and should not be taken away. Surely, no Member in this House is prepared to say, I hope, that this House should not have the authority to deal with this matter when grave international issues are involved, when something written or said continuously may endanger the peace of the world or our country. It is a very serious matter, that we cannot stop it. What steps to take and how to take them are matters for careful determination when the question arises. Unless this House has the authority to deal with it, the situation cannot be faced and we would be simply helpless to prevent a steady deterioration and disintegration of the situation.

Then the other things are public order and incitement to an offence. Again these are words which may mean more or less – it is perfectly true. If such words were used in an actual piece of legislation, they have to be examined strictly as to how far they go and what powers they confer on the executive. But when you use them here in the sense of enabling Parliament to take steps, then you should use some general phrase not limiting the power of Parliament to face a situation. But when it brings any legislation to that effect, then examine it thoroughly and carefully. It is clear that the original clause, as interpreted by superior courts in this country, has put this Government, or would put any Government, into a very difficult position. The House knows – and it is mentioned in the Statement of Object and Reasons – that one of the High Courts held that even murder or like offences can be preached. Now it is an extraordinary state of affairs if that can be done. It may be and I am quite sure it would be in the long run, as in other countries, that judicial interpretation would gradually bring things more in line with which I would beg to say is the spirit of the Constitution.

Prof. Ranga (Madras): Was it an Indian Judge who said that even murder could be preached?

Shri Jawaharlal Nehru: I do not remember his nationality; I cannot say.

An Hon. Member: It was a Punjab Judge.

Shri Jawaharlal Nehru: But I do not think we should go into that question.

Pandit Krishna Chandra Sharma (Uttar Pradesh): That position has been rejected by the Supreme Court.

Shri Jawaharlal Nehru: I have no doubt that in course of time with the help of the highest courts in the land we would develop conventions eventually which would widen the authority of the Legislature to deal with them as the United States of America has done. The unfortunate part is that we just cannot wait for a generation or two for these conventions, etc., to develop. We have to deal with the situation today and tomorrow, this year and the next year. Therefore, the safest way is not to pass legislation in a hurry but to enable Parliament to have authority to deal with such matters. Personally, I confess my own belief is that it is better in any event and always for Parliament to have a large measure of authority, even the authority to make mistakes and go to pieces. Certainly, I realize that in conditions as they exist in India today the exact form, let us say, and of the Constitution of the United Kingdom is not applicable. We are too big a country, too varied a country. We have to have a kind of federation, autonomous States and the like. Therefore, it is inevitable that we should have a written Constitution. We have got it, and it is a fine Constitution. Gradually as we work it, difficulties appear. As wise men we deal with them and change it.

Here may I say, in connection with the use of the coercive apparatus of the State to deal with these problems, it has been our misfortune in the past two or three years to have had to use it in a variety of ways? We have had to use it because, practically speaking, we have had sometimes to face a challenge which can only be comparable to the challenge of war. The challenge may have come internally, but it was a challenge to the State as a war challenge is, that is by violence and by violent effort. We had to face it – as every State has to face it – by the organized strength of the State, whether it is the police or the military strength, whether it was in Telangana[50] or wherever it may be. Yet I should like to remind the House in this connection of Telangana which I mentioned that we have recently seen – and the thing is happening today – another way of meeting this type of situation, a peaceful way, a non-violent way. We have been seeing the frail figure of Vinobha Bhave marching singly into Telangana and by his words and by his action producing a tremendous effect on the people there and possibly even in the immediate present producing much more effect than any armed force could have done and certainly, if that is so in the immediate present, taking a longer view, must certainly be doing more because the effect of the armed force is good for the time being but in the long run it may not be so good; it may leave a bad trail of memories.

Now I shall proceed with the other article, the important one, namely Article 31. When I think of this article the whole gamut of pictures comes up before my mind, because this article deals with the abolition of the zamindari system, with land laws and agrarian reform. I am not a Zamindar, nor am I a tenant. I am an outsider. But the whole length of my public life has been intimately connected, or was intimately connected, with agrarian agitation in my Province. And so these matters came up before me repeatedly and I became intimately associated with them. Therefore, I have a certain emotional reaction to them and awareness of them which is much more than merely an intellectual appreciation. If there is one thing to which we as a party have been committed in the last generation or so it is the agrarian reform and the abolition of the zamindari system.

Shri Hussain Imam (Bihar): With compensation.

Shri Jawaharlal Nehru: With adequate and proper compensation, not too much.

Shri Hussain Imam: 'Adequate' is quite enough.

Shri Jawaharlal Nehru: Now, apart from our commitment, a survey of the world today, a survey of Asia today will lead any intelligent person to see that the basic and the primary problem is the land problem today in Asia, as in India. And every day of delay adds to the difficulties and dangers, apart from being an injustice in itself. There are many ways of dealing with this problem. We have seen in many countries this problem being dealt with quickly and rapidly and without any check, either by expropriation absolute or by some middle way of part expropriation and part nominal compensation, whatever it may be. Anyhow they have dealt with it rapidly. And where they have done so they have produced a new stability. I am not going into the justice or injustice of it but am looking at it purely from the point of view of stability. Of course, if you go into the justice or injustice, you have to take a longer view, not the justice of today but the justice of yesterday also. But we adopted another method. and I think we rightly adopted that method, of trying to deal with it not in such a hurry but as adequately – after full thought and consideration of all interests – as we could, and the giving of compensation. Now, I am not going into those questions, but it is patent that when you are out basically to produce certain equality, when you are out to remedy inequalities, you do not remedy inequalities by producing further inequalities. We do not want anyone to suffer. But, inevitably, in big social changes some people have to suffer. We have to think in terms of large schemes of social engineering, not petty reforms but of big schemes like that. Now, if all our schemes like that are stopped – maybe rightly stopped, maybe due to a correct interpretation of the law and therein too the lawyers differ and even Judges have differed – again, I have no doubt that we have a generation to wait for things to stabilize. Then, we will have the help of the High Courts of the land, but we cannot wait. That is the difficulty. Even in the last three years or so some very important measures passed by State Assemblies and the rest have been held up. No doubt, as I said, the interpretation of the courts must be accepted as right but you, I and the country has to wait with social and economic conditions – social and economic upheavals – and we are responsible for them. How are we to meet them? How are we to meet this challenge of the times? How are we to answer the question:

For the last ten or twenty years you have said, we will do it. Why have you not done it? It is not good for us to say: We are helpless before fate and the situation which we are to face at present. Therefore, we have to think in terms of these big changes, land changes and the like and therefore we thought of amending Article 31. Ultimately we thought it best to propose additional Articles 31A and 31B and in addition to that there is a Schedule attached of a number of Acts passed by State Legislatures, some of which have been challenged or might be challenged and we thought it best to save them from long delays and these difficulties, so that this process of change which has been initiated by the States should go ahead. Many of us present here are lawyers and have had some training in law which is a good training and many of us respect lawyers. But nevertheless a lawyer represents precedent and tradition and not change, not a dynamic process. Above all, the lawyer represents litigation …

Shri Kamath: You have also been a lawyer.

Shri Jawaharlal Nehru: … [J]ust as, if I may say so with all respect, that in the modern system of treating disease the doctor is rightly interested in disease …

Shri Jawaharlal Nehru: Somehow we have found that this magnificent Constitution that we have framed was later kidnapped and purloined by the lawyers.

Shri Gautam (Utter Pradesh): It is a paradise for them.

Shri Jawaharlal Nehru: Yes. I do not grudge anyone entering paradise but what I do object to is the shutting of the door and of barring and bolting it and preventing others from coming in. The other day I was reading an article about India by a very eminent American and in that article which contained many correct statements and some incorrect statements, the author finished up by saying that India has very difficult problems to face but the most acute of them he said, can be put in five words and those five words were: land, water, babies, cows and capital. I think that there is a great deal of truth in this concise analysis of the Indian situation.

Shri Kamath: No lawyers there?

Shri Jawaharlal Nehru: I am not for the moment going to say anything about babies or cows, important as they are, nor do I wish to say anything about capital which is a most important question. Our capital resources are matters with which my colleague the Finance Minister and the Planning Commission are dealing but we come back to land and water. Water is connected with the land that we want to improve and we have big river valley schemes, wells and all that. Finally we come back to the land which is the most important of all and if we do not make proper arrangements for the land, all our other schemes whether they are about grow-more-food or anything else may fail. Therefore, something in the shape of this amendment that I have suggested becomes necessary. Again, if I may say so, what is intended is to give power to this House or to a future Parliament to deal with this so that it may not feel helpless when a situation arises which calls for its intervention.

Dr S.P. Mookerjee: I believe never before in the history of Parliament were we called upon to consider a matter which is so momentous and grave as we have been today on the motion of the honourable Prime Minister. The Prime Minister, in his speech, tried to clarify the position and here inferred to his own opinion that the measure is not a complicated one, nor a big one. It is, he said, a simple one; but even through a simple process very serious consequences may often ensue when it affects the rights and liberties of individuals or of a nation.

I do not want to say anything on the technical aspects of the change proposed, namely, whether this House is competent to consider this matter or not. The Prime Minister pointed out that if the Constituent Assembly was competent to pass a Constitution which has been found more or less satisfactory by all sections of public opinion in this country, obviously, if there is a need for changing the provisions of such a Constitution, Parliament, according to the Constitution itself, must be competent to deal with this matter. There may be an opinion expressed that such changes should wait until the new Parliament has been constituted, because, then, the people who would come in a more representative character representing the adults of the Indian population, would be able to judge whether the changes proposed in the Constitution are really necessary or desirable.

I shall not say much on those formal amendments which have been proposed, although I have some suggestions to make in respect of them which I may place before the Select Committee when it meets. I shall deal with the three main changes which have been proposed in the Constitution. The Constitution has been working for about fifteen months. It was incumbent upon the Prime Minister to point out in his speech what exactly have been the difficulties which have compelled the Government to come forward with the proposed changes. To my mind, the explanation which he gave was weak and halting and not acceptable, nor was it satisfactory.

He has assured the House and the country, to quote his own words, that he has not brought forward this measure in a spirit of light-heartedness, not in haste, that he has bestowed careful thought and scrutiny not he, but the Government also; and that they have consulted various people throughout the country. I accept these assertions. But, surely, any changes in the Constitution which may be considered by Parliament have to be considered not in secrecy by the Government along with certain chosen people; but opinion has to be called for on the provisions of the Bill from the people at large, by all sections of public opinion outside the House. I ask the Prime Minister what steps he proposed to take to secure public opinion on the changes that he proposes to make. We have suggested, some of us, that the Bill should be circulated for eliciting public opinion. It has not been suggested as a dilatory motion, because the date within which opinion has to be received varies from 31st May to 15th of July. It is not a formal proposal also. The Prime Minister said that there is no particular hurry about the matter. He made the strange declaration that this Government has no desire to pass any laws on the lines of the changes which he proposes to make and that these are only enabling powers which he wishes to hand over to Parliament or the State Legislatures; that he is making these changes not for the purpose of securing better administration so long as he is the Prime Minister of this country, but that he is thinking more in terms of future Parliaments and the welfare of generations yet to be born. If that is his magnanimity, if that is his great foresight and statesmanship when he tries to peep into the future and read the minds of the people that are yet to come in the sphere of Parliamentary politics, why should he not accept the proposal for circulating the Bill for eliciting public opinion? The changes proposed are not simple. The changes are fundamental and they go to the very root of some of the vital provisions of the Constitution, not only the Constitution of this country, but the Constitution of any country in which people are anxious to retain freedom and liberty of thought and action. I therefore ask the Prime Minister that he should be true to his word. If he really does not want to hurry, then, he should accept our proposal. Let the time be two weeks or three weeks;

it does not matter. But, let the public of India have this impression that when this first great step is being taken by the Government to amend the Constitution, there is no indecent or undue haste followed by the Government of the day.

How was the Constitution framed? We spent nearly four years to frame this Constitution. It was not hurriedly done. Take this Chapter on Fundamental Rights. A special committee was appointed of which the Prime Minister himself was the Chairman. How many months, how many years did we not take to weigh every single paragraph, every single sentence and every single word of that chapter? How many changes did we make at various stages of the proceedings of the Constituent Assembly? We were criticized by the people outside the Constituent Assembly that we were taking too long a time. But many of us justified this delay because we were anxious that nothing should be done hastily or on the spur of the moment. We were doing something which was unique in the annals of this country, something indeed, to which there are not many parallels in the entire civilized world. The country had attained political freedom and within a few months of attaining it, it set itself to the task of writing a Constitution and putting down everything clearly and precisely so that the people of the country belonging to all shades of opinion might have a clear idea of what exactly the country stood for. If that is so, why this indecent haste to change such a Constitution? Changes in the Constitution have been made in other countries. I was looking at the first change or amendment made to the American Constitution, and that was within three years of its first enactment. But what were the changes for? The First Amendments which were made in the American Constitution were not for curtailing freedom, not for taking away rights that had been deliberately given two and a half years ago. But every single one of those changes was made for extending the individual and the social rights of the people of the United States of America. It was a change for the advancement of the sacred policy and the principle for which the United States of America stood. And what is the sad picture that we present to the country today? Within a year and a half of enacting the Constitution, we come forward and however much the Prime Minister might attempt to say that the changes are simple, that there is no controversy about it, he knows it and knows it in his heart of hearts, champion of liberty that he has been throughout his life, that what he is going to do is nothing short of cutting at the very root of the fundamental principles of the Constitution which he helped, more than anybody else, to pass only about a year and a half ago. This is the challenge which he has deliberately thrown up to the people of India.

I do not know why he has thrown up this challenge. Is it due to fear? Does he feel that he is incapable today to carry on the administration of the country unless he is clothed with more and more powers to be arbitrarily utilized so that his will may be the last word on the subject? Or is it his doubt in the wisdom of the people whose champion he has been all his life? Does he feel that the people of India have run amuck and cannot be trusted with the freedom that has been given to them? What is it that he has in his mind? I was hearing the explanation that he was giving – explanation which, if I may say so, cannot stand the test of a moment's scrutiny. He has spoken a number of times and said that, after all, what he is doing is simply to clothe Parliament with permissive power, that he is trusting Parliament. But is he really trusting Parliament? Is he giving the Members of Parliament full liberty to decide questions? As we understand it, it is something different. He is treating this matter as a purely party question. He ought to treat this question as something different, something which affects the lives and liberties of individuals and the people as a whole and not as a party question, however big and however well-organized that party might be. He issued a circular to all the members of his party that their physical presence for the Constitution (First Amendment) Bill was necessary, even though the temperature in Delhi might go up to 110 or 112 degrees, that their presence was an imperative necessity.

An Hon. Member: That was so even when the Constitution was being made.

Dr S.P. Mookerjee: There is nothing wrong in their physical presence when Parliament is considering a matter of such vital importance. *(Interruptions)* If honourable Members will hold themselves in patience when I come to the second part, they will immediately realize what has been the second step which the honourable the Prime Minister, the Leader of the House, took in this matter. The circular has gone out that the motion of the honourable Jawaharlal Nehru is to be accepted. No amendment is to be moved by the members of the Party, and if moved by non-party Members, is to be opposed. *(Interruptions)* That is perfectly all right from the party point of view. That is quite proper. But …

Shri Naziruddin Ahmad: On a point of order. Instructions to the members of a party to the shape of a whip are private instructions and relate only to the internal working of a party, and as such they are outside the scope of the discussion here.

Mr Chairman: I was about to say that the Whip's instructions to Members are private instructions and are not meant to be alluded to and the honourable Member's point of order is accepted.

Dr S.P. Mookerjee: Then I do not know how it came to my hands inside the Chamber. In any case, my point is not about the wording of the Whip. Let me not refer to it at all. But my point is with reference to what the Prime Minister himself said, that after all what is being done is to clothe Parliament with permissive powers so that Parliament may decide what should be done and what should not be done. That is all right so far as it goes, provided vital matters like this are not looked upon as party questions. The free will of every Member of the House must be exercised without fear or expectation of favour.

Shri Sidhva (Madhya Pradesh): In that case, no Government can exist.

Dr S.P. Mookerjee: Whether any Government can exist or not is a matter completely irrelevant now.

Mr Chairman: The Whip does not bind anybody who does not belong to any party. They can take any course they like.

Dr S.P. Mookerjee: Good, and that they are doing.

The honourable Prime Minister stated in his speech that the three particular articles which are proposed to be changed by the amendments deal with vital matters concerning the welfare of the State as a whole. Let me take Article 19 in the first instance. The Prime Minister referred in detail to the freedom of the Press. Now I would like him to look at the article as it stands at present. He referred specially to two-pages or sheets-newspapers in this country which are responsible for the progressive deterioration of the moral standards of our younger folk, and he pointed out that what they are writing are immoral, untrue, vulgar, indecent, corroding. Now, what are the provisions that exist at present which authorize either Parliament or a State Legislature to pass laws for the purpose of curbing such a state of affairs? The exceptions which have been embodied in Article 19 state very clearly in clause (2):

> Nothing in sub-clause (a) of clause (1) shall affect the operation of any existing law in so far as it relates to, or prevent the State from making any law relating to, libel, slander, defamation, contempt of court or any matter which offends against decency or morality or which undermines the Security of, or tends to overthrow, the State.

Now, if there are newspapers which are guilty of these very serious acts of omission and commissions which the Prime Minister so graphically described, obviously the present Constitution arms Parliament and the State Legislatures with sufficient powers to deal with them.

Pandit Balkrishna Sharma (Uttar Pradesh): Ask the High Courts.

Dr S.P. Mookerjee: I shall ask the High courts.

Pandit Balkrishna Sharma: A person can preach murder and still go scot-free.

Dr S.P. Mookerjee: There is a proverb that the heat of the sand is sometimes greater than the heat of the Sun. Well, so far as this reference to the preaching of murder is concerned, when the Prime Minister referred to it, it was pointed out by an honourable Member that the judgment had already been reversed by the Supreme Court.

Shri Sidhva: No, no.

Shri Bharati (Madras): No.

Dr S.P. Mookerjee: So far as that decision is concerned it has been reversed by the Supreme Court. I have got with me the judgments of the Supreme Court, which is the final court of the land, in two cases, one of Ramesh Thapar vs. The State of Madras and the other of Brij Bhushan vs. the State of Delhi. When the question of interpretation of Article 19 came up, the Supreme Court held that if the maintenance of public order, or securing the public safety was something which did not affect the security of the State or the overthrowing of the State, then there could be no restriction on freedom of speech. At the same time in another case considered by the Supreme Court recently where the question of the validity of the Preventive Detention Act came up for discussion, the Court held that it was open to a State Legislature or to Parliament to pass laws in respect of matters which affected even public order and thereby detain persons. Now, let us look at the present provisions of the law. Parliament has passed the Preventive Detention Act. Its powers are sufficiently wide in character. Any person, according to that law, read with the provisions in the Constitution, can be detained for an unlimited period provided conditions are fulfilled which would make Government satisfy itself and the public that no one is being unreasonably detained. Now, supposing there are persons who are preaching murder and who are doing something of that character, supposing there is some newspaper which is doing something of that character and the writer is there, the individual can be secured under the Preventive Detention Act. So, if you want to prevent a person, or group of persons from committing acts which you consider to be against the interests of public order, you are already clothed with sufficient authority to do so.

Mr Chairman: I think that the Preventive Detention Act has laid down certain conditions under which alone persons could be detained, and these persons cannot be covered.

Dr S.P. Mookerjee: It is not the Prime Minister's intention nor Government's intention that men who are innocent should be detained. If there is some case against any one you need not even present it in the court. The only thing you are to do is to satisfy an Advisory Council that you have sufficient material which would justify you to take the person in custody and detain him as long as you like. There is no limit imposed under the provisions of the Constitution. That is the present law.

An Hon. Member: Do you advise that?

Dr S.P. Mookerjee: I am not advising it. The power is there. The Prime Minister takes upon himself the responsibility …

Pandit Thakur Das Bhargava (Punjab): Can that man be punished by the Court?

Dr S.P. Mookerjee: If you detain [a] man as long as he lives, obviously it is a very severe punishment you can give. Now that is one part of the problem. The next is that supposing a man commits an act, makes a speech and some overt act is done, then what happens? The provisions of the ordinary Penal Code or the criminal law of the land are applied. The man may be bound down under the criminal law. He makes a speech; he is arrested and put in jail. That is being done. If your intention is only to take action against a small group which is spreading venom and vulgarity throughout the country, obviously you do not have to change the provisions of the Constitution.

As the Prime Minister also hinted in his speech, there is the possibility of extending the operation of such wide powers to bona fide cases and thereby abuse the power given. Now what is the guarantee that these provisions will not be so abused? If you say public order, Parliament does not administer. Parliament passes laws.

If you say anything that offends public order then I may state that public order is an expression which is capable of the widest possible definition. You can utilize it in penalizing your political opponents. The Prime Minister said something about the legal profession not being dynamic and remaining static and preventing all sorts of things. Now it is rather strange that a member of the legal profession who happens to be a Judge of the Supreme Court in the case of Romesh Thapar, while dealing with the provisions for maintenance of the civil life of the citizen under the Constitution of India, said these memorable words:

> Thus, very narrow and stringent limits have been set to permissible legislative abridgement of the right of free speech and expression, and this was doubtless due to the realisation that freedom of speech and of the press lay at the foundation of all democratic organisations, for without free political discussion no public education, so essential for the proper functioning of the processes of popular government, is possible. A freedom of such amplitude might involve risks of abuse. But the framers of the Constitution may well have reflected, with Madison who was 'the leading spirit in the preparation of the First Amendment of the Federal Constitution', that 'it is better to leave a few of its noxious branches to their luxuriant growth, than, by pruning them away, to injure the vigour of those yielding the proper fruits'.

Here was a Judge – an Indian Judge – appointed by the same Government, which is in power today, Mr Justice Patanjali Sastri, who has interpreted the Constitution not to prove himself a man who did not know what dynamic growth was but one who gave a noble interpretation to our own Constitution for the protection of the liberty of the Indian subjects. Whether the Legislature, Parliament or Government would agree with the Supreme Court or not is a different matter. But at any rate we should feel proud that our judiciary has proved so independent. It has given expression to its opinion in interpreting the provisions of the Constitution not in a manner which goes against the interest of the country but for securing the expanding rights and liberties of the people.

Shri Sidhva: What about the independence of the country?

Dr S.P. Mookerjee: The independence of the country will remain intact if you do not try to pass coercive measures. As the honourable Prime Minister said, no country can ever be governed by force or by coercion. If the country has run amuck, if there are people who could not be kept under control without exercising very strict executive rights and powers, then you must enquire why it is that the country has come to that state of affairs. Why should these people who were swearing by you only a year ago, condemn you today and why should it be necessary to find bullets and bayonets for keeping your freedom intact?

Shri Sidhva: For political purposes.

Dr S.P. Mookerjee: Mr Sidhva says for political purposes. I have said that I do not want more heat from the sand and I would like the heat from the Sun. So far as political power is concerned, I would say with all earnestness that very often it is our inability to probe into particular situations that create difficulties. We fail miserably to solve national problems and we want to gag and coerce people. I would specially remind the Prime Minister of the happenings at Cooch-Behar a few days ago. I was myself there. I saw how India celebrated her first Jallianwala Bagh after her attaining freedom. I saw how there was [a] complete collapse of the administration there. The price of rice was shooting up from Rs 30 to Rs 70. About 56,000 *maunds* of rice were lying under the control of the local administration and not one *maund* of rice was released in time.

The order for modified rationing came two hours before the bullets were used. Even that order was not communicated to the people and young women and children were shot dead; the answer given was political exploitation by certain groups. I saw the people. There might have been some political groups here and there but the vast majority of the people were peace-loving, were anxious to co-operate with the Government. They did not know what politics was. I saw ladies, illiterate who had never seen politics and they asked: 'After attainment of freedom, is this state of affairs that is to come to our country? We cannot get our rice even when it is there and when we ask for it, we get bullets in place of rice.' If you say that you want more and more powers for curbing such situations, you will fail and hopelessly fail.

Shri Sidhva: If there was so much food, why was there any riot?

Dr S.P. Mookerjee: You come to me and I will explain it.

I therefore say that the Prime Minister has not succeeded in pointing out any reason why the amendment to Article 19 should be made as proposed.

Let me deal with foreign relations. The Prime Minister said that it was not his intention that criticism of foreign powers should be curbed. I have been trying to read the Constitution of other countries and I have also been trying to find out from case law – and in this Dr Ambedkar might be able to help us – and I have not been able to find any precedent in any part of the civilized world whereby law under the provisions of the Constitution criticism of foreign powers is taboo. Who will be the person who will be first affected if you pass this law? It will be our Prime Minister, Pandit Jawarharlal Nehru. Will he then be able to say that if Pakistan encroaches one inch more into the territory of Kashmir he will consider it as a war on India? That will offend Pakistan and he cannot make that statement.

Shri JawaharIal Nehru: May I point out that I said nothing about criticism of foreign powers being prohibited.

Dr S.P. Mookerjee: I am glad about it. We can discuss this question later on. But the way in which the wording has been suggested here – affecting friendly relations with foreign powers – is hardly reassuring. Who is to decide this question? Will our High Court decide it? Or will our Supreme Court decide whether criticism which has been made would disturb the friendly relations between India and any foreign country? Will this be a matter which will be decided by the foreign country? We may say anything about a foreign country with the utmost friendship in our hearts but if that country misunderstands and says that it offends it or it affects our friendly relations with them, you are at once bound by the provisions of the Constitution. Why should you pass such a law? I do not know whether it relates to the demand which is made in certain quarters about a possible reunion of India and Pakistan. I know the Prime Minister holds very strong views about it and he has said a number of times that any such movement or agitation is harmful to the interests of the country and that he does not like it. I do not mind it is his view. But if I hold a contrary view, as indeed I do most seriously and earnestly, that this Partition has been a mistake and has to be annulled some day or other (*An Hon. Member*: By force?) why should I not have a right to say that?

Pandit Malaviya (Uttar Pradesh): And give 40 per cent or 50 per cent representation to the Muslims everywhere all over this country.

Dr S.P. Mookerjee: Why should I not have the right to agitate for it? Pandit Jawaharlal Nehru as the leader of a big political party may oppose this view. He can appeal to his countrymen not to listen to those who today are advocating an annulment of the partition of

India. I can understand that: it will be an appeal to the logic and the good sense of the people. He wins or I win or somebody else wins. We will see what is the verdict of the people. That is a perfectly constitutional approach to the problem. I can even understand the Prime Minister of India, not as leader of the Congress party, to say that if by carrying on such agitation you create conditions in the country which lead to riots and bloodshed, he must step in and prevent it. The ordinary law of the land will then operate.

I have heard the Prime Minister speak on many occasions and I have been trying to analyse his viewpoint. But unfortunately, his statements are so contradictory to one another that I found it difficult to get at the core of them. But I would like him to explain some time or other as to what should be the attitude of Government on matters so vital to the interests of the people of India. If he says as the head of the Government that he is prepared to allow any viewpoint to be circulated within the country – and that is what we understand by democratic freedom – so long as it does not advocate chaos, I would be at one with him. If he says that because he does not like that anybody should speak about the annulment of the partition he means to prevent us and therefore wants to put these words in the Constitution and later pass some law consistent with them, then I say it is most arbitrary and if done, will lead to very serious consequences. I do not know what will happen in future. I am not necessarily thinking in terms of war. I am hoping – it may be a hope which may not be achieved in my lifetime – that this terrible mistake, which we made in partitioning the country trying to get something which we thought we were getting but which we actually did not, has to be remedied, not in communal interests but in the interests of both the Hindus and Muslims and everyone else. We have got to realize that apart from the communal aspect of it, economically, strategically, nationally and internationally we have been rendered weak and severely hit by British diplomacy. I hope that someday people will realize that this mistake will have to be rectified by the good sense of the people of both the countries.

Pandit Krishna Chandra Sharma: Were you sleeping when the country was partitioned? Why did you not revolt then?

Dr S.P. Mookerjee: I am at least revolting today, and will you also have the good sense to revolt with me?

Mr Chairman: May I appeal to honourable Members to be very calm. Everyone will have his chance to say what he likes.

Dr S.P. Mookerjee: The point that I would like to urge before the Prime Minister is that this provision is totally unnecessary. People are saying that this is being done to placate or appease Pakistan. But how long can this go on? Supposing Pakistan wants that India should be tagged on to Pakistan and we protest against it and carry on agitation, which would disturb the friendly relations between India and Pakistan, we will be guilty. It is a most dangerous clause, a clause which we do not find in any constitution in the world and there is no justification at all why such a clause should be provided. It is not a question of Pakistan only: it may be the case of other foreign countries about whose policy we may not be in agreement [with].

I have got here a book written in Chinese issued by the present Chinese Government. I have not been able to get it fully translated, otherwise I would have read it out to the House. I have a partial translation of the book with me today. The book is issued by the present Chinese Government and it is nothing but scurrilous abuse of India, her culture, her leaders starting from Mahatma Gandhi and ending by saying that England is the running dog of America and India today under Pandit Jawaharlal Nehru's leadership is the running dog of Britain. That is how that book concludes. Supposing we want to give a constructive and reasoned reply. It may affect the friendly relations between India and China and we will be committing an offence under the law. What is the necessity? What has happened here? Why are you anxious to make such a drastic provision in the Constitution itself?

An Hon. Member: Is it a Chinese Government publication?

Dr S.P. Mookerjee: It is published by the present Chinese Government in Chinese (*An Hon. Member:* When?) in 1949. It is being translated and I shall be able to bring the full translation tomorrow.

Let me now come to the important Article 31. What is the change that is being proposed? The Prime Minister talked very feelingly and quite rightly too about his great desire and ambition to introduce land reforms. There is no quarrel about this standpoint. Naturally the present land system in India is an outdated one and we cannot allow it to continue without great detriment to the interests of the people at large. When we passed the Constitution the Prime Minister would remember how he passed days and weeks in finding out a formula which would not compromise on any great question of principle but at the same time present a workable agreement. His anxiety was, as it was the anxiety of many of us, that in matters like this we should proceed with the greatest measure of agreement. He referred to the pledge which the Congress party gave for the abolition of zamindari. As he rightly pointed out the declaration was that zamindari would be abolished, for which fair compensation would be paid. Whether right or wrong, there are many parties which say that no compensation should be given and others who insist that the fullest compensation should be given. In any case the Congress stood for abolition of zamindari on payment of fair compensation.

An Hon. Member: Equitable compensation.

Dr S.P. Mookerjee: Equitable compensation. That was the pledge which was given by the Congress. Now, when you passed the Constitution after a good deal of discussion, what is the framework that you produced? We were anxious that the quantum of compensation should not at every stage, be subject to judicial decisions. At the same time, we were anxious that a certain framework should be placed before the country and the persons concerned so that the fullest measure of assurance could be given to all concerned. Now, Article 31 provides that either the actual compensation or the principles on which compensation is to be paid, or the principles on which payment is to be made, will all be determined by law. We also protected certain specific legislative measures which were passed eighteen months prior to the commencement of the Constitution.

That is how matters stand now. What has happened since then? That there has been delay is not the fault of the Constitution. There is only one party which is ruling India today. All the Governments are under the control of a centrally organized party. It is not that one particular party in one particular State proceeds in one manner and another party in another State proceeds in another manner. Why has not the Centre set down and given some sort of a formula saying: 'This is the formula which every State should adopt in effecting land reforms, making such minor changes as local conditions may necessitate.' Now, pursuant to the provisions of the Constitution several State Legislatures have passed laws. The Bihar law has been declared to be ultra vires by the Patna High Court – mind you, not on the ground of compensation but on an entirely different ground: the question of discrimination between one class and another. Well, whether that judgment is right or not is not my point. Then the UP Legislature has passed a law which the Allahabad High Court has held to be intra vires. The Nagpur High Court also has held the

Madhya Pradesh Act to be intra vires. If the Patna High Court has passed a judgment which according to Government is not correct – in fact, some aspects of the matter are already before the Supreme Court – the only way in which any Government can or should proceed, is to have a quick decision made by the Supreme Court.

Shri Bharati: How can that be done?

Dr S.P. Mookerjee: That can easily be done. You consult the Law Minister or the Attorney General, they will advise you. You get a quick decision by the Supreme Court. Supposing it takes a month, or two months even, if the Supreme Court comes to a certain conclusion which you consider to be fundamentally opposed to the basic principles on which the Constitution was framed then and only then would there be the right for you to ask for an amendment of the Constitution. That is the only logical, fair and equitable procedure which any Government which believes in the sanctity and sacredness of any Constitution, or any Parliament, which believes in such sacredness and sanctity would follow. But what is it you are doing? Will honourable Members read and re-read the clause as it has been proposed? What you say is that particular laws which are to be mentioned in a Schedule to the Constitution, no matter whether they infringe any provision of the Constitution or not, are deemed to be valid. Is that the way in which the Constitution should be amended?

Supposing a particular Legislature passes a piece of legislation which is absolutely nonsensical. By this amendment to the Constitution you are saying that whatever legislation is passed it is deemed to be the law. Then why have your Constitution? Why have your Fundamental Rights? Who asked you to have these Fundamental Rights at all? You might have said: 'Parliament is Supreme and Parliament may from time to time pass any law in any matter it liked and that will be the law binding on the people. You passed the Fundamental Rights deliberately and you clothed the judiciary with certain powers not for the purpose of abusing the provisions of the Constitution but for giving interpretations and generally acting in a manner which will be consistent with the welfare of the people. If the Supreme Court has gone wrong, come forward and say that the Supreme Court has come to such-and-such conclusions which are repugnant to the basic principles on which the Constitution was based. But the Supreme Court has not had a chance to consider this matter and you are coming forward with this hasty proposal that any law mentioned in the Schedule – there are a dozen of them there – would be deemed to be valid. Not only that. I can even understand your considering the laws which are already passed and which are before you, but you are saying that in future if any law is passed with regard to these subjects, it would be deemed to be valid notwithstanding the provisions of the Constitution. Can anything be more absurd and more ridiculous? Is Parliament being considered as a serious body? You are treating this Constitution as a scrap of paper. This is not a Constitution – it is just a piece of legislative enactment passed by Parliament. You come forward and say: 'We want to change the Constitution.' You cannot do like that. And what is the dangerous precedent that you are creating? Maybe you will continue for eternity, in the next generation, for generations unborn; that is quite possible. But supposing some other party comes into authority? What is the precedent which you are laying down? That if any particular Bill is passed by any Legislature all that you have to do is to get hold of your subservient Parliament and make it change the Constitution and provide that whatever is passed by the Legislature is valid. Let us treat the subject more seriously, more rationally.

Therefore, I would very earnestly suggest that a situation has not yet come when any change in Article 31 is called for. Let us not confuse the issue by raising the question as to whether zamindari is good or abolition of zamindari is good.

Shri D.D. Pant (Uttar Pradesh): What is your own view?

Dr S.P. Mookerjee: My own view is that zamindari must be abolished with compensation. Now will you follow me in what I am saying? You have heard my view.

The question is not today whether the zamindari system is good or bad, because merely by abolition of zamindari, you cannot improve the land system. Much more has to be done in order to improve the conditions of the peasants and also makes them produce more so that the wealth of the country may be increased. But that is neither there nor here. Today the point is not whether the zamindari system is good or bad, but the point is, what is the procedure you are following for attaining a certain objective for which you had made a specific provision in the Constitution and which, let me emphasize, you have not tried yet? If you tried it and then failed I can understand your anxiety to change the Constitution, but merely in haste you come and say: 'I cannot achieve something quickly. I cannot wait for the fulfilment of the provisions of the Constitution. Let us get hold of all the legislative enactments and deem them as legally passed.' Then do not work the Constitution. For a period of so-called emergency, you can pass a law and say that the entire task of framing, interpreting and working the Constitution will be left in the hands of Pandit Jawaharlal Nehru assisted by such people whom he may desire to consult – pass a simple amending Bill. And thus declare that for the next two years nothing more need be done in India. That we may understand. It may be dictatorship, it may be anything else, but you have then a clear-cut, straightforward way of looking at things. But do not have a camouflaged Constitution; you have declared in the Preamble of your Constitution that you have done something unheard of in history, that within so short a period of attainment of freedom you have trusted the people of this country to draft a Constitution; you have given a charter of rights to them. Now YOU come forward and stab them in the back. You are not working for the benefit of the present generation but for party ends.

Mr Chairman: May I know whether it is not the will of Parliament that is supreme over everybody? Is it not the present Parliament that is inviting the amendment? It is not Mr Jawaharlal Nehru or anybody that is doing it.

Dr S.P. Mookerjee: Since the will of Parliament is supreme, I am appealing to the sober will of Parliament not to do something which will be dangerous. Otherwise, I would not have spoken here – I might have addressed a meeting elsewhere. (*Interruption*) The honourable Member interrupts. I know in her heart of hearts she does not like this amendment. She told me yesterday definitely what she thought of it.

Shrimati Renuka Ray (West Bengal): I said that …

Shri Jawaharlal Nehru: Some of us doubt whether the honourable Member really means what he says.

Dr S.P. Mookerjee: The honourable Prime Minister apparently speaks standing before a mirror and thinks everybody is like himself.

Shri Raj Bahadur (Rajasthan): Madam, I must take objection to the honourable Member describing Parliament to be subservient.

Dr S.P. Mookerjee: The honourable Member should have known that I did not refer to the present Parliament at all. I said, supposing in future something like this happens and there is a subservient Parliament then what happens? How can I dare call this Parliament subservient when I am a Member of it? I like these interruptions, because I can feel from these interruptions that there is a real searching of the heart amongst Members of this House. What we are doing today is not the right thing. It is not necessary, it is retrograde, and I would appeal to the Prime Minister …

Mr Chairman: I was only trying to tell the honourable Member that he is saying that it is the Prime Minister and his colleagues who are trying to bring this amendment. That is not correct. It is Parliament that is now considering the amendment.

Dr S.P. Mookerjee: The reason why I was appealing to the Prime Minister especially was that I thought, my capacity being limited, if I could convince one individual, my objective could be attained. By appealing to the emotions of the Prime Minister I was appealing to all the Members of this House warning them that we are today being asked for the first time to amend our sacred Constitution. It is a great document. It is not a matter which you can take in a light-hearted way. We are anxious – no matter what our individual views may be on various matters – to retain the foundation of a good and solid Government which can work in the interest of all sections of the people of this country. That I certainly believe is the objective of all of us. Now, if we proceed in a light-hearted way to amend the Constitution, naturally we create a precedent which may lead to very serious consequences. These things, taken each one of them separately, may not mean much. But, after all, if you take them as a whole and the manner in which you are proceeding, you are doing a great disservice. If there is anything standing in your way you just come and amend the Constitution, utterly ignoring public opinion.

I would just like to refer the Prime Minister to the constitutions of England and of America. Here we have deliberately made our choice. We decided to have a written Constitution. We decided to have a Part on Fundamental Rights. Naturally when you have a Part on Fundamental Rights it obviously means that not the executive Government, not even Parliament, but the judiciary and the judiciary alone will be able to interpret and advise and decide whether the Constitution is working properly or not. That is how it is worked in different countries. As I was reading one of the judgments yesterday I came across significant remarks made by one of the Judges of America that the greatest constitutional issue in all American history was not settled by the court, not even in the halls of the Congress, but on the battlefield of America. Freedom developed in that country not by passing laws, or by the decrees of the President, because the ultimate sanction rested with the people. We have also to reckon with the people in this country. We have drawn up the Constitution with a declared desire to protect the mighty rights and interests of the people, millions of them who are downtrodden and have not the courage to speak out. But as the Prime Minister knows, even in their hearts a new awakening has come. As we move about from place to place, we can see the signs of that reawakening, which we could not have dreamt could happen so quickly.

Now, let us take the fullest advantage of that reawakening in the larger interests of this country. Let us not try to arm the executive with wider and larger powers being afraid of a Frankenstein's monster that is supposed to have raised its head in India. There may be elements in this country with mischievous intentions. But the larger section of the population of the country is well mannered and they are anxious that this country should go ahead peacefully. Therefore, their hearts being sound, we have to approach them in the proper way. We have to tackle the great problems of administration in social and economic spheres specially so as to earn their spontaneous confidence.

Talking about the Supreme Court, the Prime Minister said that while conventions may arise even in this country – I hope they will – that will take a generation, and how can you wait for a generation? Therefore, what is the remedy? Do not create healthy conventions? Let the executive decide what is to be done; let it be armed with new and arbitrary powers; and even that slow attempt at making new conventions you want to crush. Is that the way you want to preserve the sanctity and sacredness of the Constitution which is your own handiwork? Now look at this – I am reading from Beck's *The Constitution of the United States*. This is how it reads:

> This great power to curb legislatures and executives, and therefore majorities, by resort to the paramount will of a written Constitution, has been exerted for over 10 years, and while not infrequently the party whose power is thus curbed has vented its wrath and disappointment upon the Supreme Court, yet after the thunder of political debate has passed and the earthquake of party passion has spent its force, the 'still small voice' of the Supreme Court has always prevailed.

And further on:

> The most effective restraint which freemen have ever imposed upon themselves is this extraordinary power of the Supreme Court. The value of such a restraint upon precipitate action is so great that it is improbable that the American people will, at least in the near future, thus destroy the efficacy of the great balance wheel.

That is the spirit in which the Constitution has to be respected and worked. Here are a set of men who are selected by the Government. They are not foreigners coming from outside. They are our own chosen selected men holding office during their life, entrusted with the duty of seeing whether the country is being administered in the spirit of the Constitution. At the same time I do not say that the Supreme Court judges are infallible. They are after all human beings. Supposing the Supreme Court does something which goes entirely against the basic principles on which the Constitution of free India should stand. I am not suggesting that we should tie our hands and watch helplessly. Then come forward on that specific issue and amend the Constitution on that particular point. Do so after giving fullest opportunity to the public to express their viewpoints. The Prime Minister referred to three points. Has the Supreme Court given any decision with regard to foreign powers? Has anything happened in this country which necessitates that the Constitution should be disfigured with such a deplorable provision? What has happened about public order? Is not your present law sufficient? Has the Press run amuck? Even according to the Prime Minister, there may be a few news-sheets who may be shouting. Let them shout. If they shout, use the other Press; use the platform, the radio or whatever machinery you have. You make the people feel that what the gutter Press is saying is absolutely unacceptable. That is the only way in which you can nullify the activities of a small section of people who want to destroy your freedom. But do not give them the tragic importance and make them feel that if a few papers shout, you are compelled to change the Constitution. Why give them the honour which they do not deserve?

The Prime Minister himself said that a major section of the Press is all right – their heart is sound. Then sit down with the Press representatives and discuss as to how the freedom which is being abused by a small section of the Press can be combated. I do not know which section the Prime Minister has in view; but supposing there is such a section, surely it cannot imperil the freedom of the general masses of the people. Lastly, I shall read out only one quotation, and that is also a judgment from the Supreme Court, in answer to what the Prime Minister said towards the end of his speech that after all you are making only small changes and it does not vitally affect the position at all. But this warning was sounded in the last paragraph of a judgment delivered by the Supreme Court in America – the danger signal has come and let no one ignore it if he wishes well of the country.

'Do the people of this land – in the providence of God, favoured, as they sometimes boast, above many others in the plenitude of their liberties – desire to preserve those so carefully protected by the First Amendment: liberty of religious worship, freedom of speech and of the press, and the right as free men to peaceably assemble and petition their Government for a redress of grievances? If so, let them withstand all beginnings of encroachment' – and here is a beginning of the encroachment of the liberty of the people in Free India – 'for the saddest epitaph which can he carved in memory of a vanished liberty is that it was lost because its possessors failed to stretch forth a saving hand while yet there was time.'

Notes

Introduction

1. Hiren Mukerjee, *The Gentle Colossus: A Study of Jawaharlal Nehru*, New Delhi: Oxford University Press, 1993.
2. Ayesha Jalal, *The Sole Spokesperson: Jinnah, the Muslim League and the Demand for Pakistan*, Cambridge: Cambridge University Press, 1985; Jaswant Singh, *Jinnah: India, Partition, Independence*, New Delhi: Rupa, 2009; Nisid Hajari, *Midnight's Furies*, New York: Houghton Mifflin Harcourt, 2015; Narayani Basu, *V.P. Menon: The Unsung Architect of Modern India*, New Delhi: Simon and Schuster, 2020; Maulana Azad, *India Wins Freedom*, New Delhi: Orient Blackswan, 1988; Ram Manohar Lohia, *The Guilty Men of India's Partition*, New Delhi: BR Publishing, 1920. A good introductory overview would be Asim Roy, 'The High Politics of India's Partition: The Revisionist Perspective', *Modern Asian Studies*, Vol. 24, No. 2 (1990), pp. 385–415.

3. B.R. Nanda, *Jawaharlal Nehru: Rebel and Statesman*, New Delhi: Oxford University Press, 1998, p. 302.
4. Walter Crocker, *Nehru: A Contemporary's Estimate*, New Delhi: Random House, 2009, p. 27.
5. James Manor, 'Introduction' in James Manor (ed.), *Nehru to the Nineties: The Changing Office of the Prime Minister in India*, London: Hurst and Co., 1994, p. 9.
6. Sarvepalli Gopal, *Jawaharlal Nehru: A Biography, Vol. II: 1947–1956,* London: Jonathan Cape, 1979, p. 303.
7. 'Nehru, a Queer Mixture of East and West, Led the Struggle for a Modern India', *The New York Times*, 28 May 1964, New York, p. 6.
8. Shivam Vij, 'How Jawaharlal Nehru would have dealt with the Covid-19 pandemic in India', *Gulf News*, 13 May 2021, https://gulfnews.com/opinion/op-eds/how-jawaharlal-nehru-would-have-dealt-with-the-covid-19-pandemic-in-india-1.79151852 (accessed on 13 May 2021). See also, https://www.timesnownews.com/videos/times-now/india/covid-forces-nda-to-go-nehru-way-1964-order-invoked-urging-govt-staff-to-help/97376 (accessed on 13 May 2021), https://www.theweek.in/news/india/2021/05/01/opinion-blame-it-on-nehru.html (accessed on 13 May 2021).
9. Walter Crocker, *Nehru: A Contemporary's Estimate*, p. 28
10. B.D. Dua, 'The Prime Minister and the Federal System' in James Manor (ed.), *Nehru to the Nineties: The Changing Office of the Prime Minister in India*, p. 23.
11. B.R. Nanda, *Jawaharlal Nehru: Rebel and Statesman*, p. 44.
12. Walter Crocker, *Nehru: A Contemporary's Estimate*, p. 63. This is a tendency among Nehru biographers, as Jivanta Schöttli has argued in her provocative thesis *Strategy and Vision in Politics: Jawaharlal Nehru's Policy Choices and the Designing of Political Institutions*, Ruprecht Karl University of Heidelberg: Unpublished PhD Thesis, 2009, pp. 371–72.

13. Judith Brown, *Nehru: A Political Life*, New Delhi: Oxford University Press, 2003, p. 5.
14. See for example: Perry Anderson, *The Indian Ideology*, London: Verso, 2013, p. 130; Walter Crocker, *Nehru: A Contemporary's Estimate*, pp. 219–23; B.R. Nanda, *Jawaharlal Nehru: Rebel and Statesman*, pp. 203–04, 292–93.
15. Sachidananda Mohanty, 'Would China Have Won in 1962 if Nehru Had Listened to Patel?', The Quint, 6 July 2020, https://www.thequint.com/voices/opinion/sardar-patel-letters-advice-to-pandit-nehru-on-india-china-war-conflict-pakistan-expansionism (accessed on 13 May 2021).
16. B.R. Nanda, *Jawaharlal Nehru: Rebel and Statesman*, p. 293.

1: 'I fear the Pandit's articles reveal practically no acquaintance with Islam'

1. Jawaharlal Nehru, *The Discovery of India*, New Delhi: Oxford University Press, 1994, p. 352.
2. Ibid.
3. Ibid.
4. Ibid.
5. Iqbal's 'Statement on Palestine' read at the Punjab Provincial Muslim League in Lahore, 27 July 1937, as reprinted in Shamloo (ed.), *Speeches and Statements of Iqbal*, Lahore: Al Manar Academy, 1948, p. 216.
6. S. Gopal (ed.), *Selected Works of Jawaharlal Nehru*, Vol. 7, New Delhi: Orient Longman, 1972, p. 572 and p. 266.
7. See only Iqbal's support for the outcome of the Communal Award of 1932, which further entrenched separate electorates for minorities. Responding to Congress criticism to the award, Iqbal advised 'the Muslims of India to stand boldly by the Communal Award even though it does not concede all their demands.

This is the only course they can adopt as a practical people.' Shamloo (ed.), *Speeches and Statements of Iqbal*, p. 213.

8. Ibid., p. 211.
9. Ibid.
10. Ibid.
11. Ibid., p. 212.
12. Shruti Kapila, *Violent Fraternity: Indian Political Thought in the Global Age*, New Jersy: Princeton University Press, 2021.
13. Muhammad Iqbal to Francis Younghusband, 30 July 1931 as reprinted in Shamloo (ed.), *Speeches and Statements of Iqbal*, p. 167.
14. 'Local and Provincial', *Tribune*, Lahore, 16 May 1905.
15. Pervez Tahir, 'Introducing Iqbal the Economist' in *The Pakistan Development Review* Vol. 40, No. 4, (2001), pp. 1167–76.
16. The terms Ahmadis and Qadianis are used interchangeably throughout this text.
17. For the development of the movement, see Yohanan Friedmann, *Prophecy Continuous: Aspects of Ahmadi Religious Thought and Its Medieval Background*, Berkeley: University of California Press, 1989.
18. Muhammad Iqbal, 'The Doctrine of Absolute Unity, as Expounded by Abdu-l-Karim Al-Jilani', *The Indian Antiquary*, Vol. 29, (1900), p. 239.
19. Shamloo (ed.), *Speeches and Statements of Iqbal*, p. 201. For more on this aspect, see Adeel Hussain, *Law and Muslim Political Thought in Late Colonial North India*, Oxford: Oxford University Press, forthcoming 2022, Chapter 4.
20. Shamloo (ed.), *Speeches and Statements of Iqbal*, p. 99.
21. Ibid., p. 94; For more on the concept of the Finality of Prophethood (*khatm-un-nabiyyeen*), see Adeel Hussain, 'Muhammad Iqbal's Constitutionalism', *Indian Law Review*, Vol. 2, No.2, (2018), pp. 135–58.
22. Shamloo (ed.), *Speeches and Statements of Iqbal*, p. 96.
23. Ibid., p. 97.

24. For the recording of the Ahmadiyya dissent to the rejection of Jinnah's proposals, see *The Proceedings of the All Parties National Convention,* Allahabad: Secretary of the All Parties National Conventions, 1929, pp. 94f.
25. See C.A. Bayly, *Recovering Liberties: Indian Thought in the Age of Liberalism and Empire*, Cambridge: Cambridge University Press, 2011.
26. Jawaharlal Nehru, 'Orthodox of All Religions, Unite!', *The Modern Review*, Vol. 58, No. 5, (1935), p. 626.
27. Jawaharlal Nehru, 'The Solidarity of Islam', Ibid., p. 505.
28. Ibid.
29. Muhammad Iqbal to Jawaharlal Nehru, 21 June 1936, as reprinted in *A Bunch of Old Letters: Being Mostly Written to Jawaharlal Nehru and Some Written by Him*, New Delhi: Oxford University Press, 1988, p. 187.
30. Jawaharlal Nehru, 'Orthodox of All Religions, Unite!', *The Modern Review*, Vol. 58, No. 5, (1935), p. 629.
31. Nehru is referring to a letter that the Aga Khan and Syed Ameer Ali, an Indian jurist and one of the co-founders of the All-India Muslim League, wrote to the Prime Minister of Turkey in November 1923. In this letter, which was widely republished at the time, they expressed their fear of the 'disintegration of Islam' if the Ottoman caliph was deposed. They urged the Turkish assembly to protect the 'Caliph's dignity'. See 'Ameer Ali's Letter', *Times* (London), 14 November 1923.
32. The Age of Consent Committee (1928–29) was established by the Government of India to gauge public opinion regarding child marriages.
33. John Henry Newman (1801–90) was a priest and conservative academic who left the Church of England and reverted to the Catholic Church.

34. Bertrand Russell, *On Education: Especially in Early Childhood*, London: George Allen & Unwin Ltd., 1926, p. 246.
35. William T. Stead, *If Christ Came to Chicago: A Plea for the Union of All Who Love in the Service of All Who Suffer*, Chicago: Laird & Lee Publishers, 1894.

2: 'Safeguarding the rights and interests of the Mussalmans'

1. 'President of Lucknow Session of Congress: Pt. Nehru', *The Times of India* (Bombay), 27 January 1936.
2. 'All-India Students' Conference: 200 Delegates in Lucknow', *The Times of India* (Bombay) 13 August 1936.
3. S. Gopal (ed.), *Selected Works of Jawaharlal Nehru*, Vol. 7, New Delhi: Orient Longman, 1972, p. 266.
4. Ibid.
5. Ibid., p. 336.
6. 'Nehru's Speech at the All India Students Conference', 12 August 1936, UP Government, Secret Police Abstract of Intelligence No. 33, 22 August 1936, as reprinted in S. Gopal (ed.), *Selected Works of Jawaharlal Nehru*, Vol. 7, p. 336.
7. Ibid.
8. Ibid.
9. Ibid., p. 337.
10. Ibid.
11. Ibid., p. 338.
12. Ibid., p. 341.
13. Ibid., p. 339.
14. Ibid., p. 341.
15. 'Fortnightly Reports for the Month of June 1936', Home/Political, File No. 18/6/36-Poll, 17, National Archives of India, New Delhi.
16. S. Gopal (ed.), *Selected Works of Jawaharlal Nehru*, Vol. 7, p. 320.

17. 'Discussion with the India Constitution Group', 4 February 1936, as reprinted in S. Gopal (ed.), *Selected Works of Jawaharlal Nehru*, Vol. 7, p. 93.
18. S. Gopal (ed.), *Selected Works of Jawaharlal Nehru*, Vol. 7, p. 93.
19. Ibid., p. 267.
20. In his letter to Jinnah dated 6 April 1938, Nehru outright frames the 'basis and structure' of the Communal Award as 'anti-national' and that it stood 'in the way of the development of national unity'. S. Gopal (ed.), *Selected Works of Jawaharlal Nehru*, Vol. 8, New Delhi: Orient Longman, 1976, p. 235.
21. S. Gopal (ed.), *Selected Works of Jawaharlal Nehru*, Vol. 7, p. 342.
22. Sarojini Naidu, *Mohomed Ali Jinnah, an Ambassador of Unity: His Speeches and Writings, 1912-1917*, Madras: Ganesh, 1918, p. 1.
23. The concrete meaning of 'swaraj', a Hindu-revivalist concept championed by the Arya Samaj founder Dayanand Saraswati, which loosely translates to self-governance, was heavily contested. Some Arya Samajists in the Congress party, like Lala Lajpat Rai, interpreted it as a spiritual striving, while others like Bal Gangadhar Tilak understood it as a radical political project that sought to bring about an immediate rupture from colonial rule. Bipin Chandra Pal, fully aware of these multiple paths that adherence to swaraj could take, insisted that the word 'democratic' be added to swaraj to avoid that the very slogan for self-rule may not be co-opted by people who would model it as fully compatible with British colonial rule. *Report of the Thirty-Fifth Session of the Indian National Congress Held at Nagpur on the 20th, 28th, 30th, and 31st, December 1920*, Nagpur: Reception Committee, 1921, p. 57.
24. Ibid., p. 56.
25. Ibid., p. 56f.
26. *All Parties Conference 1928: Report of the Committee Appointed by the Conference to Determine the Principles of the Constitution for India*

[Nehru Report], Allahabad: General Secretary, All India Congress Committee, 1928, p.28.

27. Ibid., p. 44.
28. The Hindu Mahasabha leader, M.R. Jayakar, claimed that when promoting the Nehru Report to the Bombay Presidency Hindu Sabha, he had to personally restrain some of his colleagues 'from openly rebelling against this report'. *The Proceedings of the All Parties National Convention*, Allahabad: Secretary of the All Parties National Conventions, 1929, p. 91.
29. *The Proceedings of the All Parties National Convention*, p. 76.
30. Ibid., p. 78.
31. 'If it is conceded that Muslamáns should be enabled to secure one-third of the representation in the Central Legislature, the method which is adopted is neither quite fair to the provinces where the Muslmans are in a minority, nor does it guarantee that we shall obtain 1/3 representation in the Central Legislature. Therefore, the two Muslmans' Majority Provinces – Punjab and Bengal – will get more than their population, which means you are giving more to the rich who will, under normal conditions, get the largest number of Muslim Representations and you are depriving the Muslim minority Provinces of great importance, and restricting them to get no more than their population; whereas we wish to restrict the Punjab and Bengal according to their population and desire that the excess should be distributed among the minority Muslim Provinces.' *The Proceedings of the All Parties National Convention*, p. 79.
32. The most important resistance came from Sir Mian Muhammad Shafi, one of the founding member of the All-India Muslim League, who remained vehemently opposed to joint electorates.
33. *The Proceedings of the All Parties National Convention*, p. 88.
34. Ibid., p. 92f.
35. Ibid., p. 94.
36. Ibid., p. 93.

37. Adeel Hussain, 'The Shahidganj Mosque and Muslim Nationality in Late Colonial India: From Law to Sacrifice', *Pakistan Journal of Historical Studies*, Vol. 3, No. 2 (2018), pp. 80–106.
38. Jinnah at Town Hall: Fair and Just Solution, *Civil and Military Gazette*, Lahore, 3 March 1936.
39. Ibid.
40. Madhav Shrihari Aney (1880–1968) was a Congress politician, who was critical of what he considered the leadership's excessive accommodation of Muslim demands, from the Khilafat movement to constitutional safeguards.

3: 'Communism is no shield against imperialism'

1. Indians and Chinese are brothers.
2. H.V. Kamath, *Last Days of Jawaharlal Nehru*, Calcutta: Jayasree Prakashan, 1977, cited in Ramachandra Guha, 'The Dalai Lama's War', *The National Interest*, No. 115, p. 57.
3. See Francine Frankel, *When Nehru Looked East: Origins of India-US Suspicion and India-China Rivalry*, New Delhi: Oxford University Press, 2020, p. 105.
4. Paul M. McGarr, 'After Nehru, What? Britain, the United States and the Other Transfer of Power in India, 1960–1964', *The International History Review*, Vol. 33, No. 1, p. 120.
5. For example, https://www.thequint.com/voices/opinion/sardar-patel-letters-advice-to-pandit-nehru-on-india-china-war-conflict-pakistan-expansionism#read-more (accessed on 5 February 2021); Gautam Sen, 'Theoretical Moorings of India's Foreign Policymaking: Nehru to Modi', *India International Centre Quarterly*, Vol. 43, No. 2, p. 11.
6. For example, J.J. Singh, *The McMahon Line: A Century of Discord*, New Delhi: HarperCollins, 2019, p. 249.

7. The same George Lansbury who had presented the Commonwealth of India Bill, drafted by Mahatma Gandhi, Tej Bahadur Sapru, Sarojini Naidu and others, in the British Parliament in 1925 – the first official attempt at creating an Indian constitution drafted by Indians.
8. Paul F. Power, 'Indian Foreign Policy: The Age of Nehru', *The Review of Politics*, Vol. 26, No. 2, p. 259 and p. 266.
9. Ramachandra Guha, 'The Dalai Lama's War', p. 47.
10. Shashi Tharoor, *Nehru: The Invention of India*, New Delhi: Penguin, 2012, p. 180.
11. Jawaharlal Nehru's speech to the Asian Relations Conference, 24 March 1947, https://www.tibetsun.com/news/1947/03/24/pt-jawaharlal-nehrus-speech-at-asian-relations-conference-1947 (accessed on 1 February 2020).
12. Gautam Sen, 'Theoretical Moorings of India's Foreign Policymaking: Nehru to Modi', p. 11.
13. Diary entry, 22 August 1946, in Penderel Moon (ed.), *Wavell: The Viceroy's Journal*, London: Oxford University Press, 1973, p. 338.
14. Jawaharlal Nehru's speech to the Asian Relations Conference, 24 March 1947; see also Francine Frankel, *When Nehru Looked East: Origins of India-US Suspicion and India-China Rivalry*, p. 103.
15. A conception that received a debilitating blow in 1962, which is what made it such a shock for Nehru.
16. Francine Frankel, *When Nehru Looked East: Origins of India-US Suspicion and India-China Rivalry*, p. 103; see also Waheguru Pal Singh Sidhu, 'The Accidental Global Peacekeeper' in Manu Bhagavan (ed.), *India and the Cold War*, New Delhi: Penguin Random House India, 2019, p. 83.
17. Sumit Ganguly, *Indian Foreign Policy*, New Delhi: Oxford University Press, 2019, p. 1.
18. Francine Frankel, *When Nehru Looked East: Origins of India-US Suspicion and India-China Rivalry*, p. 101 and pp. 107–10.

19. Shashi Tharoor, *Nehru: The Invention of India*, p. 182.
20. Francine Frankel, *When Nehru Looked East: Origins of India-US Suspicion and India-China Rivalry*, p. 109.
21. Inder Malhotra, 'Nehru's Luminous Legacy', *India International Centre Quarterly*, Vol. 33, No. 3, p. 25.
22. Paul F. Power, 'Indian Foreign Policy: The Age of Nehru', p. 286.
23. The Five Principles of Peaceful Coexistence, part of the 'Panchsheel' Treaty or the Sino-Indian Agreement of 1954.
24. Gautam Sen, 'Theoretical Moorings of India's Foreign Policymaking: Nehru to Modi', p. 11.
25. Sumit Ganguly, *Indian Foreign Policy*, p. 22; J.J. Singh, *The McMahon Line: A Century of Discord*, p. 252.
26. Ramachandra Guha, 'An Asian Clash of Civilisations? Revisiting the Sino-Indian Conflict of 1962', *Economic and Political Weekly*, Vol. 46, No. 44/45, p. 58.
27. 'Matthai's Statement on Resignation', *Hindustan Times*, 3 June 1950, New Delhi, p. 4; 'Grave Misgivings on Delhi Pact: Dr Matthai's Reasons for Resignation', *The Times of India*, 3 June 1950, Bombay, p. 1; 'Cause of Dr Matthai's Exit from the Cabinet: Resignation "Demanded" by Prime Minister', *The Times of India*, 6 June 1950, Bombay, p. 1; 'Differences over Indo-Pak Agreement Too: Matthai's Reply to Nehru', *The Indian Daily Mail*, 14 June 1950, Singapore, p. 2.
28. B.R. Ambedkar, Resignation Speech, 10 October 1951, available at https://ambedkarism.wordpress.com/2011/03/10/dr-ambedkars-resignation-speech/
29. See Tripurdaman Singh, *Sixteen Stormy Days: The Story of the First Amendment to the Constitution of India*, New Delhi: Penguin Random House India, 2020, pp. 16–17.
30. Sardar Patel to Jawaharlal Nehru, 28 March 1950, in Durga Das (ed.) *Sardar Patel's Correspondence*, Vol. X, Ahmedabad: Navajivan Publishing House, 1974, p. 19.

31. B.R. Ambedkar, Resignation Speech, 10 October 1951, available at https://ambedkarism.wordpress.com/2011/03/10/dr-ambedkars-resignation-speech/
32. Shashi Tharoor, *Nehru: The Invention of India*, p. 179.
33. Ramachandra Guha, 'An Asian Clash of Civilisations? Revisiting the Sino-Indian Conflict of 1962', p. 52.
34. K.M. Panikkar, *In Two Chinas: Memoirs of a Diplomat*, London: G. Allen and Unwin, 1955, pp. 81–82.
35. Ibid. See also Francine Frankel, *When Nehru Looked East: Origins of India-US Suspicion and India-China Rivalry*, p. 155; Ramachandra Guha, 'The Dalai Lama's War', p. 48.
36. Shashi Tharoor, *Nehru: The Invention of India*, p. 180.
37. Francine Frankel, *When Nehru Looked East: Origins of India-US Suspicion and India-China Rivalry*, p. 155.
38. Ibid., p. 101.
39. Ibid., pp. 110–13.
40. Ibid., p. 115.
41. Karki Hussain, 'China's Image of India's Foreign Policy of Non-Alignment', *The Indian Journal of Political Science*, Vol. 23, No. 1/4, p. 245.
42. Michael Yahuda, *China's Role in World Affairs*, New York: St. Martin's Press, 1978, p. 50.
43. Walter Crocker, *Nehru: A Contemporary's Estimate*, New Delhi: Random House, 2009, pp. 137–38.
44. Francine Frankel, *When Nehru Looked East: Origins of India-US Suspicion and India-China Rivalry*, p. 155.
45. Paul F. Power, 'Indian Foreign Policy: The Age of Nehru', p. 274.
46. Jawaharlal Nehru to Vijayalakshmi Pandit, 30 August 1950, Nehru Papers, First Instalment, Secret & Personal, cited in Francine Frankel, *When Nehru Looked East: Origins of India-US Suspicion and India-China Rivalry*, p. 157.

47. Francine Frankel, *When Nehru Looked East: Origins of India-US Suspicion and India-China Rivalry*, p. 161.
48. Ibid., p. 126.
49. The Simla Convention in 1914 had been attended by representatives from Tibet, China and British India. It was the first time that China conceded the right of the Tibetan plenipotentiary to attend a convention and sign a treaty as an equal. Among other issues, it settled the frontier between British India and Tibet: the eponymously named McMahon Line, named after the British plenipotentiary Sir Henry McMahon. It also accepted the position of Chinese suzerainty, but not sovereignty – with Chinese suzerainty inextricably linked to Tibetan autonomy. The Chinese plenipotentiary Ivan Chen eventually did not sign the agreement.
50. Francine Frankel, *When Nehru Looked East: Origins of India-US Suspicion and India-China Rivalry*, p. 126.
51. Srinath Raghavan, 'Sino-Indian Boundary Dispute, 1948-60: A Reappraisal', *Economic and Political Weekly*, Vol. 41, No. 36, p. 3882.
52. Ibid.
53. See Qiang Zhai, 'Tibet and Chinese-British-American Relations in the Early 1950s', *Journal of Cold War Studies*, Vol. 8, No. 3, pp. 34–53.
54. Francine Frankel, *When Nehru Looked East: Origins of India-US Suspicion and India-China Rivalry*, p. 128.
55. Ibid., pp. 126–27.
56. Jawaharlal Nehru to C. Rajagopalachari, 1 November 1950, in S. Gopal (ed.), *Selected Works of Jawaharlal Nehru*, Vol. 15/2, New Delhi: Jawaharlal Nehru Memorial Fund, 1993, p. 433.
57. Dawa Norbu, 'Tibet in Sino-Indian Relations: The Centrality of Marginality', *Asian Survey*, Vol. 37, No. 11, p. 1082.
58. Francine Frankel, *When Nehru Looked East: Origins of India-US Suspicion and India-China Rivalry*, p. 133.

59. K.M. Panikkar to Foreign Ministry, 18 October 1950, Nehru Papers, First Instalment, cited in Francine Frankel, *When Nehru Looked East: Origins of India-US Suspicion and India-China Rivalry*, p. 132.
60. See Jawaharlal Nehru to C. Rajagopalachari, 1 November 1950, in S. Gopal (ed.), *Selected Works of Jawaharlal Nehru*, Vol. 15/2, pp. 433–39.
61. Maniben Patel, Diary Entry for 2 November 1950, in P.N. Chopra (ed.), *Inside Story of Sardar Patel: The Diary of Maniben Patel*, New Delhi: Vision Books, 2001, pp. 452–53. Maniben Patel was Sardar Patel's daughter.
62. See Chandrashekhar Dasgupta, 'Nehru, Patel and China', *Strategic Analysis*, Vol. 38, No. 5, p. 718.
63. The Ambassador in India (Henderson) to the Secretary of State, 10 November 1950 (Document 832) in Herbert A. Fine et al (eds), *Foreign Relations of the United States, 1950, Vol 5: The Near East, South Asia and Africa*, Washington DC: United States Department of State, 2018, p. 1475.
64. Ibid.
65. Ibid.
66. Chandrashekhar Dasgupta, 'Nehru, Patel and China', p. 723.
67. The Ambassador in India (Henderson) to the Secretary of State, 10 November 1950 (Document 832) – Herbert A. Fine et al (eds), *Foreign Relations of the United States, 1950, Vol 5: The Near East, South Asia and Africa*, p. 1475.
68. The top decision-making body of the Congress party.
69. Maniben Patel, diary entry for 21 November 1950 in P.N. Chopra (ed.), *Inside Story of Sardar Patel: The Diary of Maniben Patel*, p. 462.
70. Mir Laik Ali (1903–71) was the last Prime Minister of Hyderabad State. He was kept under house arrest after Operation Polo, but escaped to Pakistan where he lived in exile.

71. The note was obviously forwarded to Sardar Patel as it answered indirectly some of the matters raised in the Sardar's letter of 7 November 1950.
72. Famous jurist and diplomat, he was India's representative to the UN Security Council (1950–52). Before that, Rau was the constitutional advisor to the Constituent Assembly from 1946 to 1949, and later, a judge at the International Court of Justice at The Hague (1952–53).
73. The Chinese army invading and capturing the Changtu (or Chamdo) region of eastern Tibet in October 1950.

4: 'You are treating this Constitution like a scrap of paper'

1. Jawaharlal Nehru, 16 May 1951, *Parliamentary Debates*, Part II, Vol. XII, New Delhi: 1951, p. 8832.
2. Ibid.
3. Walter Crocker, *Nehru: A Contemporary's Estimate*, New Delhi: Random House, 2009, p. 40.
4. For more on the subject, see Tripurdaman Singh, *Sixteen Stormy Days: The Story of the First Amendment to the Constitution of India*, New Delhi: Penguin Random House India, 2020.
5. 'Proposed Changes in Constitution: Mr Nehru's Assurances in Parliament', *The Times of India*, 17 May 1951, Bombay, p. 1.
6. Prof. N.G. Ranga, 16 May 1951, *Parliamentary Debates*, Part II, Vol. XII, New Delhi: 1951, p. 8857.
7. Actually, Burke was a Whig or liberal, even as he was later appropriated as a conservative in more modern interpretations. His pamphlet against King George III – 'Thoughts on the Cause of Present Discontents' – and support of the American revolution and the impeachment of Warren Hastings also made him a figure of Whig adulation, and a flagbearer of classical liberalism. See, for example, Emily Jones, 'Conservatism, Edmund Burke and the

Invention of a Political Tradition', *The Historical Journal*, Vol. 58. No. 4, pp. 1115–39.

8. For example, https://scroll.in/article/811727/three-facts-about-bjp-founder-sp-mookerjee-that-a-recent-exhibition-in-delhi-wouldnt-have-revealed (accessed on 4 April 2021).
9. Mookerjee, contrary to public perception, is particularly difficult to classify as a conservative, despite being a founding figure of Hindu nationalism. See Sudipta Kaviraj, 'Contradictions of Conservatism', *Studies in Indian Politics*, Vol. 6, No. 1, pp. 1–14, especially Footnote 7.
10. See, for example, Madhav Khosla, *India's Founding Moment*, Cambridge, Massachusetts: Harvard University Press, 2019; Gautam Bhatia, *The Transformative Constitution*, New Delhi: HarperCollins, 2018; Rohit De, *The People's Constitution*, Princeton: Princeton University Press, 2018.
11. See, for example, Thomas Blom Hansen, *The Law of Force*, New Delhi: Aleph, 2020; Shruti Kapila, *Violent Fraternity: Indian Political Thought in the Global Age*, Princeton: Princeton University Press, 2021; Fali Nariman, *The State of the Nation*, New Delhi: Hay House, 2013; Ravi Ahuja, 'Authoritarian Shadows', *Social Scientist*, Vol. 46, No. 5, pp. 3–20.
12. For example, see Arghya Sengupta, 'The Book of Truths', *The Telegraph*, 18 February 2020, https://www.telegraphindia.com/opinion/anti-caa-nrc-protests-especially-the-movement-at-shaheen-bagh-has-ushered-in-a-revival-of-constitutionalism/cid/1746375 (accessed on 12 April 2021).
13. See for example, 'Indian civilization is purely under threat: Shashi Tharoor', United News of India, 10 February 2018, http://www.uniindia.com/indian-civilization-is-purely-under-threat-shashi-tharoor/states/news/1134101.html (accessed 21 March 2021).
14. Rajendra Prasad, 11 December 1946, *Constituent Assembly Debates*, Vol. I.

15. See A.G. Noorani, *Challenges to Civil Rights Guarantees in India*, New Delhi: Oxford University Press, 2012 p. 5.
16. 'The Republic of India', *The Times of India,* Republic Day Special, 26 January 1950, Bombay, p. 8.
17. 'Constitution of India Analysed', *The Times of India*, 26 January 1950, Bombay, p. B8.
18. 'The Republican Ideal: CP Ramaswamy Iyer', *Hindustan Times,* Republic Day Special, 26 January 1950, New Delhi, p. 5.
19. *Brij Bhushan vs State of Delhi*, AIR 1950 SC 129.
20. *Romesh Thappar vs State of Madras*, AIR 1950 SC 124.
21. Section 124A criminalized exciting disaffection against the state or bringing it into contempt.
22. *Tara Singh vs State of Punjab*, AIR 1951 Punj. 27.
23. Sardar Patel to Jawaharlal Nehru, 3 July 1950, Durga Das (ed.), *Sardar Patel's Correspondence*, Vol. X, Ahmedabad: Navajivan Publishing House, 1974, p. 358.
24. *Kameshwar Singh vs State of Bihar*, AIR 1951 Pat. 91.
25. Ibid.
26. *State of Madras vs Champakam Dorairajan*, AIR 1951 SC 226.
27. *B. Venkataramana vs State of Madras*, AIR 1951 SC 229.
28. See Tripurdaman Singh, *Sixteen Stormy Days: The Story of the First Amendment to the Constitution of India,* pp. 15–18.
29. Remarks at a Press Conference, 13 March 1951, S. Gopal (ed.), *Selected Works of Jawaharlal Nehru*, Vol. 16/1, New Delhi: Jawaharlal Nehru Memorial Fund, 1994, p. 153
30. C.A. Bayly, 'The Ends of Liberalism and the Political Thought of Nehru's India', *Modern Intellectual History*, Vol. 12, No. 3, pp. 605–26.
31. For more on this, see Gopal Sankarnarayanan, 'The Fading Right to Property in India', *Law and Politics in Africa, Asia and Latin America,* Vol. 44, No. 2, pp. 220–36; A.G. Noorani, 'Ninth Schedule and the Supreme Court', *Economic and Political Weekly,* Vol. 42, No. 9, pp. 731–34.

32. Granville Austin, *Working a Democratic Constitution: The Indian Experience*, New Delhi: Oxford University Press, 2003, p. 97.
33. Jawaharlal Nehru to chief ministers, 15 June 1951, G. Parthasarthi (ed.), *Letters to Chief Ministers, 1947-1964*, Vol. 2, New Delhi: Jawaharlal Nehru Memorial Fund, 1986, p. 418.
34. Tripurdaman Singh, *Sixteen Stormy Days: The Story of the First Amendment to the Constitution of India*, p. 197.
35. For a succinct overview: 'Nehru is Adamant on Curbing Press', *The New York Times*, 17 May 1951, New York, p. 8; 'Nehru Denies Aim Is a Gagged Press', *The New York Times*, 19 May 1951, New York, p. 2.
36. See Note on Amendments to the Constitution, 30 April 1951, Valmiki Chaudhary (ed.), *Dr. Rajendra Prasad: Correspondence and Selected Documents,* Vol. 14, New Delhi: Allied Publishers, 1991, pp. 273–74.
37. See Jawaharlal Nehru to G.V. Mavalankar, 16 May 1951, S. Gopal (ed.), *Selected Works of Jawaharlal Nehru,* Vol. 16/1, p. 171. Also see the footnote to the letter.
38. For greater detail, Tripurdaman Singh, *Sixteen Stormy Days: The Story of the First Amendment to the Constitution of India*, pp. 114–31.
39. Harshan Kumarasingham, *A Political Legacy of the British Empire: Power and the Parliamentary System in Post-Colonial India and Sri Lanka*, London: IB Tauris, 2013, p. 229.
40. See, for example, Gopal Sankarnarayanan, 'The Fading Right to Property in India', pp. 225–27.
41. Chief Justice of India, 1968–70, Vice-President of India, 1979–84.
42. *Sajjan Singh v State of Rajasthan*, AIR 1965 SC 845; see also Madhav Khosla, 'Constitutional Amendment' in Madhav Khosla, Sujit Chaudhary and Pratap Bhanu Mehta (eds), *The Oxford Handbook of the Indian Constitution*, New Delhi: Oxford University Press, 2016, p. 236.

43. Jawaharlal Nehru, 16 May 1951, *Parliamentary Debates*, Part II, Vol. XII, p. 8831.
44. 'Constitutional Amendment: A Denial of Democracy, 31 May 1951', Bimal Prasad (ed.), *Jayaprakash Narayan: Selected Works*, Vol. 6, New Delhi: Manohar Books, 2005, p. 135.
45. 'Note on Amendments to the Constitution, 30 April 1951', Valmiki Chaudhary (ed.), *Dr Rajendra Prasad: Correspondence and Selected Documents*, Vol. 14, New Delhi: Allied Publishers, 1991, p. 274.
46. Harshan Kumarasingham, 'The Indian Version of First Amongst Equals: Executive Power during the First Decade of Independence', *Modern Asian Studies*, Vol. 44, No. 4, p. 712.
47. 'Fundamental Rights', *The Times of India*, 12 April 1951, Bombay, p. 6.
48. 'The Rule of Law', *The Times of India*, 18 April 1951, Bombay, p. 4.
49. These included a wide range of voices: Socialists like Shibbanlal Saksena and Jayaprakash Narayan, landlords like Maharaja Kameshwar Singh, Gandhians like Acharya Kripalani, moderates like H.N. Kunzru, as well as organizations like the All India Newspaper Editors Conference. For greater detail, see Tripurdaman Singh, *Sixteen Stormy Days: The Story of the First Amendment to the Constitution of India*, New Delhi: Penguin Random House India, 2020, esp. chapters 5 and 6.
50. The armed revolt in Telangana led by the Communist Party of India, 1946–51.

Acknowledgements

THIS BOOK AND much of our intellectual journey would not have been possible without the intellectual munificence of Shruti Kapila and the late C.A. Bayly. They first put us on track to examining the complex soil of Indian politics at the University of Cambridge and nurtured our burgeoning interest in its conceptual foundations – an interest that has since blossomed through many rewarding conversations with James Manor, Faisal Devji, Javed Majeed, Tahir Kamran, Sujit Sivasundaram, Meghnad Desai and Philip Murphy. We have further greatly benefited from our respective academic homes and would like to express our gratitude to the School of Advanced Study, University of London and Leiden University for their support, as well as the British Academy for generous funding of Tripurdaman's research. Tripurdaman Singh would also like to thank Mushtaq Qureshi for having been a great source of encouragement and guidance.

We have been very fortunate in having had the excellent companionship of friends and colleagues who have been our intellectual interlocutors and helped us think through the themes and arguments of this book: Anshul Avijit, Ali Khan Mahmudabad, Amir Khan, Mariam Chauhan, Adam Lebovitz, Parul Bhandari, Alastair McClure, Saumya Saxena, Siraj Khan, Jonah Schulhofer-Wohl, Nicolas Blarel, Francesco Ragazzi, Zareer Masani, Narayani Basu and Harshan Kumarasingham.

Thanks are also due to Swati Chopra and Antony Thomas at HarperCollins India, who have been instrumental in putting this book together, and Arabella Pike at William Collins, our publisher in the UK. As ever, our agent Kanishka Gupta has been very diligent and made the whole process as smooth as possible. We would also like to thank the Navajivan Trust for allowing us to reprint the relevant extracts from Sardar Patel's correspondence.

Finally, we are exceptionally grateful for the love and support of our friends and families over a difficult period. Special thanks in this regard to Digvijay Singh Deo, Nadia Cavalletto, Kathryn Santner, William Marks, Siddhartha Chaturvedi, Aviv Fonea, Plum Schrager, Kitty Brandon-James, Simon Wolf, Imran Jumabhoy, Lucy Jacobsen, Catherine Katz and Sophie-Jung Kim.

We have split the work for this book, with chapters one and two mostly written by Adeel and chapters three and four mostly written by Tripurdaman.

Index

About the Authors

TRIPURDAMAN SINGH is a British Academy postdoctoral fellow at the Institute of Commonwealth Studies, University of London. Born in Agra, India, Tripurdaman read politics and international studies at the University of Warwick and earned an MPhil in modern South Asian studies and a PhD in history at the University of Cambridge. He is a Fellow of the Royal Historical Society, a Fellow of the Royal Asiatic Society and the author of *Imperial Sovereignty and Local Politics* (2019) as well as the widely acclaimed *Sixteen Stormy Days* (2020). He lives in Cambridge.

ADEEL HUSSAIN is an assistant professor at Leiden University and a senior research affiliate at the Max Planck Institute for Comparative Public Law and International Law in Heidelberg. He was born in Sialkot, Pakistan, and holds two degrees in German law (first and second state examination) as well as a master's and PhD from the University of Cambridge. His next book, *Law and Muslim Political Thought in Late Colonial North India,* is forthcoming in 2022. He now lives and works in The Hague.

30 Years *of*

HarperCollins *Publishers* India

At HarperCollins, we believe in telling the best stories and finding the widest possible readership for our books in every format possible. We started publishing 30 years ago; a great deal has changed since then, but what has remained constant is the passion with which our authors write their books, the love with which readers receive them, and the sheer joy and excitement that we as publishers feel in being a part of the publishing process.

Over the years, we've had the pleasure of publishing some of the finest writing from the subcontinent and around the world, and some of the biggest bestsellers in India's publishing history. Our books and authors have won a phenomenal range of awards, and we ourselves have been named Publisher of the Year the greatest number of times. But nothing has meant more to us than the fact that millions of people have read the books we published, and somewhere, a book of ours might have made a difference.

As we step into our fourth decade, we go back to that one word – a word which has been a driving force for us all these years.

Read.

Harper Collins · 4th · HARPER PERENNIAL · HARPER BUSINESS · HARPER BLACK · हार्पर हिन्दी

HarperCollins *Children's Books* · HARPER DESIGN · HARPER VANTAGE · Harper Sport